THE
FIRE
NEXT DOOR

MEXICO'S
DRUG VIOLENCE
AND THE DANGER
TO AMERICA

THE
FIRE
NEXT DOOR

TED GALEN CARPENTER

CATO
INSTITUTE
WASHINGTON, D.C.

Library of Congress Cataloging-in-Publication Data

Carpenter, Ted Galen.
The fire next door: Mexico's drug violence and the danger to America/by
Ted Galen Carpenter.
   p. cm.
Includes bibliographical references and index.
ISBN 978-1-935308-88-1 (hbk. : alk. paper)
1. Drug traffic–Mexico. 2. Drug traffic–Mexican-American Border Region.
3. Violent crimes–Mexican-American Border Region. 4. Drug control–
Mexican-American Border Region. I. Title.

HV5840.M4C367 2012
362.450972–dc23   2012027094

Cover design by Jon Meyers.

Printed in the United States of America.

CATO INSTITUTE
1000 Massachusetts Ave., N.W.
Washington, D.C. 20001
www.cato.org

To Carson and Savannah:

May the drug war and the tragic violence it has spawned in Mexico and elsewhere be nothing more than an unpleasant historical episode by the time you reach adulthood.

Contents

Acknowledgments

I owe a debt of gratitude to many colleagues and friends for their assistance in the course of this book project. My administrative assistant, Charles Zakaib, devoted considerable time and effort diligently tracking down important—sometimes elusive—sources. Justin Logan and Malou Innocent offered helpful hints and suggestions regarding developments in Mexico and the United States that were relevant to the topic of the drug war. Ian Vasquez, director of the Cato Institute's Center for Global Liberty and Prosperity, provided invaluable assistance in multiple ways. Christopher Preble, my successor as Cato's vice president for defense and foreign policy studies, helped free up my time by accepting more than his share of media interview requests on other topics.

Juan Carlos Hidalgo and Gene Healy both took many hours from their own busy schedules to provide detailed critiques of an earlier draft of the manuscript. Their contributions, as well as the excellent copyediting effort by Karen Garvin, significantly improved the final product. Any remaining errors of either style or substance are, of course, solely my own.

As usual, Cato's top management, including President Ed Crane, Executive Vice President David Boaz, and Board Chairman Robert Levy, offered their support and encouragement for this latest analysis of the destructive consequences of the international war on drugs. So, too, did the late Cato board chairman, William A. Niskanen, who viewed drug policy with the same intellectual rigor that he brought to so many other issues. Bill was an early, consistent, and incisive critic of the conventional wisdom regarding the proper strategy for dealing with the issue of illegal drugs. His massive intellectual contribution to the cause of liberty and intelligent public policy will be sorely missed.

Thanks to the leadership of those individuals, Cato experts have been in the forefront of scholarship for more than three decades, documenting both the futility and the horrific unintended side effects of drug prohibition. That effort is paying dividends as more and more opinion leaders in the United States and other countries have turned against the war on drugs. Mexico's former president, Vicente Fox, has been especially eloquent and courageous in criticizing the terrible harm that Washington's utopian crusade has inflicted on his country. So, too, has Mexico's former foreign minister Jorge Castañeda and Brazil's former president Fernando Henrique Cardoso.

Finally, I would like to thank my wife Barbara for her patient support and encouragement throughout this project. She has been my muse for more than four decades, and no amount of gratitude on my part would be sufficient to compensate her for her contribution to my success.

Foreword

Today, many prohibitions, myths, and past beliefs on numerous issues have been torn down. We now stand on the final frontier of the old approach to drug policy, as evidence mounts that the current strategy is not working. There is already an irresistible push around the world for a new, more realistic, and more constructive policy paradigm. Ted Galen Carpenter's thoughtful new book demonstrates the need for change with great clarity.

Legalization of drugs offers the best exit from the quagmire in which we find ourselves. Choosing legalization would provide substantial benefits in a number of respects. Perhaps most important, it would separate the issues of crime and violence from the issues of personal and public health. Law enforcement and security agencies could then focus their time and resources on the former, instead of treating ordinary drug users as criminals. In fact, ending prohibition would enable those agencies to strengthen their responses to a whole range of crimes.

The fear that legalization would lead to an explosion of drug use seems unfounded. Portugal's experience with its bold drug policy reforms over the past decade indicates that drug use might actually decline once prohibition is ended. In that country, drug users who might have a dependency problem can seek treatment without fear that they might run afoul of the criminal justice system. Because that fear is gone, more of them have sought treatment.

An especially important benefit from legalization is that it would greatly decrease the revenues available to the violent drug cartels. That is especially important for my country. The cartels in Mexico receive billions of dollars each year from trafficking in illegal drugs. According to the United Nations Office on Drugs and Crime, gross profits from cocaine sales in North America reached $34 billion in 2009.[1] A large majority of that amount is because those drugs are illegal and, therefore, sell for inflated prices. *Wall Street Journal* reporter David Luhnow found that a kilo of cocaine at its source in Colombia costs approximately $1,200. By the time it was in transit in Mexico, the price was $8,300. At the retail level in the United States, the price would be anywhere between $15,000 and $80,000.[2] The cartels use their vast profits to terrorize the Mexican people and to undermine the country's institutions.

Ending prohibition would enable governments throughout the world to concentrate on educating people about the potential perils of drug use. The underlying message would be that although citizens in a free country should have the right to choose—even if the choice is to use illegal drugs—some choices are much wiser than others. With freedom comes responsibility, and avoiding drug dependency is the responsible choice. Citizens are much more likely to heed such a message if the government does not criminalize unwise behavior.

That distinction is especially important with respect to young people. One of the great tragedies in Mexico—and to a significant extent in the United States as well—is that the drug gangs have tempted them to go down the wrong path. The temptation of quick riches from working for a criminal organization has all too often proven irresistible. Legalization would greatly weaken the ability of the drug cartels to entice young people into that terribly destructive career. According to the Mexican daily newspaper *Reforma*, more than 50,000 people— mostly young men in their teens and twenties—have perished in the drug-related violence in my country in recent years.[3] That is an unspeakable tragedy. Young people represent the future of the country, and they deserve a far better fate than that.

Ending prohibition and restoring peace is critical to my country. We need to divert the financial resources that are now absorbed by the drug trade to legal—and more productive—channels. That is necessary so that Mexico can move forward and not merely watch as other countries pass us by.

It is time for new and audacious ideas—for creative thinking regarding drug policy. When what we have tried doesn't work, it is time that we implement new approaches. Those approaches must place the fundamental values of peace, consensus, predictability, and legality at the forefront.

I fully agree with Ted Galen Carpenter when he says that "U.S. leaders—and those from Mexico—need to take constructive action now, before the fire consumes our neighbor's home and threatens our own." Both Mexico and the United States would be wise to adopt the strategy discussed in *The Fire Next Door*.

Vicente Fox Quesada
President of Mexico, 2000–2006

Introduction: Mexico's Agony and Washington's Worry

Jaime Zapata, a special agent for U.S. Immigration and Customs Enforcement (ICE), who dealt with issues of drug smuggling, was on assignment at the U.S. embassy in Mexico City from his normal post in Laredo, Texas. On Valentine's Day 2011, Zapata and another ICE agent were returning to the capital after meeting with law enforcement officials in the northern state of San Luis Potosí. The two agents were traveling along a four-lane federal highway in their blue Chevrolet Suburban sport-utility vehicle (SUV) when they were stopped at what appeared to be a military checkpoint. Such checkpoints have become routine, especially in northern Mexico, where the war between the government of President Felipe Calderón and several drug cartels rages with particular intensity.

In this case, though, the armed men at the checkpoint were not government troops but soldiers of one of the most powerful and ruthless cartels, the dreaded Zetas. As soon as Zapata and his partner slowed their vehicle, the gunmen opened fire, killing Zapata and seriously wounding the other agent.

The two men had become the latest victims in Mexico's increasingly chaotic and violent drug war. But they are hardly the only ones. At the time of their encounter with the Zetas, the death toll since Calderón launched his military-led offensive against the traffickers in December 2006 had already climbed to nearly 36,000. By the end of the third quarter of 2011, it would top 47,000.

The victims come from all walks of life. A majority are participants (usually at the lowest levels) in the multibillion-dollar trade in illegal drugs—everything from marijuana to cocaine to methamphetamine. But others are police officers and soldiers tasked with bringing down the cartels. Other victims include appointed or elected officials who increasingly face an ultimatum from the crime syndicates: *plata o plomo*? (silver or lead?). In other words, take a

1

bribe or risk assassination. All too many officials who refuse to be corrupted pay for that decision with their lives.

The drug gangs have become bold enough to target even the most prominent political leaders. Rodolfo Torre Cantú, the nominee of Mexico's Institutional Revolutionary Party (PRI), was the overwhelming favorite to be the next governor of the important northern border state of Tamaulipas (which is just south of Brownsville, Texas) in the July 2010 elections. He was even regarded as a rising political star with possible national ambitions. Public opinion polls gave the mustachioed surgeon a massive lead—65 percent to his nearest opponent's 31 percent. A rally on June 25, 2010, attracted some 15,000 wildly enthusiastic supporters, who cheered his call for improved security against the rampaging drug cartels.

Just three days later, gunmen ambushed his motorcade on the road to the airport near Ciudad Victoria, the state capital. The attackers sent a hail of bullets into their target, killing Torre as well as several aides and bodyguards. It was a sophisticated operation worthy of an elite military unit, but these assassins were professional killers working for one of the cartels.

That incident came on the heels of another episode that shook Mexico's political establishment. Just a few weeks before Torre Cantú's assassination, Diego Fernández de Cevallos was abducted while driving from his home in Mexico City to a ranch that he owned three hours away. His white SUV was found the next day on an unpaved country road near his ranch. Blood stains were on the front seat.

What made this abduction so frightening was the nature of the victim. Fernández de Cevallos had been the National Action Party (PAN) candidate for president in 1994. PAN is the current governing party, led by President Calderón. Despite the passage of 16 years, Fernández de Cevallos remained one of the most visible political figures in Mexico. A comparable event in the United States would be if the mafia had kidnapped Al Gore or Bob Dole.

This brazen move by the traffickers would ultimately end better than it did for Torre Cantú. After months of tense negotiations, the abductors finally released Fernández de Cevallos five days before Christmas. The sense of relief, though, was tempered by reports that his family and friends had to pay a whopping $20 million ransom to gain his release.

The Fernández de Cevallos abduction, even more than Torre Cantú's murder, conveyed a stark message that not even the highest members of the country's political elite were safe from the cartels. José Antonio Ortega, the president of the Citizen's Council for Public Security and Criminal Justice in Mexico City, concluded bitterly: "Today it is Diego, tomorrow it could be anyone. We are all exposed."[1]

Still other victims of the burgeoning violence are just civilians who are caught up in the fighting between rival cartels or between the cartels and government forces. Vicente Burciaga, a resident of El Porvenir—a small town in the middle of a major trafficking route into the United States—laments how it has become increasingly dangerous for ordinary citizens: "They are killing people over there who have nothing to do with drug trafficking. They kill you just for having seen what they are doing."[2]

Sometimes people don't even need to have witnessed anything to become targets. An especially chilling episode took place in Ciudad Juárez in late January 2010, when 16 teenagers at a birthday party for a classmate were gunned down—many of them as they fled. Several bodies were found in the street in pools of blood where they fell after desperately seeking to escape. Perhaps most terrible of all, they were apparently targeted by mistake. A neighbor allegedly gave enforcers for the Juárez cartel erroneous information that the rival Sinaloa cartel was holding a party at that address.

A similar incident occurred a few months later in the city of Torreón, in Coahuila state. A birthday party at a restaurant was still going strong early on the morning of Sunday, July 18, when gunmen burst in, yelling "kill them all." They proceeded to spray the party-goers with bullets, eventually firing more than 200 shots. When the chaos subsided, 12 men and 5 women, mostly in their twenties and early thirties, lay dead. Another 18 were wounded, many seriously. The tiles in the restaurant's courtyard were smeared with blood, amidst the chaos of overturned tables and chairs, discarded drinks, and abandoned musical instruments.

Torreón had already become a battleground between the Gulf cartel and their former enforcers, the Zetas, which led to the suspicion that this was no ordinary crime. Within 24 hours, Mexican police were confident that the bloodbath was the latest handiwork of a drug gang; they just weren't sure which one. As was the case

3

with the murders at the Juárez party, there was little evidence that any of the people at the Torreón celebration were involved in drug trafficking—and solid evidence that many of them were not.

Then there was the horrific March 2010 incident in Durango, where a group of elementary- and high-school students were on their way to receive government scholarships for continuing study. As they were being driven to the location for the ceremony, they encountered a drug cartel checkpoint. What happened then is not entirely clear, but cartel gunmen attacked the students with rifles, automatic pistols, and hand grenades. When the smoke cleared, 10 students—some as young as eight years old—were dead. Investigators could find no evidence tying any of the victims to the drug trade. In fact, they seemed to be high-achieving students—some of the least likely types to consort with criminals.

It is not certain whether such killings involve cases of mistaken identity, or even worse, if they are purely terrorist attacks designed to demonstrate the government's impotence and intimidate the Mexican people. Whatever the reason, such awful incidents are becoming an increasingly common feature of life in Mexico.

Even when innocent people are not killed in the drug violence, they are sometimes emotionally traumatized. That is especially true of Mexico's children, who have witnessed far too much slaughter. In Tijuana, children playing on the playground of their primary school saw a gun battle erupt between police and a cartel hit man. The police won that round, but pupils witnessed the exchange of gunfire and the spattering of blood. In another Tijuana drug killing, children saw police forensic investigators collect three beheaded and dismembered bodies near a shopping mall. The innocence and bewilderment of some of the country's emotionally scarred children is painful to behold. One eight-year-old girl, who had seen another dead body from a drug gang shootout, admitted "it feels awful to see it."[3]

School children are getting front-row seats to the drug war on all too many occasions. Between October 2009 and July 2010, nine major shootouts erupted in school zones. On one occasion, soldiers and cartel enforcers battled for an hour—barely 60 feet from a pre-school in the quaint jewelry center and resort city of Taxco.

And while the chaos is worst in the border cities such as Tijuana and Ciudad Juárez that lie along the main drug trafficking routes into the United States, that plague is spreading to previously quiet areas. Throughout the 1990s and the early years of the following decade, Mexico's chief industrial city, Monterrey, was thought to be virtually immune from the damage that turf fights between the drug gangs caused in such places as Tijuana and Nuevo Laredo. Television journalist Sam Quiñones, who had lived in Monterrey for a decade until 2004, recalled wistfully that it "was the safest region in the country when I lived there, thanks to its robust economy and the sturdy social control of an industrial elite."[4] An international consulting group in early 2005 even named Monterrey the safest city in all of Latin America.

How times have changed. Just how far Monterrey has descended into the abyss of drug violence became evident in July 2010 when authorities uncovered a dump site east of the city, in the township of Benito Juárez. Excavations soon revealed that there were at least 51 bodies—some intact and others in pieces—buried at the site. That made the Monterrey dumping ground the second-biggest mass grave uncovered in Mexico's drug wars. It appeared that most of the victims had been executed in groups, their bodies dumped into newly dug pits, and, in most cases, then set on fire. Fears of kidnappings swept affluent neighborhoods in the city, and orders for bullet-proof limousines and private security guards soared.

Even prominent resort areas such as Cancún and Acapulco are no longer immune. Acapulco especially is beginning to resemble the bloody border cities. Any doubt on that score evaporated in April 2010 when a wild shootout took place in broad daylight on the main boulevard in Acapulco's principal tourist area that left six people dead and dozens dashing for cover. The violence has reached the point that sarcastic residents now refer to the city as *Narcopulco*. And it continues to get worse. During a single weekend in early January 2011, police discovered 30 bodies, 16 of which were found without their heads, in and around Acapulco.

There is a growing, hotly contested debate about two important issues. First, is the carnage in Mexico reaching the point that the country is in danger of becoming a "failed state"? Second, is the drug-related corruption and violence in Mexico a problem only for that country, or is it now seeping over the border and posing a national security threat to the United States? Neither question has an easy answer.

Allegations about the possibility of a failed state infuriate Mexican officials. In a March 2009 speech, President Calderón scorned those who suggested that his country was in danger of that awful fate. "It is absolutely false, absurd that anyone indicate that Mexico does not have control over one single part of its national territory," Calderón fumed. "I challenge anyone who says that to tell me what part of the country they want to go to, and I will take that person there."[5]

Respected U.S. observers echo his views. Former Drug Enforcement Administration (DEA) chief Robert C. Bonner dismisses the failed-state theory. He acknowledges that the spike in killings during Calderón's presidency "has led some to conclude that the violence in Mexico is out of control. Others have suggested that the country is on the verge of becoming a 'failed state' (or in the words of a 2008 U.S. military report, at risk of 'rapid and sudden collapse'). The former is a gross exaggeration, and the latter is simply untrue."[6]

George W. Grayson, a prominent U.S. expert on Mexico, argues that "only a Cassandra in a deep funk could conclude that Mexico will implode as is possible in Afghanistan or Pakistan. There are too many factors . . . to let this happen." Yet in the next breath, Grayson emphasizes that "Calderón and his successors must act to prevent ungovernability in cities like Ciudad Juárez and Tijuana, and in states like Guerrero, Durango, Sinaloa, and Michoacán."[7] That's a rather large and important chunk of the country.

There are other worrisome indicators. One of the earliest warning signals that a country has at least the potential to become a failed state is when members of the business and political elites are so worried about the security environment that they send their loved ones out of the country. Mexico may have entered that stage, since there are numerous and growing examples of prominent figures protecting their loved ones in that manner. A case that received considerable attention in Mexico in late 2009 was the admission by Mauricio Fernández, mayor of the affluent Monterrey suburb of San Pedro Garza García, that he had sent his family to live in the United States. He stated that he sent his wife and children out of the country months earlier, when he first decided to run for mayor. But even after winning the office in July and being sworn in, he still was not confident enough about their safety to let them come home. They remained in the United States, he admitted, because "right now things are not safe enough for them to return."[8]

Alejandro Junco de la Vega runs *Grupo Reforma*, the largest print-media company, not only in Mexico but in all of Latin America. Yet this media mogul moved his family to Texas in 2008 because of an increase in the number of personal threats from drug cartel operatives. And in the United States they remain.

In the worst centers of violence, such as Ciudad Juárez and Tijuana, there are unmistakable signs of an even more worrisome precursor of a failed state: large numbers of upper-class and middle-class families exiting the country. Since late 2008, the number of abandoned homes in Juárez, many in previously affluent neighborhoods, has skyrocketed. The number is growing so fast that officials have trouble keeping track.

Despite these developments, fears that Mexico is on the brink of becoming a Latin American version of Somalia are overblown. The country still has a number of institutional strengths, including entrenched, well-organized political parties; a sizable, influential business community; a significant military establishment; and an especially powerful moral force—the Roman Catholic Church. Such institutions are largely absent—or at least are far weaker—in countries that have become failed states or are on the brink of doing so. Mexico's major political, economic, and religious players are not likely to implode and cede the field to the drug traffickers. Yet the overall trend is troubling. Even an outspoken skeptic of the failed-state thesis like Bonner admits that "Mexico is in the throes of a battle against powerful drug cartels, the outcome of which will determine who controls the country's law enforcement, judicial, and political institutions."[9] The prospect of violent criminal organizations controlling the principal institutions of the state is not all that far removed from a failed-state scenario.

Worries about the extent of a "spillover" impact on the United States have generated even more controversy. There is no doubt that U.S. officials are deeply concerned about such a scenario. At the moment, the greatest worry is about Americans who live or work in Mexico—including U.S. government officials. Investigators speculated that the Zetas may have targeted the vehicle carrying Jaime Zapata and his partner because they were U.S. law enforcement personnel.

An earlier incident in Ciudad Juárez raised similar suspicions. In March 2010, an American citizen, Lesley Enriquez Redelfs,

7

an employee of the U.S. consulate there, was shot to death in her car along with her husband, Arthur, also an American citizen, in broad daylight after leaving a children's party sponsored by the U.S. Consul.[10] The couple's screaming, terrified infant daughter was in the car with them when the attack took place. On the same day, the husband of another consular employee was killed and their two children seriously wounded in a separate drive-by shooting. His horrified wife, following in another car, saw the bloody incident unfold.

Two killings of individuals connected with the U.S. consulate in such a brief period suggested that the incidents were not random killings or cases of mistaken identity. The subsequent investigation, though, created more doubt than clarification. When apprehended later, one of the assassins contended that Arthur Redelfs, who was a deputy at the El Paso jail, was the real target, allegedly because he mistreated gang members in his custody.

But when Mexican authorities arrested the alleged mastermind of the hit, Jesús Ernesto Chávez, in early July, he told them Lesley was the target, and that he ordered her to be killed because she had been illegally supplying U.S. visas to members of a rival gang. U.S. officials immediately discounted Chávez's allegation, and there was no evidence that she had even been in a position to approve such visas. But if the enforcers for the Juárez cartel *believed* that she had done so, that could easily have been sufficient motive to order her assassination.

Evidence also surfaced during the investigations indicating that the attacks may have been intended to send a warning to the U.S. consulate in response to Washington's push to place U.S. drug intelligence officers within the Juárez police department. Further indications that a strategy of attacking U.S. government personnel and installations might be underway occurred in early April 2010 when assailants tossed an explosive device at the U.S. consulate in Nuevo Laredo. And then, in February 2011, the attacks on the ICE agents took place, providing the strongest indication yet that the drug cartels might be targeting U.S. diplomatic and law enforcement figures.

Ordinary American civilians also are more frequently getting caught in the crossfire when they travel or work in parts of Mexico. Kidnapping incidents, especially those involving Americans of

Mexican heritage, are on the rise. Worries that U.S. military personnel might be at excessive risk while spending furloughs south of the border have impelled base commanders to put some cities, especially Tijuana and Juárez, off-limits.

An especially horrific case of what can happen to Americans who run afoul of the cartels occurred in Ciudad Juárez, where a seven-year-old Texas boy, Raúl Ramírez, was killed while visiting his father. Gunmen attacked the vehicle his father was driving, firing at least 18 rounds from 9mm weapons. The elder Ramírez died in the vehicle. Raúl escaped the car and tried to flee, but was shot in the back. Police were uncertain whether the attackers thought that his father was involved in the drug trade, but the incident had all the characteristics of a cartel hit, and Raúl was an innocent victim in any case.

U.S. officials also fret that the cartels may be targeting Americans even on U.S. soil. Following a major nationwide anti-drug raid in June 2010, Kevin L. Perkins, assistant director of the FBI's Criminal Investigation Division, told reporters that "drug trafficking across the U.S. southwest border" was not only leading to a "surge of drugs in our neighborhoods across the country" but was leading to "increased border violence, kidnapping, extortion and human smuggling."[11]

The cartels are clearly expanding their operations north of the border, either directly or by forging ties with American affiliates. Corruption is also migrating northward. According to an Associated Press tally, more than 80 law enforcement officers at the local, state, and federal levels working along the border were convicted of drug-related corruption charges since late 2006—and the pace is accelerating.

Not surprisingly, the Customs and Border Protection agency is a high-priority target for trafficking organizations that seek to undermine or seduce law enforcement personnel. And they have achieved a considerable amount of success. James Tomsheck, the assistant commissioner for internal affairs at Customs and Border Protection (CBP), confirmed that investigators "had seen many signs that drug organizations were making a concerted effort" to infiltrate the agency's ranks. "There have been verifiable instances," Tomsheck stated, "where people were directed to C.B.P. to apply for positions only for the purpose of enhancing the goals of criminal organizations."[12] Most of those individuals were selected because they had no criminal records, which meant that they could pass a background check with little problem.

But has the violence that is so plaguing Mexico also come across the Rio Grande? The evidence is less clear on that point. The increasing Mexican domination of all phases of the drug trade in the United States certainly carries with it the risk that the turf battles in Mexico between rival cartels could become proxy wars in U.S. communities. There are some indications that such struggles may already be underway. In at least three cases, members of the La Familia cartel kidnapped competing drug dealers in Houston and held them for ransom. Similar events have occurred in Phoenix, Las Vegas, and other U.S. cities.

Some experts, though, insist that allegations of a serious spillover effect are exaggerated. Gabriel Arana, writing in the *Nation*, contends that "if media reports are to be believed, an Armageddon-like rash of drug related violence" has "crossed from Mexico into the United States." He responds that "the numbers tell a different story."[13]

Other analysts reach a similar conclusion, noting that some southwestern U.S. cities, including El Paso, Juárez's sister city, have violent crime rates lower than the national average.

Nevertheless, there are some worrisome signs. Cartel threats against U.S. law enforcement personnel are escalating. Police in Nogales, Arizona, went on heightened alert in June 2010 after receiving a threat, relayed through an informant, that officers would be targeted if they continued to carry out drug busts while off duty. Apparently, traffickers considered it within the rules of the game for police to engage in such raids as part of their job when they were on duty, but that it was a gratuitous affront to do so on other occasions. When off duty, the cartel warned, police were to look the other way and ignore any drug shipments that came across the border—if they valued their lives.

Perhaps the most jarring incident occurred in early August 2010, when reports surfaced that a Mexican cartel had put a $1 million bounty on the life of Arizona sheriff Joe Arpaio, the colorful and controversial chief lawman in Maricopa County (which includes Phoenix and many of its suburbs). The Mexican cartels have plenty of reasons to loathe the man. His department is one of the most active in the southwestern states in intercepting drug shipments. Consequently, state and federal law enforcement agencies took the threat against Arpaio's life quite seriously. They did so perhaps even more than usual in the summer of 2010, because just weeks earlier, the Drug Enforcement Administration had warned that the cartels were about to take their war from Mexico north of the border and attack U.S. law enforcement personnel.

An incident in August 2009 confirmed that cartel enforcers are already operating in the United States against other targets, even in generally peaceful El Paso. Police announced the arrest of three men and charged them with capital murder in what was apparently the contract killing of José Daniel González Galeana, a lieutenant in the Juárez cartel. Killers shot him to death in the front yard of his elegant Mediterranean-style home. And they clearly took no chances with their task—shooting him eight times at close range.

That case was especially troubling. First, González Galeana did not operate out of Juárez, but instead lived in a quiet, upscale neighborhood in El Paso, where he ran several ostensibly legal businesses. Second, one of the accused hit men was a U.S. Army private based at Ft. Bliss, suggesting that the cartels may now be infiltrating the U.S. military. Such an achievement could give the drug lords a new source of highly trained assassins—who are also U.S. citizens—and who would be especially useful for going after targets inside the United States.

For some communities directly along the border, there are already very direct spillover effects. Officials and residents in El Paso were badly shaken in late June 2010 when seven bullets struck the upper floors of city hall. Apparently, the shots came from an altercation in Juárez, and it was possible that Mexican federal agents may have fired the stray bullets. But whatever the details, the incident was a graphic reminder that Mexico's violence was no longer confined to Mexican territory.

Ranchers and farmers in the borderlands of Arizona, New Mexico, and Texas have complained for years that smugglers and illegal immigrants use their properties with impunity as routes to enter the United States. And the level of fear is rising as more and more of the uninvited seem to be involved in drug smuggling or human trafficking, rather than being ordinary people looking for work and a better life in the United States.

Matters came to a head in March 2010 when Robert Krentz, a 58-year-old rancher near Douglas, Arizona, was found murdered.

11

Authorities quickly concluded that an intruder from Mexico was the perpetrator. Tracks at the murder scene led back over the border into Mexico, and Krentz's ranch had long been an active route for illegal immigrants and drug shipments. He probably stumbled upon a scout for a trafficking shipment and paid for that encounter with his life. Since the Krentz episode, complaints from farmers and ranchers along the border have been building to a crescendo.

While the extent of a spillover effect into the United States is somewhat debatable, what is less open to dispute is that Calderón's hard-line strategy toward the cartels has led to a dramatic surge in violence without producing much in the way of positive results. That doesn't stop Calderón and his supporters from trying to apply the best spin possible to the dismal situation, however. Eduardo Medina Mora, who at that time was Mexico's Attorney General, even stated that the record-setting bloodshed in Ciudad Juárez and other cities was actually a positive sign. The increased violence did not reflect the power of those groups, Medina Mora stated, it indicated "how they are melting down." Calderón himself engages in similar optimism, which strikes critics as wishful thinking. Following comments from former president Vicente Fox in August 2010 branding the drug war a bloody failure, Calderón responded that "the number of murders or the degree of violence isn't necessarily the best indicator of progress or retreat, or if the war is [being] won or lost."[14]

But the evidence of a policy failure is hard to deny. More than three times as many Mexicans died in drug-related violence in both 2010 and 2011 as in any year before Calderón became president. The Mexican military, which had largely avoided the pervasive corruption that had tainted so many of the country's other institutions, is now showing signs of succumbing to the temptation of drug money. Equally troubling, allegations of torture and other human-rights abuses against military units are soaring—and many of those allegations appear to be true.

And as the military-led crackdown in Mexico causes inconveniences for the drug cartels, they're transferring or expanding their operations into Central America. Instead of solving Mexico's drug-trafficking pathologies, Calderón's strategy has spread those pathologies to neighboring countries. Matters have become so bad in Guatemala that then-president Álvaro Colom declared a "state of siege" in Alta Verapaz, an especially violent province near the border with Mexico, in December 2010. Colom alleged that the Zetas had overrun that province. The following month, he extended that state of siege, giving the government additional powers to combat the heavily armed cartel. The turf fights that have so plagued Mexico are now being played out with greater frequency and ferocity in Central America than that region has ever experienced before. And the gruesome trophies, especially severed heads, that characterize inter-cartel warfare throughout Mexico are now showing up in Central American countries.

Mexican critics increasingly complain about the excessive social and economic costs of Calderón's offensive against the cartels. Even some members of his National Action Party are calling for a change of strategy. Rubén Aguilar, the president's former director of communications, proposed opening negotiations with the traffickers, essentially offering to allow them to conduct their business in exchange for a commitment to halt the kidnappings, torture, and hideous murders. Aguilar was even willing to go so far as to consider wholesale legalization of drugs.[15]

Other advocates of change are beginning to speak out as well. "The people of Mexico are losing hope, and it is urgent that Congress, the political parties and the president reconsider this strategy," said Senator Ramón Galindo, a Calderón supporter, several months after Aguilar's interview.[16]

Perhaps the biggest blow to Calderón came in August 2010 when former president Vicente Fox stunned both Mexican and U.S. political leaders by advocating an end to the drug war. In a post on his personal blog, Fox called for a rapid end to the military's domestic anti-drug operations. He asserted that the rampant violence was undermining the government's legitimacy. "The first responsibility of a government is to provide security for the people and their possessions," he stressed, but "today, we find that, unfortunately, the Mexican government is not complying with that responsibility."[17]

Instead of considering a significant policy change, however, Calderón's administration insists on staying the course. Calderón himself repeatedly denounces suggestions that he back off from the offensive against the cartels. "My government," he thundered, "does not negotiate nor will it ever negotiate with criminal organizations." Instead he pledged "not only to confront them but defeat them with all the force of the state."[18] And Washington continues to back that strategy with a multiyear, multibillion-dollar aid program, the Mérida Initiative.

The Calderón administration, however, chooses to blame the United States for Mexico's escalating drug violence. And such accusations are not confined to noting that U.S. drug users constitute the biggest market for the illegal drugs produced in Mexico or transported through that country. An equally prominent criticism is that the United States is the source of the weapons that are turning some Mexican cities into shooting galleries. During his May 2010 visit to the United States, which included a summit meeting with President Obama, Calderón asserted: "If you look carefully, you will notice that the violence in Mexico started to grow a couple of years before I took office in 2006. This coincides, at least, with the lifting of the assault weapons ban in 2004."[19] A former official in his administration was even more direct, saying: "I think American [gun] laws are absurd" because "they make it very easy for citizens to acquire guns."[20]

Mexican officials repeatedly insist that some 90 percent of the weapons captured from the cartels originate in the United States. Several U.S. experts have challenged the 90 percent figure, however, and they note that even many of the weapons that did originally come from this country were not sold in gun stores or gun shows—contrary to the impression that the Mexican government fosters. Instead, they come from the flood of military ordnance that Washington sent to Central American countries and other locales during the final decades of the Cold War. And U.S. gun laws, whether they are good or bad, would have little impact on such black-market sources.

Using the gun issue as an excuse for the drug violence in Mexico is a distraction from the search for real solutions. So, too, are the panaceas that some people in the United States embrace, especially the calls for tight border security. Although some improved security measures are both possible and desirable, it's an illusion to expect that a nearly 2000-mile land border with Mexico can be sealed against ingenious, well-financed drug cartels. The only way to come even close to such an objective would be to create the North American equivalent of the Berlin Wall, patrolled by thousands of heavily-armed U.S. military personnel. And it would require bringing the multibillion-dollar legal commerce between Mexico and the United States to a crawl.

The real policy options all involve difficult choices and have potential side effects. Some experts argue that the Colombian government's achievements against the once-powerful drug organizations in that country offer a model for Mexico. "Mexico has what we had some years ago, which are very powerful cartels," Colombian President Juan Manuel Santos contends. "What we can provide is the experience that we have had dismantling those cartels."[21]

But while Colombia's hard-line policies broke the Medellín and Cali cartels during the 1990s, the long-term success is more limited than its admirers believe. The level of violence in that country has subsided over the past decade, but that development has more to do with the fading of the armed conflict between radical-leftist insurgent groups and right-wing paramilitary organizations than it does with the decline of the drug cartels. Such an ideological component is largely absent in Mexico.

Furthermore, although the trafficking enterprises that replaced the broken Medellín and Cali cartels are smaller, weaker, and more dispersed than their predecessors, the amount of drugs flowing out of Colombia and its Andean neighbors to the U.S. market has not changed dramatically. And there are even recent indications of a resurgence of drug-related violence as competition among the new trafficking gangs heats up. The Colombian model may have some superficial appeal, but it is doubtful whether that approach is a realistic answer to the problems now bedeviling Mexico.

Another option for Mexico is to attempt to return to the situation that existed under the long-governing PRI before the first PAN president, Vicente Fox, took office in 2000—and especially before Felipe Calderón became president in 2006. The PRI's approach amounted to a de facto policy of (relatively) peaceful coexistence with the cartels.

A return to the PRI-era policy of conditional appeasement was the essence of the proposal put forth in 2008 by Rubén Aguilar. Yet prospects for a successful deal along those lines are uncertain, even if Calderón or a successor would countenance it. The Mexican cartels are far more powerful than they were in earlier decades, and several of them seem intent on achieving not only dominance in the illegal drug trade but invulnerability from the authority of the

Mexican government. Reaching an agreement with such strong, violent actors would be a major challenge. It probably would buy Mexico only a precarious truce in any case. If the global (especially U.S.) prohibitionist policy regarding drugs remains intact, though, it may be the best—perhaps the only—available option.

The realization that such limited measures are not likely to dampen Mexico's violence and corruption in any significant way is causing critics of the drug war to propose the most radical option—legalizing drugs. Former president Fox has clearly reached that conclusion: "We should consider legalizing the production, distribution, and sale of drugs," he argued on his personal blog. He added a succinct, damning indictment of Calderón's drug policies, those his own administration pursued, and Washington's commitment to the policy status quo: "Radical prohibition strategies have never worked."[22]

A growing number of policy experts and political figures in the United States, Latin America, and around the world agree. Portugal's removal of criminal sanctions for the possession of small quantities of even hard drugs is serving as a model for "harm-reduction" reforms. Approval of medical marijuana initiatives in numerous states, and the relatively close November 2010 vote in California on a proposition to legalize marijuana, suggest that support for strict prohibition policies is waning in the United States as well. And the United States is the 800-pound gorilla in the international system when it comes to drug policy. Dramatic change is not likely to come in Mexico or any other drug source country as long as Washington adheres to a prohibition strategy.

Even most advocates of drug law reforms, though, shy away from endorsing the legalization of the production and distribution of drugs—especially heroin, cocaine, and other hard drugs. But it is the vast profits flowing into the coffers of the drug cartels because of the risk premium associated with operating in a black market that makes those organizations so powerful. The global trade in illegal drugs is conservatively estimated at more than $300 billion per year, and Mexico's share is something in excess of $30 billion. Vicente Fox is one of the few major political figures willing to confront the ugly economic realities of the drug trade. People should look at legalization, Fox argued, "as a strategy to strike at and break the economic structure that allows gangs to generate huge profits in their trade, which feeds corruption and increases their areas of power."[23]

Legalization, though, remains a highly controversial approach. Opponents contend that it would lead to soaring rates of drug use and a variety of other severe social pathologies. A 2010 DEA report states flatly: "Legalization of drugs will lead to increased use and increased levels of addiction." The report adds that it is "clear from history that periods of lax controls are accompanied by more drug abuse, and that periods of tight controls are accompanied by less drug abuse."[24]

The Portugal experience suggests that such an assessment is a gross oversimplification, and that fears of soaring drug use under a regime of legalization are probably overblown. Nevertheless, it will be an uphill battle to get Washington to abandon prohibition. And unless the United States does so, the factors that produce the horrific corruption and violence in Mexico will continue because of that country's proximity to the huge U.S. market and Mexico's financial stake in that market.

The deteriorating security conditions in Mexico, and the risk that the frightening violence there could become a routine feature of life in American communities as the cartels begin to flex their muscles north of the border, make it urgent that leaders of both countries reconsider their approach to the crisis. The current strategy is not working, and a wide-ranging policy debate in which all options are on the table is long overdue. The fire next door is growing—threatening to engulf our neighbor and endanger us.

1. Cast of Characters: The Mexican Drug Cartels and Their Leaders

The world of Mexico's drug cartels is a unique subculture with rules of its own. Mexican drug traffickers have long tried to strike a pose as cultural folk heroes for the masses. As *Time* correspondent Ioan Grillo points out, they "financed their own music genre—drug ballads—[and] nurtured their own fashion style-*buchones*, croco-dile-skin boots alongside designer bling." They also revere an early 20th century bandit, Jesús Malverde, "as a narco saint."[1]

In some places, that strategy has paid off handsomely. In Arteaga, a mountain town in the state of Michoacán, cartel boss Servando Gómez Martínez is widely admired for giving townspeople money for food, clothing, medical care, and other necessities. "He is a coun-try man just like us, who wears *huaraches*," (open-toed sandals) is how a farmer described one of the country's most notorious drug traffickers.[2] The same attitude was evident toward Amado Carrillo Fuentes, Mexico's leading trafficker in the 1990s, the man known as the Lord of the Skies because of his extensive use of aircraft for smuggling operations.[3] When Carrillo Fuentes died in 1997 (after a botched attempt at plastic surgery to alter his appearance to confound law enforcement agencies), residents of his home town, Guamuchilito, in Sinaloa state, lavished praise on him. Eulogies stressed that he was "a noble soul, loving with his family," a simple man who loved "enchiladas stuffed with red hot chiles."[4]

But that "simple man" worked hard to win the loyalty of ordinary citizens in Sinaloa. He was renowned for giving money, jewelry, expensive cars, and even cattle to hundreds of people. He even funded the building of the local church. Mexican politi-cal figures may have reviled him as a despicable, murderous drug dealer, but to the residents of Sinaloa, he was seen as a Robin Hood figure. Novelist and university professor Elmer Mendoza describes why Carrillo Fuentes and other drug lords enjoyed—and continue to enjoy—considerable public support in Sinaloa and other major trafficking states. "The narcos conferred jobs, then respectability and even honor." They "became community pillars, financing saint-day celebrations, paying for the bands and the beers. There was the aspect of the antihero about them."[5]

Mexican authorities are not at all pleased about the cultural glorification of drug traffickers. The drug ballads, *narcocorridos*, are a special sore point with President Felipe Calderón's government. One prominent band, Los Tigres del Norte, charged that Mexico's Interior Ministry pressured the organizers of the Lunas Entertainment Awards to urge the band not to play its most controversial song and prodded key radio stations to keep the song off the air. But trying to suppress *narcocorridos* seems a hopeless task. As musician and music historian Elijah Wald, who has written the most comprehensive treatment of the genre, points out, "it has been taken up by thousands of bands and singers in Mexico and the United States and now even as far away as Central and South America." He describes it as "a startling anachronism, a medieval ballad style whose Robin Hoods now arm themselves with automatic weapons and fly shipments of cocaine in 747s."[6]

There is little doubt that some of the songs romanticize the drug trade and its participants. A prominent song at the turn of the millennium was "What I Grew There in the Mountains," which assuredly did not refer to corn, wheat, or coffee. A few years later, a song titled "El Águila Blanco" (White Eagle) lauded Vicente Carrillo Fuentes, the head of the Juárez cartel. The song describes an incident in which police stop a group of suspected drug traffickers at a checkpoint. They release the men, though, when one of the smugglers gives the password "Carrillo Tours." The lyrics continue:

> "Why didn't you say so . . .
> Go with care
> And tell the White Eagle
> May he live for 100 years."[7]

The musical focus on drug trafficking and prominent drug lords has intensified in recent years. One tune in late 2009, "Queen of Queens," likened accused trafficker Sandra Ávila Beltrán to Cleopatra. As *USA Today* correspondent Chris Hawley points out: "In Mexican dance halls and record shops, smuggler music is hot: *Sixteen Drug Ballads,* by singer Larry Hernández, is one of the best-selling albums of the year. Another new album, *El Tigrillo Palma*, recounts the exploits of fugitive kingpin Joaquín "Chapo" Guzmán in such songs as 'The Power of Chapo.'"[8] Another band, El Compa Chuy, was nominated for a Grammy for their album, *El Niño de Oro*, which features smuggler ballads.

But it is not just the songs that glorify drug trafficking and drug traffickers that annoy the authorities. Another prominent theme of *narcocorridos* is the hypocrisy of officials who profess to want to stamp out the drug trade but are actually on the payrolls of the cartels. Two especially popular songs from a decade ago were "Por Debajo del Agua" (Under the Water—the Spanish equivalent of "under the table") and "El General" (The General), both of which skewered the rampant corruption in U.S.-sponsored anti-drug agencies in Mexico.[9]

Bitterness toward the United States, combined with affection for the drug lords, has been a *narcocorrido* theme for a long time. When Mexican authorities killed Pablo Acosta in 1987—at the time Mexico's leading trafficker—a song at his funeral perfectly combined both themes.

> Gone is Pablito, friend of the poor,
> Killed by the government
> In a world that shows no mercy
> For people like that.
> And the gringos,
> Laughing on their side of the river,
> Prayed for Pablito to die,
> Yet he had done nothing more
> Than give them what they want.[10]

The Traffickers and Their Groupies

It also appears that prominent Mexican (and even some American) celebrities, as well as politicians, congregate on the fringes of the cartels and the lifestyles they cultivate. A Mexican beauty queen created more than a little media scandal when she was seen in the company of known traffickers. And in December 2009, Texas-based *norteño* singer and accordion player Ramón Ayala was detained during a military raid on a gated community in Tepoztlán, just south of Mexico City. Three gunmen were killed in that raid, and 11 others, all suspected of working for the Beltrán Leyva cartel, were arrested. Ayala and his band, Los Bravos del Norte, were entertaining at an event in that upscale community. *Norteño* bands frequently sing about drug trafficking and are often reported to perform at drug traffickers' weddings, birthday parties for cartel leaders and members of their families, and other festive gatherings.

But Ayala is not an ordinary *norteño* singer; he is a two-time Latin Grammy winner, easily the most prominent entertainer to date to be implicated in the cartel culture. He has a large following on both sides of the U.S.-Mexico border. He is also considered a bit of a philanthropist, holding an annual Christmas festival in Hidalgo, Texas, which includes free food and a free gifts for children of poor families.

While being caught up in a drug raid may have been an embarrassment to Ayala, that was a mild problem compared with the fate of other *norteño* entertainers who have associated with the cartels. In 2006, a well-known singer, Valentín Elizalde, was shot to death along with his manager and driver shortly after a performance in Reynosa, just across the Rio Grande from McAllen, Texas. Perhaps not coincidentally, his killing followed the appearance of an online video that one cartel posted, to the accompanying refrains of one of Elizalde's songs, graphically showing the slaughter of rival gang members. A year later, an even more prominent performer, Sergio Gómez, a singer with the Grammy-nominated group K-Paz de la Sierra disappeared after a concert in Morelia, Michoacán. His mutilated corpse was found along a highway the following day.[11] That same month, vocalist Zayda Peña Arjona was killed by a gunmen while she was in a hospital recovering from previous gunshot wounds.

In August 2009, singer Carlos Ocaranza, a relative of Valentín Elizalde, left La Revancha bar in Guadalajara after giving a concert. Two men on a motorcycle approached him and fired multiple shots, hitting and killing him. Police found 12 casings from a 9mm pistol at the scene.[12]

Sergio Vega, another popular entertainer who used the stage name "El Shaka," suffered a similar fate in June 2010. Vega was driving to an engagement in Alhuey, Sinaloa, when a truck began to follow his Cadillac. According to his assistant, Sergio Montiel, who was a passenger in the car, the truck suddenly sped up and pulled alongside, whereupon an occupant opened fire, wounding

Vega and causing him to crash. Montiel climbed out of the wrecked vehicle and hid from the gunmen. Vega, though, could not do so and was dispatched with shots to the head.

Ironically, just hours before his death Vega was busy debunking rumors that he had been murdered. "It's happened to me for years now—someone tells a radio station or a newspaper that I've been killed or suffered an accident," he informed fans in a post on an entertainment website. "And then I have to call my dear mom, who has heart trouble, to reassure her."[13]

Vega was the seventh *narcocorrido* singer to die a violent death since early 2007. It has clearly become a high-risk occupation. The widespread opinion is that the cartels pay such singers substantial sums of money to write or perform ballads that tout the traffickers' achievements. But doing that puts the musicians at risk, since rival gangs take umbrage at seeing their mortal adversaries gain prominence and prestige. One way to humble a rival is to kill the singer or songwriter who has been, quite literally, singing the praises of the enemy organization or its leaders.

Given the growing body count of musical artists, singer Jenni Rivera was understandably shaken in early July 2010 when a user posted the message "You are the next one to die" on her Twitter page. Since the person used the name "Zeettas"—disturbingly similar to Zetas, the professional hitmen who once worked for the Gulf cartel and are now an independent trafficking operation—Rivera was inclined to take the threat seriously. Her own experiences added to that caution. A few weeks earlier, she had been caught in the middle of a shootout as she was beginning a concert in Tampico. Rivera recounted the episode, telling her fans later on Twitter that she had no choice but to take off her shoes and run so that she would not be hit by the bullets.[14] It had to go down as one of the shortest concerts on record.

Rogues or Psychopaths?

Oddly enough, many of the most powerful and ruthless drug lords and their henchmen seem to deliberately choose (or at least tolerate) innocent-sounding, and sometimes oddball, nicknames. Joaquin Guzmán, currently the country's most notorious trafficker, is widely known as "El Chapo" (Shorty) because of his modest, 5'6" height. Even stranger, some of the most cold-blooded, sadistic killers have benign, or even feminine, nicknames. Edgar Valdéz Villarreal, once the chief hit man for the Beltrán Leyva cartel and later a contender for its leadership position, is known as "La Barbie," an ultra-feminine moniker. Other professional killers go by such names as "Monkey," "Smurf," "Longhair," "Camel," "Nacho," and "Bunny Commander."[15]

Not all nicknames aim to sound innocent or cuddly, though. Trafficker Alfredo Beltrán Leyva, arrested by Mexican authorities in 2008, went by the name "El Mochomo," a large ant with an extremely painful bite that is found throughout northern Mexico. That nickname characterized both his personality and his treatment of anyone who got in his way. Iván Velázquez Caballero, a leading cartel enforcer, was widely known as "Taliban." Another enforcer has the nickname "Vulture."

In marked contrast to the eccentric street names of some of their competitors, the Zetas favor military-sounding designations—probably reflecting their origins as defectors from elite special-forces units in the Mexican army. Founding members had nicknames that started with a Z (the police radio code for "commander") followed by a number from 1 through 10. Later high-level commanders were given the Z designation, but with higher numbers. Operatives whose rank began with L were lieutenants—and with the higher numbers—junior enforcers or bodyguards.[16]

Throughout the world of the cartels, nicknames—even those that are humorous or bizarre—serve a serious purpose. They make it harder for police to track down drug gang suspects. Indeed, some members have multiple aliases to make investigations even more difficult.

And cuddly nicknames are merely a case of irony, given the ultra-vicious nature of these people. Take 38-year-old "La Barbie"—Edgar Valdéz Villarreal. He may have the blonde hair and blue eyes of the famous doll (which apparently is one reason why he originally got stuck with that label in high school), but this Barbie is the epitome of a cold-blooded killer. Authorities estimate that before his capture in August 2010, he was responsible for the executions of dozens, perhaps hundreds, of people, many of whom he personally dispatched. One homicide detective in Nuevo Laredo speculated: "I don't even think that he knows how many people he has killed."[17]

Unique among major Mexican traffickers, Valdéz Villarreal was born in Laredo, Texas, and grew up on the American side of the border. Also unlike most traffickers, who come from poverty-stricken backgrounds, Valdéz was the child of a middle-class family and enjoyed a comfortable upbringing. His sister was a law student, and his brother a successful, legitimate businessman. In his youth, he seemed like a typical American kid, even becoming a standout player on his high-school football team.

But during adolescence, Valdéz developed a taste for the expensive things in life and began to sell marijuana in the United States for Sinaloa cartel chieftain Joaquín Guzmán Loera (El Chapo). When a better offer came along, he broke with Guzmán and aligned himself with the Beltrán Leyva brothers, who had themselves split with Guzmán to form a rival cartel. Valdéz was especially valuable to the Beltrán Leyva organization, because with his fluent English he could often pass himself off as an American businessman. He first achieved public prominence in 2005 when he appeared on a YouTube video interrogating (and subsequently executing) four hitmen for the Zetas. Subsequent YouTube videos made him a major celebrity in Mexico—and in some Mexican-American communities in the United States. Those videos showed him as a model of success, surrounded by fancy cars and gorgeous women in posh settings.

At the time of his arrest, La Barbie was waging a bloody struggle to wrest control of the Beltrán Leyva cartel away from Hector, the last remaining Beltrán Leyva brother. Valdéz was apparently miffed that he was not given the leadership of the organization after Mexican troops killed boss Arturo Beltrán Leyva. Ironically, Valdéz's American upbringing, which had proven so valuable to his rise in the past, may have worked to his disadvantage when it came time to choose a successor to Arturo. In any case, the resulting turf fight in 2010 left hundreds dead (including a rising tally of innocent bystanders), and there was no evidence that the slaughter bothered the mild-faced La Barbie in the slightest.

If Valdéz did not fit the physical stereotype of a murderous enforcer for the drug cartels, a more recent contingent is even less typical. Some of the gangs have taken to hiring young, pretty women to conduct their hits. That technique was pioneered by Las Pantera (The Panthers), a group of women that worked with the Zetas when those gunmen served as the Gulf cartel's military arm. Many of the women would have dual assignments. They sought to entice or bribe military and civilian officials into cooperating with their employer, but failing that, they eliminated such individuals. The Panthers went to considerable lengths both to enhance their appeal and to vary their appearance to make subsequent police investigations more difficult. They would often change hair styles and color, makeup, and other factors, depending on the nature of their assignment.[18]

According to the comments of Rogelio Amaya, a member of La Línea, one of the Juárez cartel's enforcement units, about 30 young women had been hired and trained during the first half of 2010 to carry out such assignments. The rationale for using utterly atypical assassins is quite logical. "They're pretty, good-looking, to help mislead opponents," Amaya explains.[19] They're able to lull bodyguards and get much closer to their target than male killers normally could. Apparently, they've already been quite successful in their trade, killing several victims within the first few months that the new strategy was put in place.

It is difficult to overstate the prominence and power of the leading drug traffickers in Mexico. *Forbes* named Joaquín Guzmán Loera to its list of the world's richest individuals in early 2009. He came in at 701, with an estimated worth of $1 billion. He remained on that list of billionaires in late 2011.

Guzmán's life is a perverse Mexican equivalent of the Horatio Alger "rags to riches" stories so popular in the United States during the 19th and early 20th centuries. He came from a desperately poor background, and as a child, he even sold oranges on the street just to get enough money for his next meal. If he had amassed his fortune by building a legal business, he would likely be hailed today as one of the great entrepreneurs of his generation, not only in Mexico, but in the world. People would speak of him in the same breath as they do Bill Gates or Steve Jobs, or in the Mexican context, perhaps media mogul Carlos Slim. But Guzmán did not choose a legal business. And he has never been shy about using force against competitors to advance his position. *Wall Street Journal* correspondents David Luhnow and José De Córdoba aptly describe El Chapo as "part Al Capone and part Jesse James."[20]

The *Forbes* initial designation of Guzmán as a member of the global moneyed elite infuriated President Calderón. "Magazines are not only attacking and lying about the situation in Mexico but are also praising criminals," he fumed.[21] *Time* managed to irritate Mexico's political establishment further when that magazine included Guzmán in its "*Time* 100" list of powerful figures, noting that, unfortunately, criminals are sometimes quite influential in today's world. The Mexican president and his allies were irritated again with *Forbes* in November 2009 when the magazine placed Guzmán at number 41 on its list of the world's 67 most powerful people. That designation put him ahead of several heads of state, including Venezuelan president Hugo Chávez—number 67—and French president Nicolas Sarkozy—number 56.

But as much as Calderón and other Mexican political leaders might accuse the U.S. media of hyping the prominence of the drug cartels, the reality is that they have become very powerful organizations. Don Thornhill, a Drug Enforcement Administration agent who tracked Guzmán for years after the trafficker's escape from prison in 2001, conceded that "he's almost an iconic figure in the underworld."[22]

The Principal Cartels: An Ever-Changing Roster

There are approximately a dozen drug trafficking organizations that are significant players in Mexico.[23] And several of them—especially the Sinaloa cartel, the Tijuana cartel, the Juárez cartel, and the Zetas—control major swaths of territory.[24] But it is an ever-shifting competitive environment. During the early years of the 21st century, two organizations, the Gulf cartel and the Sinaloa cartel (which was a coalition of several smaller drug trafficking operations in western Mexico), gradually achieved a status at least a cut above their older competitors—and became the initial principal adversaries of President Felipe Calderón's government when he took office in December 2006.

Major changes have taken place in the power rankings during the years of Calderón's administration. The Gulf cartel has slipped badly, especially in the past two years, as the organization's one-time enforcement arm, the Zetas, became a devastating competitor. Indeed, the Zetas are the fastest-rising trafficking operation, impinging on the territories of several other trafficking operations—not just the Gulf cartel.

Another organization, La Familia, enjoyed a meteoric rise from 2006 to 2010 but has since lost its top two leaders and split into factions. One of those factions, now known as the Knights Templar,

27

openly challenges the remnant of La Familia, as well as other splinter groups in La Familia's home base, the western Mexican state of Michoacán.[25]

Such a shift in the hierarchy of power and influence among the various cartels is nothing new. To reach their positions, the current leading players had to displace other once-dominant players. And they, in turn, are now under siege by ambitious competitors. That ebb and flow of power underscores the constantly changing nature of the illegal drug trade and the position of the major participants.

Before the mid to late 1980s, Mexican drug traffickers were secondary players—largely middle men—in the hemispheric drug trade, with the exception of the cultivation and distribution of marijuana, where they had long controlled a sizable chunk of that commerce.[26] There were certainly some significant drug capos, most notably Pablo Acosta, the squint-eyed, scar-faced chieftain who established control over marijuana smuggling routes in a major swath of territory along the border near Ciudad Juárez.[27] Until his death in a shootout with law enforcement agents in 1987, Acosta was considered both the most successful, and perhaps the most ruthless, capo in Mexico. He was also a mentor to the man widely regarded as the leading drug lord of the 1990s, Amado Carrillo Fuentes.

The flow of other drugs, though, especially cocaine, was still dominated by the Colombians, principally the powerful Cali and Medellín cartels. Furthermore, the Colombian traffickers directed most of their product through the Caribbean and south Florida for distribution to the U.S. market. Mexico was merely a secondary, supplementary route.

That situation changed in the late 1980s and early 1990s with Washington's intensified effort to shut down the Caribbean pipelines. Those efforts were only partially successful, but they raised the cost and inconvenience to the Colombian cartels enough that they began to focus more on Mexico as an important trafficking route.[28] That was a classic case of the "balloon," or "push-down, pop-up" effect, which has characterized the U.S.-led war on drugs over the decades. The suppression of the trade in one area merely leads to a surge of drug production or trafficking in another region. The enormous profitability of illicit drugs—precisely because of the risk factor of their illegality—means that participants in the trade will go to great lengths to obtain product and get it to market. And since the United States is such a large consumer market for illegal drugs, the Mexican organizations were well positioned geographically to gain control of key trafficking routes when the Colombian cartels encountered difficulties in their usual routes through the Caribbean.

There also was a gradual change in payment for the Mexican wholesale distributors during this period. Instead of paying the Mexican gangs almost exclusively in cash, the Colombians began to provide part (usually about half) of that payment in drugs—increasingly at the insistence of their Mexican partners. That innovation whetted the interest of the Mexican traffickers in the retail end of the business—especially as it pertained to the voracious consumers next door in the United States.

Juan García Abrego, the head of the Gulf cartel until his arrest in 1995, pioneered that change, and his bargaining position was strong. Not only was the distribution route through Mexico direct and convenient, but the traffickers had such reliable ties to government officials that they could virtually guarantee safe passage for shipments.[29] The payment in drugs became a de facto profit-sharing arrangement, since the Mexican traffickers were able to sell those drugs in the United States and generate their own revenue flows. Consequently, the financial clout of the Mexican trafficking organizations grew rapidly. Inadvertently, the Colombians had helped to fund powerful new competitors.

If the Medellín and Cali cartels had survived, there might have been a ferocious struggle between them and the upstart Mexican organizations. But the Colombian government's crackdown on those two groups led to their demise by the mid and late 1990s. Their successors were too small to compete effectively with the Mexicans for long. Instead, in a role reversal, Colombian participants in the drug trade now became the junior partners of Mexico's cartels. In fact, their role was largely confined to providing the initial product. The more profitable wholesale and retail sectors were now mostly out of their hands.

During the 1990s, five Mexican cartels dominated the increasingly profitable cocaine trade, as well as the heroin and marijuana trade.[30] Probably the most powerful group was the Caro Quintero organization (the Sonora cartel), centered in the northern state of Sonora and headed by Miguel Caro Quintero. In some ways, it was the most traditional of the cartels, since its primary source of income remained the marijuana trade. It both cultivated marijuana in numerous locations in the interior of Mexico and developed a sophisticated internal supply and distribution chain to transport bales of the drug to (and sometimes over) the U.S. border, primarily using a fleet of small planes.

But a key change occurred during the late 1990s, when the cartel branched into the cocaine distribution business. The breakthrough came when the organization managed to bribe Mario Villanueva, the governor of Quintana Roo. Having him on the payroll gave the Caro-Quintero cartel control over a major portion of cocaine imports coming from Colombia through Cancún, Quintana Roo's main port. That coup, though, proved to be the high-water mark for the cartel. Mexican authorities arrested both Miguel Caro Quintero and Governor Villanueva in 2001, and the organization soon began to unravel.

The primary beneficiary of the Sonora group's troubles was the Gulf cartel. That organization already had a considerable presence in the northern states of Tamaulipas and Nuevo León. The Gulf cartel, under the leadership of Juan García Abrego until his arrest in 1995, and then under Osiel Cárdenas until his apprehension in 2003, gradually but inexorably expanded its turf. The organization's new ability to gain control of the cocaine flow coming through Cancún gave the cartel added prestige and power. Until the blows to the Sonora cartel, though, the Gulf cartel was smaller and less influential than three other groups—the Juárez cartel (the Carrillo Fuentes organization), the Tijuana cartel (run by the Arellano Félix family), and the Sinaloa cartel. And the Gulf cartel remained locked in a fierce rivalry with those organizations even with the gains they had achieved at the expense of the Caro Quintero faction.

Indeed, in the late 1990s and the beginning of the 21st century, both the Juárez and Tijuana cartels seemed to be emerging as the most powerful players. Their styles, though, were a study in contrasts. Under the leadership of Amado Carrillo Fuentes until his death in 1997, and after that led by his brother Vicente, the Juárez cartel quite deliberately imitated the methods of the Cali cartel in Colombia. The group developed elaborate measures to increase both security and efficiency, including using secure telephones, sophisticated codes, and highly coordinated organizational structures. Among other techniques, the cartel specialized in decentralization and compartmentalization of functions. That strategy included developing an extensive network of small drug operations within Mexico focused on different aspects of the trafficking business.

The cartel exhibited one other prominent characteristic. The Juárez organization preferred to achieve results through negotiations with rivals rather than wage all-out battles, especially under Amado Carrillo Fuentes.[31] Vicente was less adept—and perhaps less committed—to that strategy, but the Juárez cartel was, on balance, probably the least violent of the principal trafficking organizations. That history is somewhat ironic, since the Juárez organization is now regarded as one of the most ruthless and violent factions.

A reputation for ruthlessness existed for the Tijuana and Sinaloa cartels from the outset. The Arellano Félix brothers did not spurn peaceful ways of doing business when that furthered their objectives. In fact, the Tijuana cartel pioneered the practice of "leasing" portions of its claimed turf to other trafficking organizations in exchange for fees or tolls.[32] But what started out as a rational, even wise, way of dealing with competitors broke down badly in the 1990s and the following years. Some organizations balked at paying the ever-escalating charges, and when they did, the Tijuana cartel showed that it was more than willing to use violence to enforce its edicts. The Arellano Félix brothers created an extensive security apparatus, both to enforce loyalty within the organization and to collect the tolls.

The Tijuana cartel quickly became notorious for the extent and severity of its violence. It was one of the first cartels to repeatedly violate widely held taboos among the drug kingpins–for example, the taboo against attacking innocent family members of rival gangs. Two major incidents emphasized how much the Tijuana organization viewed that limitation with contempt.

The first occurred at the beginning of the early 1990s and involved a growing feud with El Chapo Guzmán and his business partner, Héctor Palma. Rafael Clavel, a Venezuelan working for the Arellano Félix organization, apparently seduced Palma's wife and took her to San Francisco. There she gave him access to some $7 million that belonged to Guzmán and her husband. Clavel's gratitude for this bonanza was short-lived. A few days after the romantic sojourn in the City by the Bay, Palma received a present—his wife's severed head in a cooler. That may have been the earliest case in which a drug gang used decapitation to terrorize a rival; it has since become a major trademark of conflicts between the cartels. Not content with that atrocity, Clavel threw two of Palma's young children off a bridge.[33]

If the gruesome treatment of the Palma family was not enough to establish the Arellano Félix gang's reputation for utter barbarity, it was reinforced in September 1998, when gunmen conducted the so-called Ensenada massacre. The target of the attack on that occasion was Fermín Castro, known to authorities as "The Ice Man" for his alleged role in the trafficking of methamphetamine. Castro seemed to be affiliated with the Arellano Félix operation, but was suspected of considering a defection to another cartel. In any case, attackers mounted a predawn assault, dragging Castro and 20 members of his extended family out of their beds and shooting them execution style. The victims included eight children.[34] During the next few years, the Tijuana cartel became even more blatantly violent, making numerous attacks on other gangs—and increasingly on any Mexican police that they could not bribe or intimidate.

The reputation for not playing by established, although implicit, rules was almost certainly a key reason why the government of President Vicente Fox, who took office in 2000, seemed to focus most of its efforts on bringing down the Tijuana cartel, while doing far less against other trafficking organizations. Mexican police killed Ramón Arellano Félix in 2002 and apprehended his brother, Benjamín, later that year. Authorities also arrested nearly another 2,000 cartel operatives between 2001 and 2005.[35] Those losses significantly weakened the Tijuana cartel and set in motion a ruthless internal struggle for control and bloody turf fights, especially with the Sinaloa cartel.

And the fast-rising Sinaloa gang was not far behind its rival in terms of brutality. Although the principal leader of that organization, El Chapo Guzmán, was arrested in 1993, he ran the organization about as effectively from prison as he did when he was on the outside. And after his celebrated escape in 2001 (supposedly hidden in a laundry cart), he moved aggressively against the Arellano Félix group. His offensive picked up steam after the demise of Ramón and the capture of Benjamín. The Sinaloa leadership saw the Tijuana cartel as a wounded and vulnerable competitor, and they sought to seize as much advantage as possible.

Although Guzmán was an especially ruthless kingpin, he was also a very adept innovator when it came to the business side of the drug trade. Not only did he intensify direct connections with Colombian suppliers, which both assured a more reliable flow of product for his organization and made it more difficult for rivals to get access, Guzmán also worked the angles regarding the domestic phase of the trafficking business. He especially countered the Fox administration's efforts to disrupt the drug trade, both by making his operations more mobile, so that they needed less protection, and by expanding his campaign to develop an extensive network of corrupt local officials.[36] The latter tactic meant that even when portions of the federal government's bureaucracy were characterized by brief episodes of reduced corruption, Guzmán's hirelings at the state and local levels could usually circumvent Mexico City's anti-drug measures with ease.

The Sinaloa cartel also worked diligently to open new product lines. During the 1990s, a smaller trafficking organization in northwest Mexico, headed by Jesús Amezcua and his brothers, began using contacts that he had developed in East Asia to import large quantities of the precursor chemicals needed for the production of methamphetamine, a drug that was becoming popular in the United States. The Amezcua brothers developed an impressive supply chain that ran from their production facilities in the Sierra Madre region in western Mexico, where the chemicals were converted into a saleable product, to distribution centers in the border cities of Tijuana and Mexicali. This move, however, meant an intrusion onto the turf of the Tijuana cartel.

Guzmán's Sinaloa cartel saw huge new profit-making potential in the methamphetamine trade and moved to gain control. Ultimately, the Sinaloa organization absorbed or displaced the Amezcua operation, and by the early years of the new century had become the principal player in that trade. Guzmán assigned one of his top allies, Ignacio "Nacho" Coronel, to take charge and professionalize the methamphetamine trafficking business. Coronel was so successful in his assignment that he became known as the "king of ice" or "king of crystal." He made the Sinaloa cartel utterly dominant in the methamphetamine trade until his death in a shootout with Mexican federal authorities in the summer of 2010.

The fighting between the Sinaloa and Tijuana gangs produced some of the worst violence Mexico had ever seen in the drug wars before the Calderón years. During the period between 2002 and

2006, the maneuvering for advantage also became increasingly complex. The bloodiest turf fight centered on securing control of Nuevo Laredo, one of the biggest single-access portals to the United States. Until late 2002, the Tijuana cartel, in alliance with two smaller local trafficking operations, controlled most of the illegal drugs flowing through the city. But the weakening of the Tijuana cartel following the removal of the Arellano Félix brothers created a power vacuum.

Osiel Cárdenas's Gulf cartel made the first move to try to displace the Tijuana organization, but that effort faltered when Cárdenas was arrested. Ever the skilled opportunist, Guzmán then sought to move in, taking advantage of the temporary disarray of his two main rivals. He might have succeeded rather easily had not Cárdenas and Benjamín Arellano Félix not formed a strategic alliance while in prison.[37] The struggle for control of the trafficking routes through Nuevo Laredo then became more complex, and Guzmán seemed outgunned. He responded, though, by forming a competing alliance between his Sinaloa cartel and the Juárez cartel. The war between those two coalitions caused the violence in Nuevo Laredo to explode in the next few years (see chapter 2), until a peace accord of sorts was reached.

Another factor causing a steep rise in the level of violence was the emergence of more professional enforcers for the rival blocs. The Gulf and Sinaloa organizations were the earliest to develop sophisticated enforcement units. Gulf leaders bribed members of elite special forces in Mexico's military to desert the government and pursue the much more lucrative option of being enforcers for the cartel. Those military deserters became the feared Zetas, and that organization quickly acquired new recruits from other Mexican security agencies. Indeed, Gulf and Zeta leaders focused on enticing personnel who had military training and experience. The Zetas became the most feared enforcement unit and contributed greatly to the Gulf cartel's growing power—until they turned against their employer in late 2008 and early 2009. Just as serving as hit men for drug traffickers was more profitable than being soldiers for the Mexican government, being traffickers in their own right proved to be more profitable—and therefore irresistibly tempting—for the Zetas.

Although the Zetas became the most notorious and effective killers, other cartels did not stand idly by while the Gulf cartel upped the ante regarding the professionalization of intimidation and violence. The Sinaloa cartel quickly responded by developing its own group of hitmen, the Negroes. The Juárez cartel lagged a bit in the lethality competition, but that group eventually professionalized its own enforcement arm, called La Línea, and later gave some assignments to competing operatives in the Ciudad Juárez region—operatives who became known as Barrio Azteca.

The growing reliance on paramilitary units gave the most violence-prone elements of the various cartels more influence than they had exercised in earlier eras. In addition, the arrests of senior (and somewhat more conciliatory) leaders such as Osiel Cárdenas created power vacuums filled by younger traffickers who lacked both the long-standing relationships with competitors that kept the rivalries within at least some bounds and who were temperamentally less inclined to compromise. All of those factors led to the increase in violence during the first decade of the 21st century–even before the additional surge in response to Felipe Calderón's broad offensive against the cartels.

It would be a mistake, though, to assume that during the Fox administration the trafficking organizations solely resorted to violence, combined with the bribery of government officials, to secure their power. They also launched public-relations offensives toward the populations in their respective base areas. The Sinaloa and Gulf cartels were especially astute at using that tactic. They provided gifts and charitable assistance to residents in their core regions, at a minimum to procure their silence when the authorities sought information on cartel activities. In several cases, cartel leaders funded multimillion dollar projects to build hospitals, schools, recreation centers, and facilities to provide better water and sanitation. Understandably, that generosity created a considerable amount of gratitude on the part of poverty-stricken populations, and much of that good will persists, despite the soaring violence and increasingly sadistic killings that have taken place since 2006.

In the power struggles of the late 1990s and early 21st century, the Gulf and Sinaloa cartels emerged as the most powerful players, eclipsing their Juárez and Tijuana competitors—and even more so, several smaller, largely local trafficking operations. It is clear, though, that the Gulf cartel's stature has badly eroded, and the Sinaloa cartel is under siege from multiple rivals. Just as those cartels took

advantage of government crackdowns that weakened powerful players such as the Arellano Félix and Juárez cartels, new
rivals are taking advantage of the Calderón administration's campaigns against leading organizations—especially the government's
zferocious attacks on the Gulf cartel. Several top Gulf figures
have been arrested or killed since the current offensive began in
December 2006.

The main problem for the Sinaloa cartel was a split that emerged
between Guzmán and a long-time lieutenant, Arturo Beltrán Leyva,
alias "El Barbas" (The Beard), in 2008. Much of the violence in and
around the state of Sinaloa appeared to reflect feuding between the
Sinaloa cartel and that splinter group, the Beltrán Leyva organization, rather than the older turf fight between the Sinaloa and Gulf
cartels.[38] However, the main challenge to Guzmán appears to have
receded following the death of Arturo Beltrán Leyva in a shootout
with the Mexican military in December 2009. Indeed, there seemed
to be as much factional fighting within the Beltrán Leyva cartel itself
during 2010 and early 2011 as there was between that group and the
Sinaloa organization.

The splintering of the Gulf Cartel seems to be even more pronounced and devastating than the factionalism in Sinaloa, with the
organization's one-time unit of enforcers, the Zetas, emerging as an
independent trafficking operation. Indeed, by the end of 2011 the
Zetas had emerged as a player comparable in power to the Sinaloa
cartel, thereby eclipsing the Gulf cartel and other groups.

The evolution of the Zetas demonstrates both the complexity of Mexico's drug trade and the many pitfalls (if not outright
futility) of trying to suppress it. Heriberto Lazcano, alias "The
Executioner," the leader of the Zetas, enlisted in the military as a
young man and was later selected to be a member of Mexico's elite
and highly trained Special Forces Airmobile Groups (GAFEs). That
unit, created in the mid-1990s, received enhanced training from
U.S. and other foreign instructors (primarily Guatemala's Kabiles,
an elite counter-insurgency unit notorious for its human rights
violations against Guatemalan peasants). Most training from
U.S. instructors came from the 7th Special Forces Group, the
"Snake Eaters," at Fort Bragg, North Carolina. According to Craig
Deere, a former special-forces commander and now a professor at
the National Defense University, more than 500 GAFE personnel

probably went through the Fort Bragg program.[39] The training included instruction in aerial assaults, rapid deployment, ambushes, intelligence collection, and sophisticated communications. The GAFEs then were deployed to battle the drug gangs, especially the Gulf cartel, in northern Mexico near the U.S. border.

Unfortunately, the financial incentives that the Gulf cartel was able to offer proved irresistible. Lazcano and other GAFE personnel defected en masse. Estimates of the number of defectors vary, but the total could be as high as 200. In a final insult to their former employer, the defectors named their new drug army Los Zetas, after a code designation that the Mexican military used for its units. Ironically, the Mexican and U.S. militaries trained the people who would become the most notorious and effective hit men in Mexico's drug wars. That special training made them especially lethal—and therefore an especially valuable asset—in those struggles.

Because they were ex-military, the Zetas have also been extraordinarily successful in inducing other soldiers to defect to their ranks. The Mexican army had suffered more than 99,000 desertions during the administration of Vicente Fox, and a sizable percentage of that number ended up in the ranks of the Zetas or other enforcement arms of the various drug cartels.[40] And that pace of defections has not diminished since the Fox years. Furthermore, the GAFE desertion rate—some 25 percent—was high even by Mexican military standards. None of this comes as a surprise to Craig Deere. The Mexican government doesn't pay those elite troops nearly enough, he states bluntly. "I'm not saying that they have to pay as much as the cartels," but such forces "must be paid decently if they aren't going to be susceptible to corruption."[41]

Since the late 1990s, the Zetas have set up several training camps of their own. There, army defectors, as well as former federal, state, and local police officers, have their skills honed. And the lethality that the Zetas have shown confirms that they've learned their lessons all too well.

But the same huge financial incentives that caused Zeta personnel to defect from law enforcement to the drug trade led them to abandon their Gulf cartel employer and go into business for themselves. The Gulf cartel is reacting furiously to what it considers a betrayal. Indeed, in early 2010, it appeared to forge an alliance (dubbed the New Federation) with two of its previous mortal adversaries,

La Familia and the Sinaloa cartel, in a campaign to crush the Zetas in the state of Tamaulipas, through which pass some of the most valuable trafficking routes. That alliance, shaky from the beginning, has apparently proven insufficient to preserve the Gulf cartel's position. By the summer of 2011, the Zetas were clearly the dominant trafficking organization in Tamaulipas. Indeed, that cartel's clout there rivaled that of both the state and national governments.

The Zetas rise to power threatens the operations of all three incumbent trafficking groups in Tamaulipas and elsewhere in northern Mexico. Even though there is no love lost among the three members of the new alliance—and that cooperation will likely not last—they are held together by that most classic of factors binding diverse allies: a common enemy. "The Zetas have become too powerful," College of William and Mary professor George Grayson, a long-time expert on Mexico, concludes. "The Zetas have taken over probably 70 to 80 percent of Tamaulipas. The Gulf cartel simply couldn't handle the Zetas by themselves."[42] The willingness of the three trafficking rivals to make common cause against a more threatening interloper suggests a degree of sophistication more common to effective political organizations and nation states rather than criminal gangs. That alliance also was a prelude to an upsurge in fighting that threatened to make Tamaulipas into the kind of bloody battleground that such places as Ciudad Juárez and Tijuana had already become.

The Weirdest Group: La Familia

The Zetas are not the only trafficking organization to have appeared on the scene in recent years. A relative newcomer—and definitely the strangest outfit—was La Familia.[43] That group first burst on the scene in 2006 with a gruesome incident, when they rolled the severed heads of five rival traffickers across the dance floor in a disco in western Mexico.[44] Subsequently, La Familia became a serious competitor to both the Gulf and Sinaloa cartels, as well as some smaller operations. It was especially prominent in President Calderón's home state, Michoacán. At the height of its power, in 2009 and 2010, La Familia reportedly employed several thousand people, paying them far more than they could earn in alternative occupations.

The organization was more notable for its other characteristics, though. It emerged as one of the more violent players in an already especially violent industry, and it did not flinch from initiating major assaults on police and military forces. An episode in July 2009 was typical of La Familia's behavior: within hours after federal police arrested the cartel's number-two leader, La Familia gunmen launched a series of bloody attacks throughout Michoacán and neighboring states against the authorities, ultimately killing 18 law enforcement agents (see chapter 2).

Far more than most of its competitors, however, La Familia tried to seize the moral high ground in its fight with Mexican authorities and rival cartels. Murders of competitors were portrayed as cases of "divine justice."[45] Just hours after the July attacks subsided, a caller claiming to be one of the organization's capos, Servando Gómez, contacted a Michoacán television news program and asserted that the attacks were justifiable defensive measures. "Our fight is with the federal police because they are attacking our families," the caller insisted. "If someone attacks my father, my mother or my brother, then they are going to hear from me."[46]

Such a brazen use of the media became a La Familia trademark. The cartel even bought ads in newspapers and gave an interview to a leading Mexican magazine. One marked aspect of the cartel's effort to portray itself as a moral organization was the stress on its own alleged purity. Although they trafficked in drugs, members insisted that they abstained from using drugs (as well as alcohol) themselves and were dedicated to the betterment of their families and communities. In fact, spokesmen for La Familia told the media that the organization's primary aim was to protect Michoacán from the Zetas.

Even more than the other drug trafficking organizations, La Familia provided an array of social welfare services in Michoacán— which, whatever their other motives, was a good public-relations strategy. Ricardo Ravelo, an investigative journalist based in Mexico City, describes that approach. "It's a cartel, but it also has a social component, as if to say: 'We're not bad. We also worry about people.'"[47] Rafael Pequeño García, chief of anti-drug operations in Mexico's Public Security Ministry, conceded that La Familia filled a vacuum in social services throughout Michoacán, and increasingly in other portions of the country. "When you needed help, you didn't go to the government. You went to the narcos," he stated.[48]

La Familia members even claimed to be evangelical Christians, and new members had to undergo a program of rigorous religious indoctrination. But if so, they were evangelical Christians of a very odd sort. Members were required to study a special supplement to the Bible authored by the cartel's founder, Nazario Moreno González, whose alias was "El Más Loco" (The Craziest One). That's a rather unusual appellation for someone who purports to be a religious leader, but it did not seem to bother La Familia's rank-and-file members. Indeed, with Moreno's death during a shootout with Mexican authorities in December 2010, there is a possibility that he may have become a martyr for the organization and its followers.

Moreno's writings themselves are a weird amalgam of Christianity and Mexican political populism.[49] In 2008, federal agents seized a copy of Moreno's book, *Pensiamientos* (*Thoughts*), which had become La Familia's bible. Passages printed by various newspapers illustrated that unusual mixture of theology and peasant revolutionary ideology. One Moreno passage emphasized the former: "I ask God for strength and he gives me challenges that make me strong; I ask him for wisdom and he gives me problems to resolve; I ask him for prosperity and he gives me a brain and muscles to do work." Yet, later in those same writings, he thundered revolutionary slogans, such as "it is better to be a master of one peso than a slave of two; it is better to die fighting than on your knees and humiliated."[50]

For all their cultural posturing, including cultivating images of modern-day Robin Hoods, most drug kingpins and their followers have remained, first and foremost, economic actors, not quasi-religious figures—although La Familia appeared to be at least a partial exception. Ioan Grillo noted that the effort by La Familia "to forge their own religious sect is new, proof of a cultural autonomy to match their fearsome ability to defy Mexico City and Washington with impunity."[51] There were indications that the cartel was even trying to establish itself as a moral and institutional rival to the Catholic Church. Pequeño García charged that La Familia was shrewdly trying to exploit the religious nature of the Mexican people, seeking to become "a parallel institution [to the Church] to satisfy the social demands of the people." Parish priest Father Miguel López, though, scorned the cartel's religious trappings: "It's just something they have applied to themselves, like varnish."[52] But it seemed to be a bit more than that. Among its other actions, La Familia helped finance the building of evangelical Protestant churches in Michoacán.[53] That made La Familia a rival of the Catholic Church in a very direct sense!

For all of its quasi-religious qualities, La Familia was quite sophisticated about its economic activities. It was the first cartel to establish a horizontal business structure, with branch "offices"[54] throughout the country.[55] It also became a commercial conglomerate. According to a Michoacán state intelligence agent, the group not only trafficked in drugs, it was also involved in "bootlegging, kidnapping, and even hotels, informal car lots, real estate sales, [and] bars."[56]

The Mexican government was elated following the death of Moreno González. And for a time it appeared that the celebration might be warranted, as La Familia hung banners throughout Michoacán in early January 2011 announcing that the cartel was disbanding. However, as with everything else involving that group, the reality appears to be much less predictable. Just weeks after the appearance of the banners proclaiming the demise of La Familia, new banners appeared announcing a previously unknown gang, the Knights Templar.[57]

Some observers quickly concluded that the Knights Templar was merely La Familia under a different name. The very choice of that name reinforced the suspicion, since it so perfectly corresponded with La Familia's self-proclaimed status as religious protectors. Indeed, the Knights insisted that they would "be carrying out here the altruistic activities previously provided" by La Familia. "We will be at the service of the people of Michoacán," the banners pledged, with a commitment to, among other goals, "protect the state" from depredations by "rival organizations."[58]

Subsequent evidence indicated that the Knights Templar was not just a new name for La Familia. Instead, it seemed that, upon the death of Moreno González, the cartel began to splinter into several factions. One of those factions was the rump La Familia operation headed by Moreno Gonzalez's right-hand man, José de Jesús Méndez, known as "El Chango" (The Monkey). The principal rival faction was directed by Servando "La Tuta" Gómez Martínez, and that's the group that took the name Knights Templar.

Fighting between operatives loyal to El Chango and those who followed Gomez Martínez became especially nasty during the spring and summer of 2011. In June alone, some 50 bodies, killed execution style, showed up in Michoacán. A majority of them had signs left on them by the Knights Templar.[59] With El Chango's capture on June 21, 2011, by Mexican federal police, the future of La Familia became more uncertain than ever. In any case, there appear to be several candidates eager to erode or take over the cartel's profitable and strategic Michoacán home base.

Beyond Gangs: Sophisticated Business Enterprises

Most of the surviving cartels in Mexico are sophisticated business enterprises. Reuters correspondent Robin Emmott describes their operations: "The organizations have the equivalent of chief executives and accountants. They also use outsourcing and run offices to coordinate logistics, money laundering, and murders. . . . As in legitimate commerce, the gangs employ business models and strategic planning to manage and expand their operations, make acquisitions and seek alliances."[60]

The Gulf cartel exhibits many of those characteristics. Mexican officials contend that the cartel is operationally split into three divisions. One handles international drug distribution and logistics; another is in charge of finances and money laundering; the third division (until recently, the notorious Zetas) deals with security and enforcement. For obvious reasons (the dangers associated with operating in a volatile, illegal business environment), the Gulf cartel's security and enforcement personnel have an importance—and acquire far more internal power and influence—than do their counterparts in legitimate businesses. Indeed, in the case of the Zetas, by late 2008 and early 2009 they had become too powerful to remain under the Gulf cartel's control.

The Barrio Azteca (which has affiliates in both Mexico and the United States whose members serve as contract killers for the Juárez cartel) and the Zetas show impressive degrees of internal organization, specialization, and sophistication. As the *Washington Post* reported, some of Barrio Azteca's strikes were "brazen ambushes involving multiple chase cars, coded radio communications, coordinated blocking maneuvers and disciplined firepower by masked gunmen in body armor. Afterward, the assassins vanish, back to safe houses in the Juárez barrios or across the bridge into El Paso."

In short, it is a very professional operation. David Cuthbertson, special agent in charge of the FBI's El Paso office, notes the extent of specialization, with the hit squads having "surveillance people, intel people, and shooters."[61] Oddly, they don't seem to demand a high price for their services. DEA intelligence suggests that some hits are made for as little as $100.

The cartels have become so potent that members routinely conduct business even while in prison. *New York Times* correspondent Marc Lacey notes: "Mexico's prisons, as described by inmates and insiders and viewed during several visits, are places where drug traffickers find a new base of operations for their criminal enterprises, recruit underlings, and bribe their way out for the right price."[62] Jail breaks are so frequent as to be almost routine. In early August 2009, a suspected trafficker in a Sinaloa prison disappeared during a party (complete with a band) held for the inmates. Perhaps the most famous episode occurred in 2001 when Joaquin Guzmán made his escape by being smuggled out in a prison laundry cart. He was already one of Mexico's top traffickers, and after his prison break, he became the country's most-wanted fugitive.

Drug traffickers typically are celebrities in prison, with other inmates becoming their eager followers. Even guards sometimes become their employees. Cartel leaders stay in contact with operatives on the outside by using newly released inmates as couriers. At least, that was the most common method until the last few years. Now, they usually just use cell phones.

Lacey describes the situation in one prison where many of the top drug lords are held. "The prisoners are a privileged lot, wearing designer clothing and enjoying special privileges ranging from frequent visits by girlfriends to big-screen televisions in their spacious cells."[63] Not exactly what one would call doing hard time. Pedro Arellano, an expert on Mexico's prisons, states succinctly: "The authorities no longer control the prisons—the drug lords do."[64]

These are the people and organizations that have turned significant portions of Mexico into killing fields. And they now pose a major challenge to the authority of the Mexican government and are creating major worries in neighboring countries. That concern is growing in the United States, but the uneasiness is even more pronounced—for very good reasons—in the fragile states of Central America.

2. Calderón's War and the Surge of Casualties

Rodolfo Torre Cantú, the nominee of Mexico's Institutional Revolutionary Party (PRI), was the odds-on favorite to be the next governor of the northern border state of Tamaulipas in the July 2010 elections. Public opinion polls gave him a massive lead—65 percent to his nearest opponent's 31 percent. A rally on June 25, 2010, attracted some 15,000 wildly enthusiastic supporters, who were especially animated when he called for improved security against the rampaging drug cartels.

Just three days later, Torre Cantú became a victim of Mexico's skyrocketing drug violence. Gunmen ambushed his motorcade on the road to the airport near Ciudad Victoria, the state capital. One vehicle blocked the motorcade's path while others cut off any retreat, thereby creating a perfect free-fire zone. Multiple attackers then sent a hail of bullets into their helpless target, killing Torre Cantú as well as several aides and bodyguards.[1]

Except for the prominence of the victim, though, the incident was typical of the violence that has claimed at least 47,000 lives—and according to some estimates, 51,000 lives—since President Felipe Calderón decided in December 2006 to wage a military-led offensive to crush the drug cartels. Not only is the overall level of killings alarming, but the trend is ominous. The number of killings in 2010 was a stunning 60 percent higher than during the previous record year, 2009.[2] The 2010 slaughter reached a crescendo in early June, when nearly 170 people perished in just a five-day period—but the rest of the year was not much better.

Matters did not improve during 2011. On January 11, 2012, the Attorney General's Office (AGO) in Mexico City released the latest casualty figures in the government's war against the drug cartels. During the first nine months of 2011 alone, 12,903 people died in the violence, compared with 11,583 during the same period in 2010.

Thus, not only was the carnage taking place at an alarming pace, but the annual toll was still getting worse. According to the Mexican government, though, the news was actually somewhat encouraging. Why? Because, as the AGO statement stressed: "It's the first year (since 2006) that the homicide rate *increase* has been lower compared with previous years" (emphasis added).[3] In other words, although the already terrible situation may be getting worse, it is getting worse at a slower pace. It is truly a case of grasping at straws when Mexican authorities have to cite that development as the principal sign of progress in the war against the drug cartels.

It is not as though drug-related violence was unknown in Mexico before the Calderón era. During the early 1990s, a vicious rivalry between the Tijuana and Sinaloa organizations for control of the main trafficking route into southern California convulsed Tijuana and the surrounding area. There were also suspicious assassinations during that decade that may have been committed by the drug gangs. One of those incidents was the murder of PRI presidential candidate Luis Donaldo Colosio in 1994. Another incident, even more shocking to the Mexican people, was the assassination of Cardinal Juan Jesús Posadas Ocampo in 1993.

The precise circumstances surrounding the latter incident remain murky to this day. The government's official account asserted that gunmen linked to the Tijuana cartel were trying to kill Sinaloa kingpin Joaquín Guzmán at the Guadalajara Airport, but missed and instead hit Cardinal Posadas Ocampo. However, suspicions have lingered that the Cardinal was the real target because of his outspoken criticism of the growing power of the drug lords. Given that he was in full clerical garb and wearing a large cross around his neck when he was shot, there is understandable skepticism about the "mistaken identity" explanation. And it was not as though the killers fired from a distance—circumstances that would have been consistent with that theory. Gunmen yanked open the door of his limousine, and pumped 14 slugs into him at close range.[4] And Posadas Ocampo didn't even look that much like El Chapo Guzmán.

The extent of violence began to grow worse after the turn of century and had already reached a troubling level by 2002 and 2003.[5] Since then, though, the situation has dramatically deteriorated, especially during Calderón's presidency. Drug cartels, especially the Gulf and Sinaloa organizations and the Zetas, battle law enforcement agencies and one another with ever greater ferocity to gain or retain control over various access corridors to the hugely profitable U.S. market for illegal drugs.

The multiyear tally is now on a par with some countries in the throes of civil war, but it is not just the raw body count that is so worrisome. Even more troubling is the growing arrogance of the cartels. An incident in Nuevo Laredo in April 2008 illustrates how bold the traffickers have become. The Zetas, at the time the enforcers for the Gulf cartel, openly sought recruits to their ranks, posting help-wanted signs and hanging a giant banner across a major thoroughfare. The banner's message: "The Zetas want you, soldier or ex-soldier. We offer a good salary, food and benefits for your family. Don't suffer any more mistreatment and don't go hungry."[6]

On a single day later in that year, August 26, the Gulf cartel hung dozens of *narcomantas* (drug banners), typically a dozen feet long and three or four feet high, around parks and plazas in Monterrey and eight other Mexican cities. Journalist Sam Quiñones, who once lived and worked in Mexico for a decade, observed that "the narcobanners were a chilling reminder of how openly and brazenly the drug gangs now operate in Mexico, and how little they fear the police and government."[7]

Even supposed victories by the Mexican government in the war against the cartels prove to be mixed blessings at best. As Stratfor, a risk-assessment consulting organization, noted even before Calderón's presidency, "inter-cartel violence tends to swing upward after U.S. or Mexican authorities manage to weaken or disrupt a given organization. At any point, if rival groups sense an organization might not be able to defend its turf, they will swoop in to battle not only the incumbent group, but also each other for control."[8]

President Felipe Calderón's decision in December 2006 to have the military launch a full-scale offensive against drug trafficking organizations, though, is a major reason why violence has spiked. Calderón was not the first Mexican president to employ the military against the drug lords, but previous efforts were limited, isolated affairs. His campaign was a massive, militarized attack on the trafficking empires. Not surprisingly, the cartels have struck back. Critics charge that Calderón used a baseball bat to strike a hornet's nest, and then seemed unprepared when the hornets swarmed out and attacked.[9]

But there is an even more important, although less apparent, perverse effect of Calderón's strategy. It has damaged the established cartels just enough to weaken their dominance of the drug trade without eliminating them as serious players. The result is that the once relatively stable division of turf and markets that characterized Mexico's drug trade in earlier decades has turned into something very different and far more dangerous.

As several of the established cartels fracture, there is a growing free-for-all among a larger number of organizations for control over the trafficking routes. Sylvia Longmire, a former senior intelligence analyst on drug trafficking and border violence for the California state government, muses that it is "tough to gauge who is spilling more blood in Mexico: cartels fighting the authorities or fighting each other."[10]

Rafael Pequeño García, chief of anti-drug operations for Mexico's Public Security Ministry, was surprisingly candid about the negative consequences of the fragmentation. "When a cartel is divided into smaller pieces, the pieces become more violent," he admitted. "Because when you break up a big cartel, the people with access to command are the *sicarios*, the hit men. Now the killers are running the organizations. That is why they are so violent. They don't know anything about negotiation. Everything is about force and fear."[11]

Such an astonishing admission from a top Mexican law enforcement official begs the question of why Calderón thought—and continues to believe—that the military offensive against the cartels is a good strategy. Whatever the explanation, the people of Mexico are bearing the ugly consequences.

Tragedy in Tijuana

What is happening in Tijuana confirms Pequeño García's grim assessment. Although violence there was bad even in the 1990s and the early years of the new century, matters became worse once the dominant Arellano Félix cartel split into factions after the founding brothers were arrested or killed. Two rival trafficking organizations emerged to try to control the Tijuana supply route into the United States. Fernando Sánchez Arellano attempted to hold together what was left of the Arellano Félix family operation. But Teodoro García Simental, a one-time cartel lieutenant, challenged Sánchez Arellano for control, a struggle that culminated in an April 2008 gun battle that left 14 gang members dead.

García Simental, known as "El Teo," then broke away and formed a competing cartel that began to solidify control of eastern Tijuana. That rivalry led to more than 400 murders just during the final three months of 2008. Bodies were often left with messages directed to the opposing gang. A typical missive was: "Here are your people, pick them up."[12] The situation in just one neighborhood showed both the surge in slayings and the gruesome nature of killings. During September 2008, 12 bodies were dumped in a lot across from a school; 7 of them had their tongues cut out. Two months later, 9 severed heads, with their eyes and mouths wrapped in tape, were found in a nearby vacant lot. One resident commented that "it smelled like a graveyard."[13]

The bloodletting seeped down to the lowest echelons of the trafficking business–street-level sales to Tijuana's own growing population of drug users. Associated Press correspondent Elliott Spagat's account of the fate of one minor pusher in Tijuana is all too typical of what is happening in many areas of Mexico today. That dealer, Héctor Rodríguez Estrada, controlled a small distribution ring for methamphetamine in an eastern Tijuana neighborhood. Ironically, it was a much-ballyhooed crackdown on meth production in the United States in the 1990s that led to a massive surge of meth labs in Mexico that created trafficking opportunities for people like Rodríguez Estrada.

He understood the extreme danger of his business, and his sense of foreboding grew worse in the final months of 2008 as the Sánchez Arellano–García Simental rivalry heated up. His boss turned up beaten to death and dumped in an empty lot, his teeth and fingers missing. Shortly thereafter, one of his own underlings turned up in a soccer field, with his severed head placed carefully next to his body. Rodríguez Estrada then talked about getting out of the illegal drug trade. Whether he would have done so or not will never be known. On the morning of January 10, 2009, his family found his lifeless body in his house. "He was shot dead in his sleep, along with his pregnant girlfriend, their blood spattering the walls" of the bedroom.[14]

There is no doubt that the turf fights are becoming increasingly ferocious throughout Mexico. Indeed, the battles between

49

rival gangs extend into Mexico's prisons. In November 2008, 5 prisoners died in a shoot-out in a jail in Mazatlán. That was merely one incident in a wave of killings in Mexican jails during the summer and autumn of 2008. A week earlier, 7 people were killed in fighting between cartel inmates in a prison in the state of Durango, and in October, 21 men perished in fighting among rival drug gangs in a prison in Reynosa on the border with Texas. The prison battles continued in 2009 and 2010. In August 2009, 20 inmates were killed and another 25 wounded in a prison brawl at a prison in Durango, and a fight among knife-wielding prisoners left 24 dead and another 20 injured in January 2010. Both battles were apparently between members of the Sinaloa and Gulf cartels.

Epicenter of the Violence: Ciudad Juárez

During the period from 2008 through 2010, Juárez became the biggest arena for bloodshed, and it has fully retained that status.[15] The situation became so bad that the mayor sometimes slept across the border in El Paso to avoid assassination. Even the ongoing presence of 5,000 troops seemed unable to quell the violence in Juárez. Matters did improve briefly in early March 2009, after President Calderón dispatched an additional 7,500 troops as well as 2,500 police reinforcements, but the killings there soon reached—and then exceeded—the pre-deployment levels.

It grew worse in 2010, with fatalities topping the 3,000 mark.[16] The overall pace for homicides in Juárez during 2009 and 2010 was truly astonishing. New York City, which has more than five times the population of Juárez, tallied 464 murders in 2009 and 530 in 2010. If New York were experiencing violence at the same rate as Juárez, it would expect to have more than 15,000 homicides a year.

No one could have any expectation of safety in Juárez, despite Calderón's assignment of additional troops. In late July 2009, gunmen assassinated federal prosecutor José Ibarra Limón, who was investigating a high-profile cartel hit the previous year on a prominent journalist, Armando Rodríguez, who covered crime issues for the newspaper *El Diario*. Ibarra Limón's assassination was just one of 11 drug gang killings that evening. One of the other murders occurred less than a hundred yards from the hotel where Interior Minister Fernando Gómez Mont was staying.[17]

Even during the brief period of spring and early summer 2009, when relative peace returned to Juárez, other regions actually experienced an increase in deaths. The cartels had simply moved their operations temporarily from Juárez to areas in which the Mexican authorities had a more limited presence. That pattern is nothing new.

Prelude to the Juárez Turmoil: Nuevo Laredo

During the years 2004–2006, the city of Nuevo Laredo was one area where the violence was especially bad–so bad that Vicente Fox's administration sent forces to occupy the city and quell the disorders–much as his successor did with Ciudad Juárez. As National Public Radio (NPR) reporter John Burnett emphasizes, it is hard to overstate how bad the bloodshed was in Nuevo Laredo.

> The new police chief was murdered hours after he was sworn in. Rival cartel gangs used rocket-propelled grenades in street battles. Thugs murdered the editor of the largest daily, *El Mañana*, in 2004, because they didn't like its coverage. And two years later, they attacked the newspaper's newsroom.

> "They started shooting with automatic weapons in the direction of the receptionist. And after that, one of the shooters threw a grenade; it exploded right in the hall in front of the editorial director's office," says current editor Daniel Rosas. A bullet hit a reporter, who remains in a wheelchair to this day.[18]

Ultimately, though, the violence did drop in Nuevo Laredo. In 2006, 180 murders took place, while in 2008 the total was 55. That decline was due at least as much to a de facto truce between two coalitions—the Sinaloa and Juárez cartels on one side, and the Gulf and Tijuana cartels on the other—as it was to any action that the Mexican government had taken. But whatever the reason, the city did become a more peaceful place. Unfortunately, as the violence dropped in Nuevo Laredo, it rose in other cities, one of which, it turned out, was Juárez. What occurred in the aftermath of a truce between the two cartels in Nuevo Laredo was that the Sinaloa traffickers moved up the Rio Grande and tried to wrest Ciudad Juárez from their one-time allies in the Nuevo Laredo turf fight, the incumbent Juárez cartel.

51

Even the relatively peaceful interlude in Nuevo Laredo may be coming to an end. Incidents were again on the rise during the last half of 2010 and the first half of 2011. The situation became especially tense in July 2010 when late-night gun battles between police and drug gangs took place at several major traffic intersections across the city. Gang members forced citizens out of their cars and then used the vehicles to erect barricades against advancing police units. Nuevo Laredo city officials posted messages on Facebook warning civilians to stay away from the affected areas.[19] Once again, Nuevo Laredo was beginning to become a battleground like Tijuana and Ciudad Juárez.

The Multi-Sided War

Most victims of the violence throughout Mexico seem to be participants in the drug trade, and far more are killed by rival gangs than by the police or military. Calderón administration officials invariably stress that relatively few civilians have been slain. According to Calderón, 93 percent of the killings in 2008 occurred among the criminal organizations themselves. In early 2010, he reiterated that about 90 percent of the casualties were gang members. While that may be true (and some analysts dispute Calderón's figures), the number of non-drug gang casualties is not trivial, especially for the military and law enforcement agencies. Following back-to-back ambushes of government security convoys in April 2010, Gómez-Mont conceded that the cartels were directing more and more of their attacks against police and military personnel: "In the last few weeks the dynamics of the violence have changed. The criminals have decided to directly confront and attack the authorities."[20] Gómez-Mont was merely stating what had been obvious to most people for well over a year.

The most unsettling aspect of the April ambushes was the scope and sophistication of the operations. In one incident, gunmen attacked the motorcade of the top state-security official in Michoacán, Minerva Bautista. The attack was well coordinated, using a tractor-trailer to block the motorcade and then having assailants on both flanks open up with AK-47s and fragmentation grenades. Four members of Bautista's entourage were killed and another 11 wounded, including Bautista herself.[21] The attack had all the earmarks of a professional military-style operation.

Still, fighting among the cartels accounts for the bulk of the bloodshed. The intergang conflicts are especially bad in areas where no single cartel has a dominant position. That was the principal factor producing the carnage in both Ciudad Juárez and Nuevo Laredo. It was also the primary reason for the abundance of killings that plagued Tijuana. The spike in casualties in Tamaulipas throughout 2010 and 2011 was primarily because of the ferocious turf fights between the Gulf cartel and the Zetas.

Drug gang members are the most likely victims of the violence, but they are hardly the only ones. As of early 2011, more than 1,300 police officers and soldiers had also died in the fighting, including some high-ranking members. In May 2008, an assassin killed the acting federal police chief, Edgar Millán, inside his own home in Mexico City. An especially nasty series of attacks on the police occurred in February 2009 in Zihuatenejo, a resort city on the coast of the state of Guerrero. The day after the army deployed troops to the city, an attacker fired a rocket-propelled grenade into the main police station. Four days later, hit men attacked four policemen with gunfire and grenades as they patrolled an area in a pickup truck. The police burned to death in their vehicle. A week later, assailants killed another officer in a quiet residential area, and left behind a sign that warned that they would "kill every single cop, an eye for an eye, a tooth for a tooth."[22] Cartel executioners are not subtle in their messages of intimidation to police. One favorite tactic is to display dead officers with their badges stuffed into their mouths.

Since Calderón began using the military against the cartels, the number of attacks against soldiers, as well as police, has risen. During 2008, the army intensified its efforts in Guerrero, killing several traffickers and arresting dozens of others. But that success was quickly followed by a flurry of attacks on the military, culminating when nine soldiers were abducted. Their decapitated bodies were displayed a short time later in the state capital.

Both current and former high-ranking military officers are increasingly targets. One spectacular episode involved Brigadier General Mauro Enrique Tello Quiñones, who retired from the army in January 2009 and promptly went to work for the mayor of Cancún to try to neutralize the drug gangs in that important resort city. Previously, Tello Quiñones had served as commander of army forces in Michoacán, so the cartels knew him well. They also knew that he had a reputation for—at times brutal—incorruptibility. In other words, even before he arrived in Cancún, the traffickers regarded him as a mortal enemy. Cancún's mayor, Gregorio Sánchez, hired Tello to set up an elite police unit to focus on drug crimes. The 100-man unit was to be equipped like SWAT forces but would also have robust intelligence-gathering capabilities. Tello Quiñones intended to recruit trusted former federal police agents and military personnel.

Whether he could have succeeded in executing his plan will never be known. On the evening of February 2, 2009, Tello Quiñones, along with his driver and bodyguard, was kidnapped in downtown Cancún. The bodies of all three men were found the next day in a pickup truck outside of the city; all had been shot in the head. They had been systematically tortured, as well. An autopsy showed that the general's arms and legs had been fractured in multiple places.[23]

Calderón ordered the military to give a massive show of force in response. Military units were deployed to Cancún and set up roadblocks and patrols throughout the city. Yet weeks went by without the perpetrators being caught. Given the area of the country and the sheer brutality of the assassination, the Zetas became the primary suspects; but given the complexity and murkiness of Mexico's drug underworld, they were hardly the only ones.

An episode eerily reminiscent of the Tello assassination occurred later that same year in the upscale town of García, near Monterrey. Retired Brigadier General Juan Arturo Esparza had been appointed to head the municipal police force at the beginning of November. On November 4, Esparza, accompanied by several bodyguards, drove to meet Mayor Jaime Rodríguez, who had been receiving death threats. On route to the meeting, a heavily armed convoy of some 30 assailants launched an attack on Esparza's motorcade. When it was over, Esparza and four bodyguards lay dead.[24] The message seemed all too clear: retired military officers would be wise to consider second careers in something other than directing police forces in areas where the drug cartels have a major presence. Otherwise, such officers could expect an extremely brief retirement.

As bad as the violence against Mexican authorities has been, the drug organizations now seem to be escalating their attacks on police and military personnel.[25] An example of that increased aggressiveness toward law-enforcement personnel occurred in early July 2009 in Michoacán. Authorities had captured Arnoldo Rueda Medina, reputed to be the closest associate of Nazario Moreno González, the founder of La Familia. Although La Familia was not yet as large or powerful as the Sinaloa and Gulf cartels, it was already second to none in its penchant for brutality. Indeed, Moreno González fully earned the nickname "El Más Loco" (the craziest one), since his trademark was masterminding torture-slayings that featured the branding of victims before their decapitation.

As authorities were interrogating Rueda Medina in the Michoacán capital, Morelia, La Familia gunmen struck with attacks in eight cities throughout the state, using grenades and high-powered weapons. Before that bloody Sunday ended, three federal police officers and two soldiers were dead, and more than a dozen others wounded. But that toll was mild compared with what would follow. On Tuesday morning, the bodies of 12 more federal police were found along a rural road in Michoacán. The corpses of the 11 men and one woman, who had been engaged in criminal investigations in the area, were stacked like firewood and all bore signs of torture. Notes were left near the scene bearing such messages as "La Familia, join its ranks or leave," and the far more chilling "let's see if you try to arrest another one."[26] A video showing the victims being stripped, brutally beaten, and finally executed apparently was posted on YouTube for a brief period before it could be removed. Authorities attributed the atrocities to La Familia.

Before the spasm of violence subsided, attacks had taken place in at least 10 cities, mostly in Michoacán, but also in the neighboring states of Guerrero and Guanajuato. But the Michoacán assaults had the greatest political symbolism, since they occurred in President Calderón's home state. La Familia was sending a message that no area was safe, and that Calderón's political allies had better watch their backs.

But Calderón showed no inclination to back down in his campaign against La Familia, sending another 2,500 troops to reinforce the 1,500 federal police and 1,000 soldiers already deployed in Michoacán. A little more than a week after the slaughter of the 12 investigators, Mexican police announced the capture of 11 suspected cartel members and the seizure of a major meth lab. La Familia was not backing down, either. In early September, assassins took down José Manuel Revuetas, who had become deputy director of security in Michoacán just two weeks earlier. Gunmen intercepted his car in the southern part of Morelia—an area where La Familia was especially strong—and riddled it with bullets, killing Revuetas and his two bodyguards.[27]

There were other incidents elsewhere in Mexico during that especially nasty three-day period in July. A hit squad assassinated Hector Ariel Meixueiro, the mayor of Namiquipa, in northwestern Chihuahua near the U.S. border. The assassins certainly took no chances. No fewer than 15 gunmen accosted Ariel Meixueiro, who was shot multiple times. It was not entirely certain which drug organization was responsible for that incident, though, which was also the case with the killing of 11 men in Ciudad Juárez. In both of those instances, it seemed more likely that the Gulf or Sinaloa organizations, rather than La Familia, was behind the slayings.

The breadth of the July 2009 attacks that La Familia launched against police and military personnel over such a short period of time shook even veteran anti-drug fighters in Mexico. One newspaper columnist went so far as to describe the attacks as a Mexican version of the Tet Offensive, the stunningly large communist offensive against U.S. and South Vietnamese government forces during the lunar new year in 1968. That offensive, although ultimately repelled, marked the start of a rapid and irreversible decline in American public support for the Vietnam War. Some observers, both in Mexico and the United States, wondered whether the July incidents would have a similar impact on public support for Calderón's confrontational strategy. Those attacks were not just examples of gang violence, said Professor Bruce Bagley, a long-time scholar on the drug war in Latin America, "They have a much more profound impact on the public psyche." In particular, such attacks "erode confidence in Calderón's strategy and the legitimacy of the state response."[28]

Equating the July incidents with the vastly larger Tet Offensive was a bit over the top, but they were an especially graphic warning that the cartels were prepared to take the authorities head on. Although Calderón described the attacks as a desperate reaction to his administration's anti-drug campaign, that spin seemed to be a case of wishful thinking. The drug gangs may have been angry and violent, but there was little sign of desperation. If anything, the episode seemed to convey unprecedented determination and boldness.

Sadism Run Amok

The violence often takes on gruesome characteristics, and victims typically bear signs of extensive torture. In late March 2009, two male bodies were discovered in Michoacán, chopped into several pieces and with the eyes ripped from their sockets.[29] In October 2009, officers in Guerrero found the bodies of nine men in the cargo bed of a pickup truck. All nine had been decapitated and their bodies chopped up and stuffed into 18 plastic garbage bags.[30] Such incidents have now become all-too-frequent occurrences across Mexico.

Atrocities occur in nearly all armed conflicts, but this degree of sadism is unusual. Normally, such extreme barbarism takes place only in wars where the sides are motivated by ethnic, religious, or racial hatred. Yet those factors are not present in the drug wars now raging in Mexico. The adversaries are fighting over access to wealth and power. While such struggles have led adversaries in other settings to kill opponents, sometimes even on a large scale, those stakes have rarely provoked the worst forms of sadistic torture as a normal feature of warfare, as they apparently have in Mexico.

La Familia differed in subtle ways from other cartels in its use of torture, as it did in many other respects. Insisting that it was meting out "divine justice" to its enemies, the group sometimes conducted lengthy executions that resembled perverse religious rituals. Typically, the executioners carved cryptic initials into the foreheads of victims—initials that apparently had some special meaning to La Familia. There were other incidents in which that organization killed rivals by thrusting ice picks through their skulls or boiling the victims while they were still alive.[31] The Knights Templar, the principal secessionist faction when La Familia started to fragment in late 2010, has apparently embraced the tactics of its parent.

One tactic many of the cartels use when they wish to make an emphatic point is to behead their victims and display those heads in a highly visible place. In one incident, the heads of a murdered police strike-force commander and one of his agents were left jammed onto a fence in front of the police station in the prominent Pacific seaside resort of Acapulco. A short time later, five severed heads were tossed across the dance floor at the Sol y Sombra (Sun and Shade) disco in Uruapan, a city in Michoacán.[32]

There have been numerous other incidents in which severed heads have been left near schools, courthouses, and other government facilities. And although La Familia deservedly gained a reputation for being especially fond of such displays, other drug gangs also use that tactic. In January 2009, three severed heads were found stuffed inside a cooler outside the town hall of Guadalupe, a small community not far from Ciudad Juárez, far outside La Familia's base in Michoacán. Those three beheadings occurred less than a week after the beheading of the police chief of the nearby town of Praxedis, whose head was also deposited outside the entrance to that community's town hall.[33] In June 2009, Mexican police discovered 11 bodies stuffed into an SUV that had been stolen in Arizona and driven across the border to the small town of Caborca, in the northwestern state of Sonora. Most of the corpses had both their hands and feet cut off.[34]

The killers seem to be exploring the outer limits of sadistic creativity. On January 2, 2010, 36-year-old Hugo Hernández was kidnapped in Sonora, apparently as part of a feud between the Sinaloa and Juárez organizations. (There were indications that he may have had some connection to the latter group.) A few days later, his body was left in seven pieces on the streets of Los Mochis, in neighboring Sinaloa. His torso was discovered in a plastic container in one location, while a box left at another place contained his legs, arms and skull. But the interesting twist was that the skull contained no skin from his face. That, authorities discovered in a bag left near city hall. Hernández's face had been painstakingly sewn onto a soccer ball.[35]

A close second to decapitation in popularity is cutting out the tongues of victims. That is an especially graphic way of conveying the consequences to any gang member who might be tempted to become an informer for law enforcement authorities. But it is not just an intragang method of discipline. The same stark message is used to intimidate civilians who might think of providing information on trafficking activities to police or the military. And the strategy of intimidation works. A supervising investigator in the federal attorney general's office laments: "Nobody cooperates with anything. They're too afraid. Nobody wants to say what they saw."[36]

The most grisly revelation to date occurred in January 2009, with the arrest of a drug gang enforcer, Santiago Meza, near Tijuana. He would soon gain the moniker "the stew maker," for an especially repulsive reason. Meza confessed to police that over the previous 10 years he had received the corpses of some 300 members of gangs competing with his employer, a breakaway faction of the Arellano Félix cartel, and then dissolved their bodies with corrosive chemicals. "They brought me the bodies and I just got rid of them," he told police. "I didn't feel anything." Although the bodies mostly dissolved within 24 hours of being dosed with caustic soda, a small amount of residue typically remained, which Meza then dumped into a nearby pit. That was a key reason the police believed his confession. They had previously recovered traces of human remains that had been burned with acid in and around Tijuana.[37]

Drug Terrorism in the Digital Age

The hideous quality of many of the killings is not the only way the cartels emphasize their power and brutality. They also use technology to drive home their points and sow terror among their adversaries. Videos of torture and executions are finding their way onto YouTube and other sites. That development began in 2005 and seemed to emulate the videos that Islamic terrorist groups in Iraq and Afghanistan distributed showing prisoners being beheaded. Soon, Mexican-produced videos were incorporating similar scenes.

Even the earliest videos were rather professional products, and the more recent ones are decidedly high quality. A typical example would feature professional singers praising the leaders of a specific cartel, while graphic pictures of executed enemies—law enforcement figures or rival gang members—appear on the screen. One video, apparently produced by the Sinaloa cartel, begins with credits proclaiming: "This is what happens to all my enemies." What follows is a montage of slain police officers, bullet-riddled police cars, and other scenes depicting the cartel's power.[38]

Reuters correspondent Mica Rosenberg points out that the format for many of the videos is the same: "Captives, many bloodied from beatings, are tied up, blindfolded and posed in front of a draped sheet in an anonymous setting. Surrounded by heavily armed captors in ski masks and guided by questioning from an off-camera voice, the captives are forced to confess allegiances to [rival] cartels or corrupt officials. Many are then murdered on camera." Some of the scenes are extremely graphic. "In one video, a man with a black eye is tethered to a chair in his underwear and appears to be strangled to death with a tourniquet by his captors. There is a 'Z' scrawled across his chest for Zetas."[39]

The rival drug gangs have also taken to online chat rooms to conduct their propaganda wars. In December 2008, one Mexican-based chat room featured a vitriolic exchange between a member of the Juárez cartel and a competitor. That exchange included a warning from the Juárez participant: "Wait for the little gift we're going to leave for you tomorrow morning." The next day, two decapitated heads were found in a cooking pot just outside the Juárez city limits.[40]

A Spreading Plague

Pamela Starr, an international relations scholar at the University of Southern California, concludes that the death toll in Mexico is now similar "to a country in the throes of a civil war."[41] The U.S. State Department warned American travelers as early as April 2008 that battles between drug trafficking gangs (and between those gangs and Mexican military and police) in portions of northern Mexico were so severe that they constituted "the equivalent of military small-unit combat and have included use of machine guns and fragmentation grenades."[42] That warning remains in effect.

The adverse impact of the fighting has been most pronounced in Mexican cities along the border with the United States. Tijuana merchants concluded in June 2008 that tourism had declined as much as 90 percent from 2005, when an estimated 4 million people visited the city. Half of the downtown businesses—some 2,400 enterprises—had closed their doors during that period. *Washington Post* correspondent Manuel Roig-Franzia found that matters were not much better in the other border cities. Empty markets "have become the norm in Ciudad Juárez," he observed in June 2008, and in Nuevo Laredo, five major hotels had shut down.[43] Writing in July 2011 about the situation along the border between El Paso and Juárez, *New York Times* contributing writer Andrew Rice observed that "few El Pasoans venture across the bridge anymore, if they can help it."[44]

The negative economic impact of the turmoil in Ciudad Juárez has become steadily greater since the summer of 2008. "Six thousand businesses have closed during the last nine months," Daniel Murguia Lardizabal, the head of the local chamber of commerce, confirmed in April 2010. "Downtown is dead."[45] He's right. Signs with "closed" "and "for rent," often in both Spanish and English, saturate the main business district. Juárez is a city where the legal economy seems on the verge of entering a death spiral, even as the drug trade flourishes.

Less prominent border cities are also taking a financial hit as worried American tourists keep their distance. Carol Cullar, a resident of Eagle Pass, Texas, laments the changes in Piedras Negras across the river. "We always take out-of-town visitors to their elegant restaurants for a taste of Mexico. Or we did." She goes on to mourn the passing of one of the city's most venerable restaurants. "A few months ago, El Restaurante Moderno in Piedras, known locally as 'Modernos,' closed its doors, another victim of Mexico's raging drug wars. Its quirky elegance and four-star menu had served four generations of luminaries and film stars."[46]

Cullar echoes the arguments of many residents in the southwestern states, contending that Mexico's problem is becoming our problem. It's "not just the fear that the violence will seep across this man-determined boundary (which I suspect it will), but the despair that as my Mexican friends lose their way of life, I'm also losing mine. As Piedras is lacerated, Eagle Pass winces in pain."[47]

Elsewhere, the situation is not yet as bad as it is in the border cities, and the Mexican government is incensed at allegations that the country is unsafe. Local and state officials go beyond mere denials about the danger. Officials from the Acapulco city government, the Guerrero state government, and the Mexican attorney general even signed a statement in March 2009 assuring college students who were considering going there on spring break that authorities were taking extra measures to ensure their safety.

Nevertheless, areas once thought safe are increasingly caught up in the conflict. Throughout the 1990s and the early years of this century, Mexico's chief industrial city, Monterrey, was thought to be virtually immune from the damage caused by the turf fights between the drug gangs in places such as Tijuana and Nuevo Laredo. Sam Quiñones, who had lived in the city during that period, recalled wistfully: "Monterrey was the safest region in the country when I lived there, thanks to its robust economy and the sturdy social control of an industrial elite."[48] An international consulting group in early 2005 named Monterrey the safest city in all of Latin America.[49]

61

But events in the spring of that same year shattered the illusion of calm, when two reputed traffickers were gunned down in a Dave and Buster's restaurant as they were dining with their families. In August, state police arrested 23 apparent cartel hit men in another restaurant. Marcelo Garza y Garza, the commander of the state police investigation unit, was widely credited for the raid, and he encouraged the belief that it had struck a major blow against the foothold that the cartels seemed to be trying to establish in Monterrey and the rest of Nuevo León. Barely a year later, the traffickers struck back, assassinating Garza y Garza as he strolled along a street in a wealthy Monterrey suburb. He was hardly the only victim. During 2006, hit men assassinated six municipal police chiefs in Nuevo León, along with two federal prosecutors tasked with investigating narcotics cases.

The trend grew worse the following year, and the homicide rate in Monterrey became double the already heightened toll in 2006. The murders included a state legislator who was shot in broad daylight in front of the city hall. There was also a proliferation of lesser-known victims. In one incident, traffickers attached a note to the body of a victim with a message apparently directed to Nuevo León attorney general Rogelio Cerda: "Look, fool, even with all of your body guards you will die . . . together with your family, all the officials who are with you, and the Sinaloa Cartel. P.S. This will continue until you get it."[50]

By 2010, Monterrey had become one of the main theaters in the spiraling warfare among the cartels. In July of that year, authorities uncovered a gruesome dump site east of the city, in the township of Benito Juárez. Excavations soon revealed that there were at least 51 bodies—some intact and others in pieces—buried at the site, making the Monterrey dumping ground the second biggest mass grave uncovered in Mexico's drug wars.[51]

The awful discovery underscored—as if any further evidence was needed—that Monterrey was now a major battlefield in the armed conflicts, with the struggle being especially intense between the Gulf cartel and its former allies, the Zetas. And that fighting was clearly escalating. Most of the burial pits at the Benito Juárez site were freshly dug, and the vast majority of bodies found in those mass graves had been executed within the previous two weeks. The days of Monterrey being a safe and peaceful city were nothing more than a quaint memory.

When Edelmiro Cavazos, the mayor of Santiago, a prosperous suburb, was abducted and murdered in August 2010, the frustration of Monterrey's commercial community boiled over. Business leaders took out full page ads in several major local and national newspapers calling on President Calderón to send more troops into Monterrey and the surrounding state of Nuevo León, specifically three army divisions and a division of marines. "Enough Already!" the ads proclaimed.[52] The reinforcements requested would create a military presence even larger than that in Chihuahua, which because of Ciudad Juárez, was seen by everyone as the main theater in the drug wars. Such a request indicated the level of panic in Mexico's principal economic metropolis.

But an enhanced presence of security personnel has done little to restore Monterrey's safe environment. That point became undeniable in late August 2011 when cartel gunmen burst into the Casino Royale and torched the building. Fifty-two patrons, mostly middle-age and elderly women playing bingo, were unable to escape and perished in the blaze. In the weeks leading up to the attack, the casino owner had apparently refused to comply with extortion demands. Three days after the killings, Mexican police arrested five of the alleged hitmen—all apparently affiliated with the Zetas.[53]

Mexico's main tourist locales, such as Cancún, Acupulco, and Los Cabos, have fared better than the border areas—and even cities such as Monterrey. So far. The Mexican government assures travelers that the most prominent resorts are quite safe. Privately, though, both officials and business leaders seem nervous as reports proliferate about the bloodshed afflicting other areas. And even cities such as Cancún and Acapulco are no longer immune. That point became apparent in early June 2009 when a four-hour shootout between Mexican soldiers and drug gang members erupted in Acapulco. The battle raged from 8 o'clock on a busy Saturday night and did not subside until after midnight. During the course of the fighting, some 3,000 shots were fired and 50 grenades exploded. Hundreds of tourists, some from the United States, cowered in their hotel rooms as the fighting raged. When the smoke cleared, 17 people lay dead, including two soldiers and two innocent bystanders (a father and son). At least nine other people were wounded, including three bystanders.[54]

Fortunately, that firefight did not occur in Acapulco's main tourist venue but in a secondary tourist area that had once been a mecca for the Hollywood set in the 1950s and 1960s and had since faded badly. Elizabeth Taylor held one of her many weddings nearby, and such stars as John Wayne once held posh parties at the Flamingo Hotel, about 100 yards from the main scene of the fighting. Acapulco's current high-profile tourist strip, built primarily over the past decade or so to revitalize the resort's appeal to foreign visitors, was located several miles across the city. The bloodshed did take place, though, barely a mile away from the site used by the famous Acapulco cliff divers—a major tourist attraction. Cindy Pelaquin and Michelle Johnson, travelers from Boston, were both watching the diving show and encountered military roadblocks on their return. "We were just lucky, I suppose," Johnson stated, apparently realizing that they could have been closer to the scene when the fighting broke out.[55]

Nor was the weekend shootout the end to Acapulco's troubles. A little more than a day after that incident, gunmen killed two police officers. Just hours later, attackers shot and wounded two other officers. Acapulco was rather quickly beginning to resemble the bloody border cities.

In April 2010, a wild shootout took place in broad daylight on the main boulevard in the principal tourist area that left six people dead and dozens dashing for cover in a full state of panic. The violence in Acupulco has reached the point that sarcastic residents refer to the city as *Narcopulco*.[56] And the environment continues to get more dangerous. During a single weekend in early January 2011, police discovered 30 bodies in and around Acupulco, 16 of which were found without their heads.[57] Such an orgy of violence is not likely to go over well with prospective visitors.

Other important resort areas are no longer immune from the bloodletting either. In late November 2009, a 19-year-old woman was found beheaded in a sports stadium in Cancún. She apparently had a relationship with a police officer who had been murdered the previous week in the trademark style of cartel executions. Two months later, police in Veracruz state found the body of a federal court official, Nayeli Reyes, who had been kidnapped a few days earlier. A note from the Gulf cartel was left on her corpse.

The overall security environment in Cancún is showing signs of deterioration. In August 2010, eight people died when six men tossed Molotov cocktails into a local bar, the Castillo del Mar. The resulting fire quickly consumed the building, causing numerous injuries in addition to eight fatalities. Police reported that the owner of the bar had previously rebuffed two extortion attempts by the Zetas.[58] Although the bar was in an area not generally frequented by foreign tourists, the incident certainly did not enhance Cancún's reputation for safety.

That was especially so given an ugly atrocity that occurred two months earlier, when police discovered six bodies, four men and two women, in a cavern near the city. Three of the bodies had their chests opened and their hearts cut out. The corpses also had the letter "Z" carved into their abdomens, an apparent calling card left by the Zetas.[59] A short time later, authorities discovered another 12 decomposing bodies stuffed in sink holes near the resort city.

A shootout at a disco in the beach resort of Mazatlán in early February 2010 left six people dead. Four armed men entered the nightclub and promptly shot two waiters and a patron. They then seemed prepared to leave, but when they reached the door, they turned and killed three more people.[60]

The brutal turf war between rival factions of the weakened Beltrán Leyva organization became an all-too-prominent feature of life in Cuernavaca, an hour's drive from Mexico City. Cuernavaca has long been a favorite retreat for Mexico's political and economic elite, and it has been an appealing (although secondary) destination for knowledgeable American and European tourists who regard such places as Cancún, Acapulco, and Cabo San Lucas as too commercialized. The appeal of Cuernavaca faded as the body count rose in the war between Edgar "La Barbie" Valdéz Villarreal and Hector Beltrán Leyva. In the first six months of 2010 alone, more than 120 people in Cuernavaca died in the fighting. When three bodies were found hanging from pedestrian bridges in early July, with notes from the Southern Pacific cartel (the Hector Beltrán Levya–led faction) accusing the executed men of working for La Barbie, some Cuernavaca residents might be excused for wondering if they lived in Ciudad Juárez instead of the quiet tourist town they had previously known.[61]

Less famous tourist destinations are also taking a hit. The previously quiet silver town Taxco, in Guerrero state, has long been a prime attraction for tourists seeking good buys on silver jewelry and other products. Its quaint cobblestone streets added to its peaceful, romantic image. But as the drug wars have reached Guerrero, tourism has suffered. In late May and early June 2010, hotel occupancy rates were down to a depressing 16.5 percent. And that was before authorities discovered dozens of bodies, in various states of decay, dumped into an abandoned silver mine outside of town.[62] Autopsies indicated that many of the victims were alive when they had been hurled down the mine shaft. But more worrisome, a number of heads found in that cavern of horrors did not match any of the headless bodies–suggesting that even more corpses might lie elsewhere.

Even before the bloody April 2010 incident in Acapulco and the subsequent toll in Cuernavaca, Cancún, Taxco, and other resort areas, rumors and reports of drug violence in Mexico were beginning to cause some tourists to choose other destinations. The impact thus far on Mexico's tourist industry, outside the bloody border cities, has been fairly limited, but that could easily change if the overall violence continues to intensify and spread. Foreign tourists who do still come to Mexico are noticeably more cautious. Ralph O'Donnell, a 42-year-old tourist from North Carolina visiting Cancún, was clearly skittish. "I'm afraid to go out at night, and we prefer to stay in the hotel," he admitted.[63]

Mexico's Tourism Board seems utterly tone deaf regarding the growing expressions of fear about safety issues. McClatchy correspondent Tim Johnson notes that the "beautifully crafted ads on cable televisions and in mass marketing magazines" in the United States show no hint at all of the "bloody war between drug cartels that's made parts of northern Mexico more akin to Afghanistan than a tranquil holiday destination."[64] A prominent feature on the VisitMexico website was "Routes of Mexico"–a list of 10 off-the-beaten-track itineraries for tourists. But several of those routes would take travelers through the states of Michoacán, Chihuahua, and Sinaloa, which are central theaters in the drug wars, and which the U.S. State Department has repeatedly urged Americans to "use extreme caution" when traveling in those states. The tourism board's attitude was one of apparent indifference regarding the safety issue, with one official saying bluntly that it isn't the board's duty to advise travelers on safety.

The epidemic of killings in the urban hot spots is spreading even into previously placid rural areas, including portions of Chihuahua far outside Ciudad Juárez. Some residents contend that the heightened military presence in the border areas merely pushed the gangs into the countryside. Certainly, there has been an upsurge of assassinations and kidnappings throughout the state since the summer of 2008. One municipal police chief was killed in November of that year, while another chief and a senior commander in his force went missing in October. Gunmen also killed the town treasurer and mayor of Namiquipa, a small city in central Chihuahua.

On August 20, 2009, the president of the legislature in Guerrero was murdered. The following month, the PRI candidate for a legislative seat in the southeastern state of Tabasco was killed, along with his wife and two children, in his own home. The bodies of José Francisco Fuentes Esperón and his wife were found shot in the head. Their two sons, ages 8 and 10, had been asphyxiated.[65] The probable motive for the hit was retaliation for the recent arrest of minor drug traffickers, and Fuentes Esperón's own negative comments about the cartels.

A struggle for control of the smuggling routes through the previously quiet northwestern state of Durango killed 235 people in just the first four and a half months of 2009, and matters grew worse later in the year. The U.S. State Department issued an updated travel alert in February 2010, adding both Durango and Coahuila to the list of states with areas that Americans should avoid visiting because violence had reached the point of posing an acute danger. This alert repeated the comment from warnings involving other Mexican states, which noted that much of the fighting resembled small-unit combat operations.

Because President Calderón deployed so much of the army in such places as Tijuana, Ciudad Juárez, and Nuevo Laredo, there are only a few hundred troops in Durango. As a result, drug hit men, primarily from the Gulf cartel, are taking over towns, attacking government offices, and killing rival traffickers. Noel Díaz, Durango's deputy state attorney general, stated that there had been a 600 percent increase in violence during 2009, and that authorities did not "have the resources to attack these groups." Olivero Reza, the number-two official in the state government, admitted: "There is a long list of police killed and official buildings raided and attacked with grenades, with AK47s, and burned down."[66] There are several Canadian-owned gold and silver mining operations in Durango, which has long been a center of mineral wealth, but local mayors now report that the security environment is so bad that several of the mining concessions are now too dangerous to explore.

Shortly before Calderón replaced him as Interior Minister, Gómez Mont insisted: "We are committed to enduring this wave of violence."[67] But such pledges of endurance are being put to an excruciating test. The recurring spasms of violence are raising concerns both in the United States and in Mexico about the stability of the country. If matters do not improve significantly under Calderón's successor, those worries are certain to intensify.

3. Carnage in Mexico: The Innocent Victims

In addition to the casualties among the drug gang members, the police, and the military, the toll of civilian victims is rising dramatically. Some of those victims appear to be on the fringes of the drug trade themselves, or at least have questionable backgrounds. Others are entirely innocent parties who run afoul of the cartels.

People on the periphery of the drug trade court considerable danger, and from sources that are not always clear. Silvia Raquenel Villanueva, a lawyer who routinely represented accused drug traffickers, survived four assassination attempts—on one occasion being hit by eight bullets—between 1998 and 2009. During that period, she became a heroine of sorts within Mexico's criminal community and even in the broader culture. Songs were written about her with such titles as "The Bulletproof Lawyer" and "Lady of Steel."[1] Her luck ran out on August 9, 2009. As she was shopping in Monterrey, three assailants shot her multiple times.

There was a long list of suspects. Rivals of cartel leaders she had defended over the years had repeatedly threatened her. And the Mexican authorities were none-too-fond of her pit-bull courtroom tactics on behalf of accused traffickers. She also may have known about the numerous linkages between the drug lords and prominent officials and political figures. There were a lot of powerful people who wanted Silvia Raquenel Villanueva dead.

People on the fringes of the drug trade also include patients in drug treatment centers, which are increasingly the target of attacks. One such incident occurred in September 2009 when four hooded assailants armed with automatic weapons broke down the door of the *Aliviane* drug rehabilitation center in Ciudad Juárez, lined 18 people up against the wall, and shot them at point-blank range. Apparently they wanted to make sure of their work, since nearly 100 bullets were fired. It was the third attack on a Juárez drug rehab facility in 13 months and the fifth attack on such facilities in Mexico as a whole. The string of killings began with an August 2008 incident when several armed men barged into a pastor's sermon at a treatment facility and opened fire, killing eight people and wounding several others. Two weeks after the attack on the *Aliviane* facility, gunmen burst into the *Anexo de Vida* rehabilitation center in Juárez just before midnight and killed another 10 people.[2]

Suspicions that some treatment facilities had become inter-cartel battlefields deepened in late September 2009 when Mexican police arrested five men for dozens of murders in Ciudad Juárez, including the attacks on the *Aliviane* and *Anexo de Vida* centers. All five were apparently members of the Sinaloa organization. Mexican authorities boasted that with those arrests, they were able to account for nearly 300 of the 1,720 murders that had occurred in the city that year.

It is not surprising that such centers have become yet another arena for the bloody inter-cartel rivalries. Both U.S. and Mexican officials contend that drug rehabilitation facilities in Juárez and elsewhere have become hideouts for drug gang members on the run. The trafficking organizations also allegedly use the centers as places to identify and recruit new foot soldiers. According to Public Safety Secretary Genaro García Luna, Mexico's top law enforcement official, Rafael Cedeño, a major figure with La Familia, supervised numerous private, nonprofit drug rehabilitation centers, primarily in Michoacán. Cedeño's centers allegedly held retreats to train new recruits. That may be true, but many of those recruits were apparently not willing volunteers. It was common practice in Cedeño's facilities to execute recovering addicts who declined to join the cartel.

Another incident illustrates the murky backgrounds of the victims in attacks on drug treatment centers. Just before midnight on June 10, 2010, trucks carrying a group of more than 30 heavily armed men pulled up in front of a blue concrete building that housed the Templo Cristiano Fe y Vida (Christian Faith and Life Temple) in Chihuahua City. They stormed the building and climbed to the second floor, where they rousted people out of their beds and then opened fire on patients and employees alike, killing 14. On their way out of the building, they executed another five people. Police speculated that some of the dead were members of the Mexicales, an enforcement arm of the Sinaloa cartel and the mortal enemies of the Aztecas, hit men for the Juárez cartel. But others appeared to be innocent bystanders, including one blind man.[3]

Later that month, attackers opened fire in a treatment center in Gómez Palacio in Durango, killing nine people, including the director. The gunmen were relentless in their pursuit, since bodies were found in all parts of the center, including the gymnasium, dorms, and patio. Another nine patients were wounded in the assault.[4] Once again, at least some of the victims appeared to be drug abusers who were just trying to turn their lives around. There was no credible evidence that they were drug gang members.

Civilians Who Run Afoul of the Cartels

The second category of victims is the most tragic, because they are not involved with the drug traffickers, and in some cases they may loathe the gangs. Yet they are sometimes on the front lines of the drug war, and they suffer the consequences. On Mexico's national day in September 2008, drug gang assailants tossed two grenades into a packed crowd celebrating the holiday in the city of Morelia, killing eight and wounding dozens.

That sort of intimidation and terror, as well as the bloodshed itself, has become a way of life for ordinary citizens of Juárez. Citizens court fatal risks if they cross the traffickers in any way. One man who had the temerity to call a police hotline to report probable drug sales near his home was later found inside an SUV that had crashed into a tree. He had been tortured so badly that he had lapsed into a coma and later died of his injuries. A note attached to the battered body read: "This is what happens to those who ring 060 [the hotline tip number]." Store clerk Luisa Rivera voiced the frustration and fear of many Juárez residents, "What good are 10,000 soldiers and federal police if we don't have any security at all, if we are too afraid even to go to the corner shop?"[5]

Some fed-up residents are fleeing the increasingly chaotic areas of Mexico for safer locales. Anna Maria Salazar, a U.S. deputy assistant secretary of defense during the Clinton administration, states that "many people fearing for their lives in border towns are moving to big cities within Mexico."[6] She adds that if the violence becomes worse, there will be more and more pressure for refugee status in the United States as well.

In many cases, it is evident which cartel is responsible for a particular attack or atrocity. Indeed, the perpetrators often boast publicly of the deed. In other cases, though, the identity of the guilty party is not clear. An example of the latter situation occurred in Chihuahua just two weeks before the bloodletting in Michoacán, in July 2009. Benjamín LeBaron, the leader of a Mormon enclave in Chihuahua, had antagonized drug traffickers by resisting extortion demands and creating an armed protection force in his local community. In the early morning hours of July 7, several pickup trucks, containing 15 to 20 heavily armed men, converged on LeBaron's home outside the town of Galeana. According to eyewitness accounts, they smashed windows and demanded that he open the door. Le Baron's brother-in-law, Luis Widmar, who lived across the street, ran to help him, something that proved to be a fatal mistake. The gunmen threatened to rape LeBaron's wife in front of their five terrified young children unless the two men surrendered and cooperated. Widmar and LeBaron did so, but they were then taken outside of the town, tortured, and shot in the head.[7]

Afterwards, a video camera captured the departure of the murderers at a nearby highway tollbooth. The videotape recorded not only the make, model, and year of their vehicles, but the license numbers. As is so often the case with killings that the drug gangs commit, weeks later there were still no arrests. In fact, the authorities seemed uncertain which gang was responsible. Chihuahua's state attorney general, Patricia González, contended that La Línea, a key enforcement arm of the Juárez cartel, committed the deed. Yet just a few months earlier, González had boasted that La Línea, which consists primarily of former police officers, had been devastated by arrests and in-fighting and was now an ineffective remnant. After the LaBaron and Widmar murders, her credibility was more than a little suspect.

The Juárez cartel clearly did not appreciate being fingered by González as the culprit in the LeBaron-Widmar killings. A few days after she made her comments, banners appeared in Ciudad Juárez with the message, "Mrs. Prosecutor, avoid problems for yourself, and don't blame La Línea," also asserting that the rival Sinaloa cartel was responsible.[8] Such is sometimes the murky nature of the armed turmoil in Mexico.

Attacks on the News Media

Casualties among law-abiding civilians, while still relatively low, are growing. And members of the news media appear to be increasingly high-priority targets for the cartels, especially in the main trafficking areas along the border with the United States.[9] In the past few years, numerous journalists have been killed—most of them execution style. Not only is the roster of media victims mounting, but the pace is accelerating. A July 2009 report issued by the Manuel Buendía Foundation, named after a Mexican journalist who was assassinated in 1984, found that six journalists were murdered during the entire presidency of Ernesto Zedillo from 1994 to 2000. Six more were killed during Vicente Fox's presidency from 2000 to 2006.

The death count spiked dramatically in 2007, when five reporters died. And the hazards to journalists have become greater since then.[10] On July 29, 2009, Juan Daniel Martínez, a newscaster for W Radio in Acapulco, became yet another victim. Police discovered his body partially buried in a vacant lot. He had been beaten and gagged. A spokesman for the New York–based Committee to Protect Journalists lamented: "Juan Daniel Martínez joins a sickeningly long list of journalists who have fallen victim to the lawlessness plaguing Mexico."[11] The toll climbed higher during 2010, and by August 2011 human-rights groups reported that more than 60 journalists had been killed since 2000. The last week of August 2011 was an especially bad period, when three members of the media died execution style.[12]

Attacks have taken place in major media centers and in backwater communities alike. In late September 2009, five suspected drug hit men burst into a radio station in the small town of Nuevo Casas Grandes, in a rural section of Chihuahua. They shot reporter Norberto Miranda Madrid in front of his colleagues. "His body was found full of bullets," stated Vladimir Tuexi, a spokesman for Chihuahua's attorney general's office.[13] Just days earlier, Miranda Madrid had told Mexico's Center of Journalism and Public Ethics that he had received death threats for publishing details about the September 4 arrest of José Rodolfo Escajeda. Not only was Rodolfo Escajeda allegedly a top lieutenant of the Juárez cartel, he was linked to a high-profile 2006 incursion by armed traffickers into Texas.

José Bladimir Antuna, a reporter for *El Tiempo de Durango* (a major paper in that state), met a similar fate in November 2009. Antuna wrote repeatedly about violent drug crimes and had told his colleagues that he had received multiple telephone death threats. Matters escalated in June 2009 when he filed a complaint with the state attorney general's office that gunmen had fired shots at his house. The Durango authorities dismissed the case, concluding that the shots had not been directed at Antuna, but were "merely" stray bullets from a fight in the street. Five months later, Antuna's body was found in a vacant lot in the state capital. He had been beaten and strangled. Next to his lifeless body investigators found a message claiming that he had been killed for giving information to the military.[14]

Until 2011, Mexico City itself seemed to be an exception to the perils that journalists elsewhere experienced. But that has changed. An especially jarring incident occurred at the end of August 2011 when the bodies of Ana Marcela Yarce Viveros, founder of the feisty news magazine *Contralínea*, and her friend Rocío González Trapaga, a freelance writer who formerly was a reporter for Mexico's dominant television network, Televisa, were found bound and strangled.[15] They were the first journalists to have been the victims of gang slayings inside the environs of the national capital.

In addition to the murders, there have been hundreds of threats or assaults on media personnel. Many reporters—and in some cases, entire newspapers—now flatly refuse to cover stories involving the cartels.[16] In early January 2010, a major regional newspaper, *Zócolo*, based out of the northern city of Saltillo, announced that it would stop covering drug violence entirely. That decision was made after the body of one of its reporters, Valentín Valdés, was discovered with a threatening message attached. Valdés had recently written several stories about the arrests of accused drug traffickers. "As of today we will publish zero information related to drug trafficking," the paper told the Associated Press. The reason was "to avoid situations like the one we experienced today."[17] Other publications have not retreated quite as far as *Zócolo*, but they often limit themselves to printing, with no comment, government press releases. Investigative reporting on the drug trade has diminished dramatically over the past four years.

And there are instances in which the news blackout reaches astonishing proportions. The border city of Reynosa and the surrounding area in Tamaulipas was a veritable battlefield between the Zetas and the Gulf cartel in February 2010. Gunfights and executions went on for days at a time, producing hundreds of deaths. But Carlos Lauría, head of the Americas program for the Committee to Protect Journalists, points out that there was not a single report in newspapers or on radio and television about the bloodshed. In fact, the first media reports of the extent of the casualties appeared in a U.S. paper, the *Dallas Morning News*. Gerardo Albarrán, a reporter with the weekly magazine *Proceso*, warns that such timidity is not confined to Tamaulipas. Especially in northern Mexico, Albarrán contends, "residents have a war raging around them complete with grenades and cartel members setting up their own road blocks in the streets, yet the local media are reporting on weddings, *quinceañeras* and fender benders."[18]

There is little doubt that Albarrán is right. *Washington Post* correspondent William Booth reports a similar news blackout in Nuevo Laredo. "Two weeks ago Mexican soldiers clashed here with drug cartel gangsters in running gun battles that lasted five hours. The outlaws hijacked vehicles, including a bus, for use as barricades and battering rams. Terrified residents scrambled for safety. At least a dozen people were killed, including bystanders. Children were wounded in the crossfire. Not a single word about it appeared in the local news media."[19] That was an astonishing omission, since Nuevo Laredo has four daily newspapers, three television news channels, and a half dozen radio stations that devote at least some portion of air time to news. But in a country wracked by drug wars, a failure to report dangerous news is now becoming the norm.

According to the editor of a daily newspaper in Tamaulipas, the Zetas have become the the de facto news editors in that state, "The Zetas send word on what they want and don't want published."[20] That editor declined to have her name used in a National Public Radio segment on Mexico's drug war. There is evidence that the Zetas have a press chief and a deputy press chief whose jobs are to monitor what news outlets in Tamaulipas are reporting and to ensure that there are no negative accounts of the cartel.

Much of the information about the depredations of the gangs doesn't come from the conventional news media at all, but from freelance bloggers. One blog in particular, *Blog del Narco*, has been especially active in providing coverage. Associated Press correspondent Olga R. Rodríguez contended that "operating from behind a thick curtain of computer security, *Blog del Narco* in less than six months has become Mexico's go-to Internet site at a time when mainstream media are feeling pressure to stay away from the story." She was not exaggerating about the degree of electronic concealment that *Blog del Narco* employed. When the Associated Press wrote to the blog's e-mail address, the blogger called back from a disguised phone number. He identified himself as a college student majoring in computer security. And he clearly understood the risk he was taking, even with the elaborate cyber-security precautions. "For the scanty details that they (mass media) put on television, they get grenades thrown at them and their reporters kidnapped," he told the Associated Press (AP). "We publish everything. Imagine what they could do to us."[21]

But just as dictatorial regimes around the world are finding it difficult, if not impossible, to thwart information getting out on the Internet, the Mexican drug traffickers are discovering that they are unable to identify and silence *Blog del Narco* and similar sites. Some of the cartels apparently have decided to make the best of a frustrating situation and even use the sites to post some of their own videos. Those often gory posts aim to send a message of intimidation to rivals and police.

The main objective of the trafficking organizations is clearly to suppress troublesome news stories. Sometimes, though, a cartel will employ extortion tactics to force the mainstream news media to become conduits for propaganda. That was apparently the motive behind a kidnapping episode in July 2010. The *Milenio* newspaper and television network reported that one of its cameramen, along with three other journalists, including two other cameramen from Televisa, had been kidnapped in Durango. They had been covering a huge scandal that had broken just a few days earlier, in which the director and guards of a prison were accused of letting drug drug gang enforcers, who were supposedly locked up in the facility, come and go freely to carry out killings—often using government weapons and vehicles (see chapter 4).

Initial speculation was that the kidnapping was yet another attempt by the traffickers to silence nosy journalists and intimidate their colleagues. But that proved not to be the case at all. Instead, the Sinaloa cartel wanted the employers of the cameramen to broadcast unedited videos of police captives and others who were accusing the Durango state government of being under the control of the Sinaloa gang's bitter rivals, the Zetas. The Milenio network complied with that demand rather than risk having its abducted employees executed. Televisa might have gone along with the demand, as well, if Mexican police had not conducted a successful rescue mission on July 31.[22]

That kidnapping incident had a relatively happy ending. But the journalists had not been treated gently. When they appeared in newscasts shortly after being rescued, they were bruised and bleeding. "They intimidated us all day and night," said cameraman Alejandro Hernández. "They hit us in the head with a board."[23] Most galling of all, the kidnappers escaped when the police closed in— although authorities did announce the arrest of three suspects a few days later. Given the previous incidents in Mexico's criminal justice system, it was anyone's guess whether those suspects were the real perpetrators, and if they were, whether they would actually be tried, convicted, and punished.

And despite the rescue, the cartel had succeeded in intimidating a prominent news outlet to serve as its propaganda distributor. Experts immediately worried that this was an escalation in the campaign by drug lords to demonstrate their power, and that it was a new tactic to try to control the flow of information. Javier Oliva, a security expert at Mexico's National Autonomous University, contends that the cartels have a big incentive to intensify their blackmail strategy. "It is free publicity. A company has to pay thousands of pesos to promote their products. But for these criminal groups, it just takes a threatening phone call or grenades chucked at a television station."[24]

Media watchdog groups charge that Mexico has now become the most dangerous country in the world for reporters and editors— especially those who seek to do their jobs regarding the drug crime epidemic afflicting that country.[25] In fact, the number of casualties is reaching—or exceeding—the number in full-fledged war zones like Afghanistan.

As with their recruiting efforts, the traffickers are becoming bolder in their attacks on the news media. Even Televisa is not immune to such coercion. On the evening of January 6, 2009, the network's offices in Monterrey came under attack in the form of a commando-style raid. Hooded gunmen fired Kalashnikov automatic rifles at the front door of the building and then lobbed a grenade into the adjacent parking lot, not far from where a reporter and her cameraman were standing. Although no one was injured in the attack, the incident unsettled the news organization and its reporters. The attackers left a message warning Televisa to stop focusing its coverage on the drug cartels.[26]

That the traffickers would go after Televisa was especially significant. Televisa is the world's most popular Spanish-language network and has an enormous presence throughout Mexico. The network rakes in an astonishing 75 percent of all broadcast advertising revenue—some $3.5 billion a year—in the country, and it has long had a powerful influence on Mexico's political affairs. "Televisa has the equivalent political clout of ABC, NBC, and CBS combined," according to Mexican media analyst Raúl Trejo. "When the narcos threaten this organization, they are showing that they have no limits to their power."[27]

That point was driven home again with the July 2010 kidnapping of Televisa cameramen, and yet again a few days later when assailants tossed a grenade at the building housing the Televisa affiliate in Nuevo Laredo. Typically, no Mexican news outlet, including Televisa itself, reported that attack.[28] Just a few weeks after those incidents, a car bomb exploded outside the Televisa studios in Ciudad Victoria, in Tamaulipas. That explosion was so large that it was felt blocks away, and it damaged the studio sufficiently to knock the station off the air for several hours.[29] Although Televisa journalists avoided death or serious injury in all of those attacks, many other reporters throughout Mexico have not been so lucky.

The Catholic Church: A New Target?

People involved in movements that might challenge the growing hold of the cartels over the public in the affected states run the risk of being eliminated. Even the Roman Catholic Church may have become a target. In June 2009, a priest and two seminarians were driving through the town of Arcelia, near Acapulco, on their way to organize a spiritual retreat in the nearby city of Ciudad Altamirano, when gunmen ordered them out of their vehicle and shot them to death. It was probably not a coincidence that the killing occurred in the state of Guerrero, one of the most active drug growing regions in western Mexico.

The incident did not come as a great surprise to members of the clergy, who had complained that they were increasingly the targets of attacks and extortion demands from drug traffickers. A few weeks earlier, priests in northern Mexico were urged by the Church hierarchy to take extra precautions for their safety after an archbishop infuriated the drug gangs by commenting on where the nation's most-wanted trafficker might be hiding out. The Archbishop of Acapulco, Felipe Aguirre Franco, lamented in response to the Arcelia murders: "We have become hostages in the violent confrontations between the drug cartels living among us."[30]

Explicit attacks on the clergy may be yet another new phase in an effort by the drug capos to eliminate or intimidate potential adversaries. There have been suspicious incidents in the past, most notably the killing of Cardinal Juan Posadas Ocampo in 1993, although the official investigation of that episode concluded that it was a case of mistaken identity rather than an assassination. True, many people in Mexico said at the time—and continue to believe—that the investigation was a blatant cover-up, and that the mistaken identity theory doesn't even pass the straight-face test. Nevertheless, there was no clear evidence that Posadas Ocampo was the victim of a drug gang hit. No one could say that about the 2009 murders of the churchmen in Arcelia.

The Catholic Church has always had a murky and, at times, somewhat ambivalent relationship with drug traffickers.[31] Officially, of course, the church condemns their illicit activities, and many church leaders do seem to genuinely detest the drug trade and the people who profit from it. But in certain areas of the country, the condemnation lacks intensity. Furthermore, prominent drug lords openly provide money to build or refurbish churches all across Mexico, and large contributions from tainted sources routinely find their way into collection plates in many locales. And, perhaps not coincidentally, church personnel have seemed to be off-limits, even as members of other professions are threatened, kidnapped, or gunned down on a regular basis.

If that implicit truce is ending, it would have profound implications for the drug war in Mexico. The cartels would be provoking an extremely powerful institution, and thereby transforming a relatively passive adversary into an angry and determined one. If they do that, knowing the risks, it suggests either that they are short-sighted and clumsy, or that they fear no adversary any more, and that their already large appetite for power is growing.

Just Being in the Wrong Place at the Wrong Time

And there are the innocent bystanders who are caught in the crossfire when fights erupt between the drug gangs or between gang members and the authorities. *Newsweek* correspondent Michael Miller noted that innocent victims, in just one brief period in 2008, included a little girl in Ciudad Juárez, six people in front of a recreation center in the same city, a 14-year-old girl in Acapulco, two small children in Tijuana, and other victims who were simply in the wrong place at the wrong time.[32]

As the fighting heats up, civilians sometimes need to worry about the police and army—as well as cartel gunmen. The tragic case of the Almanza family confirms the danger.[33] They left their home in Nuevo Laredo in April 2010 for a holiday on the Gulf coast. They drove east along the Rio Grande in their Chevrolet Tahoe toward Matamoros. That route took them through areas of Tamaulipas that were heavily infested with drug gangs and military patrols trying to root out those gangs. On a stretch of highway between Ciudad Mier and Nueva Ciudad Guerrero they saw a convoy of army vehicles parked along the road. What happened next is a subject of great dispute.

The military contends that the family was caught in a crossfire between the military patrol and gunmen during a major battle. Family survivors insist that there was no firefight. Instead, they contend that, as their vehicle passed the parked convoy, they slowed down until a soldier motioned for them to continue. Seconds later, soldiers opened up on the Tahoe with rifle fire and rocket-propelled grenades. According to the Almanzas, the military later planted evidence, including bullet-riddled SUVs, weapons, and a few dead traffickers, to cover up a huge blunder. Whatever the truth of the matter, one point was indisputable: two children, Martín Jr., 9, and Brayan, 5, lay dead, and their uncle and aunt were seriously wounded.

A similar tragedy occurred in early September 2010 when soldiers at an army checkpoint on the main highway linking Monterrey and Laredo, Texas, in an area with extensive drug trafficking activity, opened fire on a vehicle.[34] Patricia Castellanos, a 45-year-old tamale vendor, was on her way back to Monterrey after visiting her sister in the small town of Salinas Victoria. With her in the car was her husband, Vicente León; their 24-year-old daughter, Iliana; their 15-year-old son, Alejandro; their son-in-law; and two grandchildren. As in the case of the Almanzas killing, there is a huge difference between the account that the family gives and the official military version of events.

According to Patricia Castellanos and other family members, they had just passed an army convoy when shots rang out and riddled their vehicle, killing Alejandro instantly. Vicente was mortally wounded and would die a short time later at a hospital. Three other family members suffered wounds ranging from minor to serious. The military contends that soldiers shot at the car when it failed to stop at a military checkpoint, arguing that the tragedy resulted from the family's own blunder. Yet according to Patricia, the military commander of the unit later visited the survivors at the hospital and apologized for his men. And the state government of Nuevo León offered to pay both medical and funeral expenses. That is not the typical response if the authorities believed that the soldiers were acting properly and that the family had either made a mistake or had engaged in a reckless action.

Despite incidents like the Almanzas and León Castellanos tragedies, innocent civilians need to worry more about the traffickers than they do about the military. Sometimes victims of the cartels almost seem to be chosen at random. A student athlete in Ciudad Juárez was kidnapped in January 2009 by gunmen disguised as soldiers. His body was discovered a few hours later. At roughly the same time, a local butcher, who had survived an attack on an auto repair shop two months earlier, was shot to death. Apparently neither victim was involved in the drug trade. One of the casualties in Ciudad Juárez, during an upsurge in killings in November 2009, was a three-year-old child. And on one especially bloody day that saw 15 people killed in that border city later that month, victims included a seven-year-old boy, three women who apparently had no connection to the drug trade, and an unassuming university professor.[35]

The mounting toll of innocent civilians is hardly surprising. As the turf fights between rival trafficking gangs and between various

81

cartels and the Mexican military become more intense, the danger of "collateral damage" also increases. Furthermore, the ranks of cartel enforcers are rapidly expanding beyond the usual professional assassins; newer and more amateurish hit men, some of whom are willing to whack a target for $100 or even less, are becoming far more numerous. They are indifferent about whether innocent civilians get caught in their fusillade of bullets. "To kill one person, they shoot hundreds of rounds and maybe hit the person [their target] with five," said Enrique Torres, spokesman for the joint police-military command in Ciudad Juárez.[36]

Vicente Burciaga, who lived in El Porvenir—a small town in the middle of a major trafficking route southeast of Juárez—laments how it has become increasingly dangerous for ordinary civilians. "They are killing people over there who have nothing to do with drug trafficking. They kill you just for having seen what they are doing."[37]

Sometimes people don't even need to have witnessed anything to become targets. The horrible attacks on teenagers at the birthday party in Ciudad Juárez in late January 2010 and the July 2010 attack on the birthday party at the Italia Inn restaurant in Torreón (both discussed in the Introduction) confirms that depressing reality.

Journalists and others immediately began to compare the Torreón slaughter to the January bloodbath in Juárez. Because the party announcement had been posted on a gay website (among other places), there was some initial speculation that the attack may have been a homophobic hate crime. But that theory was quickly discarded. The weapons used—multiple AK-47s—strongly suggested a drug cartel hit. So did the coordination with heavily armed assailants converging on the scene in a convoy of SUVs. The fact that Torreón had already become a battleground between the Gulf cartel and the Zetas added to the suspicion that this was no ordinary crime—or even a hate crime. Within 24 hours, Mexican police were confident that the bloodbath was the latest handiwork of a drug gang; they just weren't sure which one.

As was the case with the murders at the Juárez party, there was little evidence that any of the people at the Torreón celebration were involved in drug trafficking—and solid evidence that many of them were not. Police were baffled about a possible motive. And people recalled two earlier, very troubling attacks in local bars where the motives were equally unclear. At the end of January, gunmen had killed 10 young people, and in May another attack took the lives of 8 more. In both cases, several of the victims were students who had no obvious ties to drug gangs.[38]

The same was true of the March 2010 incident in Durango, in which cartel gunmen at a checkpoint attacked a group of elementary- and high-school students on their way to receive government scholarships for continuing study. Vehicles in the student convoy were hit by hand grenades as well as bullets from rifles and automatic pistols. The grenades were especially deadly, tearing gaping holes in their vehicles. Investigators could find no evidence tying any of the victims to the drug trade.

Were all the killings cases of mistaken identity, as the January assault on the party in Juárez appeared to be? Or even worse, were they purely terrorist attacks—and were such incidents now becoming a frequent feature of life in Mexico? Either way, the proliferation of such bloodbaths is causing mounting worries. The Torreón massacre, occurring just three days after a car bombing in Juárez (the first time that tactic made an appearance in Mexico's drug wars), especially added to public uneasiness.

The ranks of innocent victims also are swelling as the cartels branch into other activities, especially kidnapping, to generate revenue.[39] One practice that is becoming increasingly common is to "tax" migrants from Mexico or Central America that are trying to go to the United States. Since cartels control the drug trafficking routes, it is not a big challenge for them to gain control over the routes for illegal immigration as well. Often, the routes are virtually the same. The Zetas have been especially active in that new enterprise, either extorting money directly from the migrants or threatening them until they reveal the names and telephone numbers of relatives in the United States (or in some cases, back home) who are able to pay a ransom via wire transfer so that the migrants can continue on their way.

Sometimes, though, what starts out as simple financial shakedown turns far more tragic. An especially ugly incident took place in Tamaulipas, now the principal battleground between the Zetas and the Gulf cartel. On August 25, 2010, police discovered 72 bodies (58 men and 14 women) stacked in a cinder-block building on a ranch about 100 miles south of the U.S. border. Most victims had been blindfolded and had their hands tied behind their backs before being shot execution style. One survivor, an Ecuadorean migrant named Luis Freddy Lala Pomavilla, staggered to a police checkpoint despite a bullet in his neck. He told of the horrific massacre and said that comments by some of the gunmen indicated that they were members of the Zetas.[40]

Why the slaughter occurred was not clear. One theory was that too many of the migrants were both destitute and lacked relatives with funds in the United States or in their home countries. Another possibility was that police patrols in the vicinity spooked the gunmen, and they decided to quickly eliminate witnesses and make their escape. A third possibility, which the Ecuadorean survivor's sketchy testimony seemed to support, is that the Zetas wanted to compel the migrants to become indentured foot soldiers for their trafficking operation and killed those who refused.[41] Whatever the reason, 72 innocent souls paid the ultimate price for being unlucky.

Even when innocent people are not killed in the drug violence, they are sometimes emotionally traumatized. That is especially true of Mexico's children, who have witnessed far too much of the slaughter. In Tijuana, children were playing on the playground of their primary school when fighting erupted between police and a cartel hit man. The police won that round, but pupils witnessed the exchange of gunfire and the spattering of blood from the fatally wounded gunman. The terrified kids ran screaming and crying back inside. Laura Elena Carrión, a teacher at the school, later admitted to reporters: "Children are scared, and we have pupils with very serious emotional crises."[42] In another Tijuana drug killing in March 2009, children witnessed police forensic investigators collect three beheaded and dismembered bodies near a shopping mall. The innocence and bewilderment of some of the country's emotionally scarred children is painful to behold. One eight-year-old girl, who had seen a dead body from a drug gang shootout, admitted "it feels awful to see it." Puzzled, she asked church counselors: "Didn't anyone tell them that killing is wrong?"[43]

School children are getting front-row seats to the drug war on all too many occasions. On June 15, 2010, soldiers and cartel enforcers battled for an hour barely 60 feet from a preschool in Taxco. Later that month, gunfights occurred near public schools in the northern city of Apodaca and in Bellavista, a small town in the western part of Mexico. Following the Taxco incident, school officials in the state of Guerrero ordered special training for all 54,000 teachers about how to keep their students from becoming casualties in a drug war crossfire. Several schools went beyond mere training and held special "shootout drills," instructing students how to "duck and cover" if a gun battle started while school was in session. Other schools systems throughout Mexico are holding similar drills, and several states are circulating manuals to teachers about how to respond to shooting incidents that might put their young charges at risk.

Another lesson plan included admonishing students not to try to take photos or videos of the fighting with their cell phones. Erika Arciniega, director of Crime Prevention for the Guerrero state police, noted that "the first thing the kids want to do is take pictures to post on their social networks."[44] But such a move would instantly make them a target of drug gang members—who tend to be camera shy.

"We're in a situation like nothing we've ever lived through before," Juan Guardo, director of school safety in Tamaulipas, lamented. "And we need to keep the kids safe."[45] Some parents worry that shootout drills scare children unduly, but given the events of the past few years, the caution of school administrators seems warranted—and perhaps even a little belated.

The growing recklessness of the drug gangs about possible collateral damage was graphically demonstrated in April 2010, when a wild shootout took place in Acapulco that left six people dead. Three things were notable about the episode: it occurred in broad daylight, it took place on the main boulevard in the principal tourist area, and many of the victims were innocent bystanders. Among the dead were a mother, her eight-year-old daughter, and a taxi driver. The woman had apparently just picked up her daughter from school and was taking her home. Both the brazenness of the attack and the utter indifference of the warring cartel gunmen regarding civilian casualties produced immediate panic. Terrified motorists tried to drive over the median to escape the gunfire, and there were several crashes in the process. Their escape efforts proved only partially successful, though, as more than a dozen vehicles ended up riddled with bullet holes. In addition to the three innocent people that were killed, another five were wounded.[46]

The body count of innocent victims is rising, and the Mexican people are beginning to exhibit the characteristics of a terrorized population. Ordinary citizens who never thought that they would be involved in the drug wars now find themselves caught up in the maelstrom of violence that is afflicting more and more portions of the country. Minding your own business and staying on the right side of the law is no longer reliable protection against becoming a casualty statistic. That fear has an alarming, corrosive effect on society, and all signs suggest that the situation may get even worse.

4. "Silver or Lead?" The Sources of the Cartels' Power

The main reason the Mexican drug cartels wield such alarming power and can inflict terrible violence on government officials, business people, and innocent civilians is that they have a vast reservoir of money at their disposal. The global trade in illegal drugs is a huge, extremely profitable enterprise, estimated at $320 billion a year or more. Mexico's share of that trade is generally thought to be at least $30 billion to $35 billion, and some estimates place the figure as high as $60 billion.[1]

The overwhelming majority of the drug trade's value is because the drugs in which the cartels are involved are illegal, thereby creating a massive black-market premium culminating in an inflated retail price. Participants along every portion of the supply and distribution pipeline profit from that premium. For those organizations willing to incur the risks, financial and physical, of trafficking in marijuana, cocaine, methamphetamine, and other prohibited drugs, the profit margins are far greater than they would be in any legal enterprise. Without the black-market premium, which exists largely because Washington's determined commitment to a prohibitionist policy has maintained a consensus against legalization among the world's governments, the drug trade in Mexico would likely be only a $3 billion to $5 billion a year industry. Although that amount is not trivial, it is very modest compared with the current situation under a system of prohibition.

Moreover, the illegality of the drug trade guarantees that most participants will be individuals who have no qualms about breaking not only the laws against illicit drugs, but the laws against other actions, including kidnapping, torture, and murder. Prohibition has channeled commerce in mind-altering substances into the hands of violent trafficking organizations, most notably the Mexican cartels. And it has provided those cartels with wealth and power beyond their wildest expectations—wealth and power that they use extensively to penetrate Mexico's political system.

Such enormous sums in the coffers of the cartels create an ideal climate to intimidate or corrupt Mexican government officials. Those twin strategies are captured in the alternative that traffickers reportedly give to police, judges, business people, and political figures: *plata o plomo?* Silver or lead? In other words, will you take a bribe, or will we have to kill you?

The former technique was in evidence when scandal enveloped the July 2009 elections for the Chamber of Deputies (the lower house in Mexico's Congress), several governorships, and several hundred mayoral posts. One candidate who found himself in a less than desired spotlight was Mario Aguiano, a candidate for governor of Colima, a state on the Pacific coast directly west of Mexico City. The Zetas, at the time the enforcers for the Gulf cartel, hung a banner on a busy highway overpass praising Aguiano: "The Zetas support you, and we are with you to the death."[2] In a normal political setting, someone running for office would probably regard that endorsement as about as politically helpful as an endorsement by Nancy Pelosi for a candidate in a Utah Republican primary. Predictably, Aguiano denounced the Zetas's banner as a "dirty trick" by a rival candidate.

Other political figures have also adopted the "dirty tricks" defense when embarrassing evidence surfaces. Fresnillo mayor David Monreal, in the state of Zacatecas, accused his political enemies of planting a huge stash (some 14.5 tons) of marijuana that police discovered in a chili-pepper drying facility owned by his brother. Skeptics mused that Monreal's political adversaries had to be really motivated to go through the difficulty of buying and then storing such a vast quantity of drugs in a facility they didn't control.

Allegations of political dirty tricks have some plausibility. Yet in Aguiano's case, the family has disturbing, indisputable ties to drug trafficking. The candidate's own brother is serving a 10-year prison sentence in Mexico for trafficking in methamphetamine, and another family member is serving a 27-year sentence in Texas for running a large meth ring. Such ties stoked suspicions that the Gulf cartel's campaign embrace may have been genuine, albeit indiscreet. Perhaps more troubling, the drug links miasma surrounding Aguiano apparently did not seem to dent his popularity with Colima voters. Indeed, in the days following the display of the Zetas's banner, his level of support in pre-election polls actually went *up*. At the very least, that reaction suggested a rather blasé public attitude about allegations of drug-related corruption. Martha Sosa Govea, the PAN candidate against Aguiano, conceded that her efforts to highlight the issue had been less than successful, noting that the reaction of many voters was, "Poor guy, why don't they leave him alone."[3]

The apparent involvement of the cartels in the 2009 election was an escalation of their financial focus on the political process. Until the beginning of the 21st century, drug organizations directed most of their bribes to law enforcement personnel, since they were in the best position to impede or facilitate trafficking operations. That strategy has gradually shifted in recent years, with the traffickers devoting more and more resources to influencing the political process itself in an attempt to elect pliable candidates. The erosion of the seven-decade, one-party dominance by the Institutional Revolutionary Party (PRI) and the emergence of a multiparty system with hotly contested elections facilitated the entry of the cartels as major political players. James McDonald, an expert on Mexico's politics, notes: "In this newly competitive, moderately democratic system, it takes serious money to run a political campaign."[4]

Another scholar, Shannon O'Neil, reaches a similar conclusion in the pages of the prominent U.S. policy journal *Foreign Affairs*:

> Mexico's Achilles' heel is corruption—which in an electoral democracy cannot be stabilizing the way it was in the days of Mexico's autocracy. Under the PRI, the purpose of government policy was to assert power rather than govern by law. The opacity of court proceedings, the notorious graft of the police forces, and the menacing presence of special law enforcement agencies were essential elements of an overall system of political, economic, and social control.[5]

She adds that as today's democratic political system struggles to overcome that history, "it faces a new threat: increasingly sophisticated, well-funded, and autonomous criminal organizations intent on manipulating the rule of law for their own benefit."

The Political Clout of the Cartels

Professor Edgardo Buscaglia, an expert on Mexico's politics, concludes that the cartels either control or heavily influence better than

70 percent of the country's municipal governments. He notes that in most of those jurisdictions, the drug enterprises operate openly, with little or no interference from political officials or law enforcement agencies.[6] Virgilio Mendoza Amezcua, a PAN chamber of deputies candidate in Colima, was caught on tape acknowledging the financial temptations the traffickers put in front of aspiring politicians. "You don't imagine how many 'nice' people have relations with those drug-trafficking bastards," he fumed. "They try to seduce you. They got close to me like they get close to half the world, and they sent me money."[7] He did not indicate whether he had accepted that money.

A more focused investigation that the Mexican government conducted in 2010, with regard to Michoacán, seemed to support Buscaglia's pessimistic thesis. That investigation concluded La Familia controlled 83 of the state's 113 municipalities. Even more worrisome, the report contended that the cartel controlled a third of Michoacán's "formal" (i.e., legal) economy.[8] And that's just one drug organization. Granted, Michoacán was the citadel of La Familia, but rivals, especially the Sinaloa cartel, also have a presence there. That suggests the degree of cartel control of the state's government and economy may be even more pervasive.

A September 2007 intelligence assessment by the U.S. Federal Bureau of Investigation (FBI) accused governors of two states, Veracruz and Michoacán, of collusion with the Gulf cartel. According to the FBI report, the cartel agreed to dampen the violence in the former and fund the municipal candidacies of cooperative political figures in the latter. In exchange, Veracruz governor Fidel Herrera allegedly allowed the cartel to secure a trafficking route through the state, and Michoacán governor Lazáro Cárdenas Batel supposedly gave the cartel free rein to control a key port and to collect a "tax" on drug shipments from other cartels. Both men emphatically denied the allegations, as did Cárdenas Batel's successor, Leonel Godoy. There is one interesting feature, if the FBI report is accurate: Herrera is a member of the PRI, while Batel and Godoy are members of the leftist Party of the Democratic Revolution, suggesting that the drug traffickers adopt a somewhat nonpartisan approach to bribery.

In Godoy's case, the scandal was just beginning to heat up. Ten months after the FBI assessment, Monte Alejandro Rubido, a senior security official in Calderón's administration, openly accused

Godoy's half brother, Julio César, of being in charge of "institutional protection" for the operations of La Familia. Later, the authorities would allege that he had accepted more than $2 million from the cartel. Julio César Godoy had been elected to the Chamber of Deputies in July 2009 but fled the authorities following Rubido's allegations. He did not return to take his seat in the Chamber for more than a year, eventually returning to be sworn in—and thereby receive an automatic immunity from prosecution. His arrival was something out of a cheap suspense novel—managing to evade police who had the building surrounded in an effort to apprehend him before he could take the oath of office.

Whether the charges were accurate or merely part of the vicious political rivalry between the PAN and the PRD was difficult to determine. However, additional damaging allegations about César Godoy surfaced in October 2010, when federal prosecutors leaked a taped conversation between Servando Gómez, a top La Familia lieutenant, and the congressman. The voice identified as that of Gómez pledged to support Godoy in the upcoming election, stating "I want you to win, and you can count on all the help you need." Equally damaging, the two men appeared to be close friends. They referred to each other as "compa," a slang term for *compadre*. "Compa" is an especially affectionate term, usually reserved not merely for good friends, but the godfather of one's child—the very closest of friends.[9]

The drug cartels' lack of partisanship in their financial generosity appears to exist in other areas of Mexico. Mauricio Fernández, the mayoral candidate of President Calderón's party in San Pedro Garza García, an affluent Monterrey suburb, was recorded telling supporters that the Beltrán Leyva drug gang controlled security in the town. "Penetration by drug traffickers is for real, and they approach every candidate who they think may win," he stated bluntly. Then, in a comment that would spark a firestorm of speculation, he added: "In my case, I made it very clear to them that I didn't want blatant selling."[10] Opponents immediately raised two issues. Why was Fernández speaking to known traffickers? And did he reject "subtle" as opposed to "blatant" selling?

More and more questions exist about the nature and extent of ties between political figures and drug kingpins. Such questions surfaced in a spectacular fashion in early November 2009, when Fernández, now the newly re-elected mayor of San Pedro Garza García, shared exciting news with the crowd of cheering supporters attending his acceptance speech. He announced that Héctor Saldana, known as "Black Saldana," reputed to be the local head of the Beltrán Leyva organization, had been found dead in Mexico City.

There was just one problem. Mexico City authorities wouldn't discover Sadana's mutilated corpse for another three and a half hours, and it wouldn't be identified for another two days. Barring a major case of extrasensory perception, it seemed odd that Mayor Fernández had the knowledge of Saldana's demise long before the authorities did. Inquiring minds wanted to know how that was possible. Fernández initially tried to brush off such queries by observing that sometimes "there are coincidences in life; it's better to look at it this way."[11] When that explanation did not fly, he contended that U.S. intelligence sources had first alerted him to Saldana's plan to kill him and then to the trafficker's own death. U.S. authorities, though, did not back up the mayor's story, refusing to comment on the matter.

It is possible that Fernández was telling the truth about being briefed by a DEA source, especially if the agency had information that he was a cartel target. Another possibility is that the Saldana incident was a case of a vigilante group executing a violent drug trafficker. Indeed, an article in *Reforma* engaged in precisely that speculation with the headline "Death Squads?" Fernández himself fueled speculation along those same lines during a radio interview on November 3, announcing the establishment of a group to "clean up" crime in his city. When asked whether that "cleaning group" would act outside the law, he replied that in "some form that's correct."

But there is an even darker possibility: that a competing cartel executed Saldana, and that Mayor Fernández had links to that cartel. Fernández's comments on the leaked recording, six months earlier during his campaign, caused many people to believe it was a plausible explanation. One portion of the recording now seemed even more disturbing than it did at the time. In that passage, he admitted that major drug traffickers lived in the town, but urged supporters not to worry because such individuals had a vested interest in keeping the place quiet. When the recording originally surfaced, Fernández charged that those remarks were taken out of context, but the Saldana episode revived suspicions that he was cozy with at least some drug lords.

Efforts to curtail the financial clout of the drug capos in Mexico's political system have been strikingly ineffective. The federal government has tried to make it difficult for drug money to infiltrate campaigns at all levels. The centerpiece of that effort is a program of lavish public financing of campaigns, including free radio and television ads for candidates. Such generous public financing is combined with extremely tight restrictions on private donations.

On the surface, it would appear to have worked. No candidate has been convicted of receiving illicit campaign donations since Calderón became president. Indeed, as of early 2011, no candidate had even been charged with that offense. But appearances are deceiving. For one thing, cartel donations are very hard to trace. The drug capos generally do not use bank drafts, personal checks, or wire transfers for any purpose, since those can easily be traced. For them, cash is still king, and any contributions given to political aspirants or incumbents would invariably be under the table. And cash payments are inherently difficult to track.

Moreover, it seems that traffickers have moved away from direct contributions in favor of indirect support. Money flowing from such sources now benefits the businesses, homes, or other private ventures of candidates, rather than going directly to their campaigns. That technique makes it very difficult for even honest law enforcement agencies—much less agencies that are themselves thoroughly compromised by drug money—to trace the source of funds. "There is no way in Mexico to control this," stated Manuel Clouthier, a PAN congressman from drug-ridden Sinaloa state. "This supervision of funding is just another sham." He added that while "narco-politics goes back many years," it seemed to be getting worse. Referring to July 2010 local elections, Clouthier concluded that narco-politics was "looking for its coronation in these elections."[12]

The law enforcement system and the political system are not the only institutions that the cartels have penetrated extensively. Indeed, it is not certain that any institution in Mexico has remained uncontaminated by the drug trade. There are even allegations that the Catholic Church has willingly received contributions from known drug traffickers. The administration of President Vicente Fox launched an investigation of money laundering that included inquiries into the role of the Church. Cardinal Juan Sandoval of

Guadalajara even had his bank records subpoenaed during the course of the investigation.[13]

Bishop Ramón Godínez, of the central state of Aguascalientes, caused an uproar in October 2005 when he conceded that donations from traffickers were not unusual and argued that it was not the Church's responsibility to investigate the source of donations. "Just because the origin of the money is bad doesn't mean that you have to burn it," Godínez said. "Instead, you have to transform it. . . ." The money, he said, was "purified" once it passed through the parish doors.[14]

In October 2010, federal prosecutors launched a probe to determine whether Heriberto Lazcano Lazcano, the head of the Zetas, funded the renovation of a church near the city of Pachuca. Manuel Corral, an official with Mexico's bishops' council, stated that money for the restoration apparently came from Lazcano's mother, who served on the church's restoration committee. If the priest knew of the source of the donation, Corral stated, his action should be sanctioned. There seemed little doubt that the money did come from the Zetas leader. When a plaque was unveiled following the renovation, Lazcano's name was on it as one of the principal donors. A statement that the local diocese put out once the scandal broke contended that "it came as a considerable shock to the community, especially now that the media has linked this person to organized crime." One can speculate whether Church officials were really that innocent and whether Corral's contention that he was unaware of any other cases of drug traffickers donating money to the Church has credibility.

The "Silver or Lead?" Dilemma

There are indications that the cartels increasingly give the silver or lead "choice" to key personnel outside of the law enforcement and political arenas. One doctor, who worked for the Arellano Félix organization in Tijuana, summed up his personal dilemma: "You can't say no to these people. You take what they are offering or they kill you."[15] The doctor had been pressed into service on numerous occasions to treat senior hit men who had been wounded in gunfights.

The underlying message from traffickers is very simple. The cartels will conduct their business without interference, one way or the other. The problem, though, for police personnel and other government officials (and even lawyers, doctors, and others who deal with the traffickers, voluntarily or involuntarily) is that even agreeing to accept the offer of silver does not guarantee safety. If the drug lord offering the bribe becomes dissatisfied with the performance of the bribe taker, or concludes that perhaps the individual knows too much about the organization's internal workings, he might still order an assassination. Even if that does not happen, rival traffickers may resent the assistance that the official has given and order a hit.

An incident in Tijuana illustrated how selecting silver over lead can still leave a corrupt official in an insecure—even fatal—position. At 5:30 in the morning on October 9, 2009, factory workers arriving for their shift in an industrial area found the mutilated body of Rogelio Sánchez hanging from a bridge. He had been kidnapped as he left his home two days earlier. A police investigation concluded that Sánchez, a Baja California state official in charge of driver's licenses, had been selling them to drug traffickers and other members of organized crime. The criminals apparently didn't have much gratitude for his services. Despite such incidents, though, most people given the silver or lead option deem it far safer to accept bribes than to attempt to defy the cartels.

Pervasive Official Corruption

Drug related corruption, ranging from low-echelon police officers to the highest-level officials, has a long history in Mexico. Robert C. Bonner, who headed the U.S. Drug Enforcement Administration under President George H. W. Bush, describes how the then-powerful Guadalajara cartel had thoroughly penetrated the Jalisco police force in the 1980s:

> In February 1985, when Enrique 'Kiki' Camarena, a U.S. Drug Enforcement Administration agent, was kidnapped, tortured, and killed, the U.S. government began to grasp the full extent of the problem in Mexico. . . . The DEA's investigation of the killing uncovered widespread corruption and complicity in drug trafficking at all levels of the Mexican government. A large portion of the Jalisco state police force, it turned out, was on the payroll of the Guadalajara cartel. Indeed, it was Jalisco state police officers who had abducted Camarena at the behest of the Guadalajara cartel.[16]

Bonner goes on to describe how the financial and ethical rot was by no means confined to just one state police force:

> "The corruption extended beyond the state police and into the governor's office and even into the federal government, including the principal internal security agency, the Federal Directorate of Security. The [DEA's] investigation revealed that the *comandantes* of the Mexican Federal Judicial Police, who at the time oversaw all federal police in each state, had been bought off by the drug cartels; *comandante* positions in the northern Mexican states were going for several million dollars each. The 'bagman' was a senior official in the attorney general's office.[17]

It became clear during the following decade that nothing had changed for the better. The National Police Commander was caught with $2.4 million in the trunk of his car. Later he was convicted of giving more than $20 million to another government official to buy protection for a notorious drug lord.[18] Perhaps the most embarrassing incident prior to the 2008–2009 arrests of high officials in the Attorney General's office occurred in the mid-1990s when President Ernesto Zedillo appointed General José de Jesús Gutiérrez Rebollo to be Mexico's new drug czar. The general seemed to have excellent drug-fighting credentials, having personally led a much-publicized raid against the Tijuana cartel. U.S. officials greeted Gutiérrez Rebollo's appointment enthusiastically. U.S. drug czar Barry McCaffrey gushed: "He has a reputation for impeccable integrity. . . . He's a deadly serious guy."[19] Three months later, the Mexican government announced that its new drug czar was in a maximum-security prison, charged with taking bribes and protecting the nation's largest drug trafficker. The general had indeed been tough on drug trafficking—tough, that is, on organizations that competed with his patron's cartel.

Matters have gotten progressively worse since that episode. In February 2000, Tijuana's police chief was assassinated—the second such assassination in less than six years. A short time later, seven men, including two former members of the Tijuana police force, were arrested for the chief's killing. The men confessed to working for the Sinaloa cartel. In another incident, a bloody gun battle ensued in downtown Tijuana when police attempted to stop a drug trafficker's armed motorcade. The commander of the police unit and three officers were killed by the trafficker's bodyguards. Those bodyguards, it turned out, were local police officers.

The government of President Vicente Fox made a serious effort to crack down on police that had been co-opted by the drug cartels. At one point, more than 700 officers were charged with offenses, ranging from taking bribes to instances of drug-related kidnapping and murder. Yet most knowledgeable observers believed that those arrested represented only the tip of a very big iceberg of corruption.

Both violence and police corruption in Nuevo Laredo reached the point in June 2005 that Mexico's national government suspended the entire Nuevo Laredo police force and sent in the federal police to patrol the streets. For President Fox's administration, the final straw came when Nuevo Laredo's new police chief was assassinated just hours after his appointment, apparently because he was serious about rooting out internal corruption.[20]

Federal authorities proceeded to purge the city's police force. After being required to take polygraph exams, 305 of the 765 police officers were dismissed. Indeed, 41 of them were arrested for attacking the federal police when those units arrived in the city. The "new and improved" Nuevo Laredo police were put back on the streets in late July, wearing new uniforms with white shirts. The white color was chosen deliberately, according to Mexican federal authorities, to demonstrate that they were a trustworthy new entity.[21] Those officials apparently were serious.

The fiasco with the Nuevo Laredo police was just one indication of the steadily mounting corruption within Mexico's political and law enforcement systems. Several of the most egregious episodes of violent drug turf struggles, including one in and around the popular resort city of Cancún, involved present or former police officers. In March 2005, prosecutors charged 27 state, federal, and local police in Cancún with running a drug ring or aiding in the murder of fellow police officers.[22] In another case, a state police commander and 12 other officers in the state of Chihuahua were arrested in connection with the killing of 11 people near Ciudad Juárez. "Instead of protecting and guaranteeing the safety of the population," they were "openly working with organized crime," said Mexico's deputy attorney general.[23]

There is no indication that the corruption of police forces has diminished under the Calderón administration. In September 2009, the city of Cancún fired another 30 officers because of corruption concerns. Two months earlier, nearly 80 police officers were arrested in 18 towns across Nuevo León after soldiers found their names on an organizational roster that had been captured from traffickers. Just before Christmas 2009, soldiers discovered a list of dozens of police in Monterrey who were apparently on the payroll of traffickers. Many of them received up to $1,500 a month to assist the Zetas, in some cases working as actual hit men, but more often by tipping off the organization about any state security operations that might impact them.[24]

The corruption problem was so severe among Mexico's 2,022 municipal police departments (some 40 percent of Mexico's police forces) that Public Safety Secretary Genaro García Luna recommended that all of them be abolished and their personnel combined with state police forces. He argued that local police were an especially "easy target for corruption" by the drug gangs, since more than 60 percent of them received salaries of barely $300 per month.[25] Incorporating them into state forces, García Luna contended, would reduce the potential for corruption.

But his proposal was, at best, a Band-Aid solution. Municipal police are hardly the only law enforcement personnel who have been seduced by drug money. Indeed, the record of state police departments, and—as García Luna himself acknowledged, the federal police he inherited—is scarcely better. An embarrassing incident that underscored the problem occurred in August 2010 when some 200 federal police rioted in Ciudad Juárez and took one of their commanders hostage. Their grievance? They alleged that the commander and three other officials with that rank were on the payroll of one of the cartels. Whatever the truth of that particular allegation, police forces at all levels in Mexico are riddled with corruption. And given the enormous sums of money available to the cartels for that purpose, such a result should come as no surprise.

Although the Mexican military has a reputation for being significantly less corrupt than local, state, or federal police forces, the generals still fret about the danger of their troops succumbing to financial temptation. In 2007, the military raised the salary for members of the elite commando units to $1,100 per month in an effort to induce soldiers to stay loyal and not defect to the cartels—as the unit that became the Zetas had done years earlier. How much of an uphill struggle that strategy confronted, though, was apparent when the cartels promptly doubled the salaries they were paying their own troops, thus creating an even bigger incentive for government commandos to join the other side.[26]

Even when cartel leaders are arrested and imprisoned, that appears to do little to impede the operation of the criminal enterprises. Indeed, all too often, the authorities have been implicated in those illicit activities. Time and again, drug capos have been able to control trafficking operations from their prison cells with impunity. Lower-level personnel sometimes have to wait until a prison break can be arranged, but even that is little more than a minor inconvenience. A typical incident occurred in May 2009 when 53 inmates, many them members of the Zetas, escaped from Cieneguillas prison in Zacatecas state without encountering any resistance. Security-camera footage showed that guards at the prison simply stood by as an armed gang led the escapees away. It was not immediately clear whether the guards had been bribed or intimidated, but federal authorities jailed the prison director and all 44 guards pending an investigation about their possible complicity.[27]

The degree of collusion involving that prison break, though, was minor compared with the scandal that broke in July 2010. Guards and officials at the prison in Gómez Palacio in Durango state allegedly did a lot more than allow prisoners to escape and resume their lives of crime on the outside: they supposedly let inmates out temporarily so that they could carry out assigned killings on behalf of their employer. After completing their assignment, the hit men would return to their prison cells. In essence, the prison served the drug gangs as little more than a dormitory or hotel—paid for, of course, by Mexican taxpayers.

But the prison authorities may have done more than merely allow the inmates to have weekend passes for their work. The killers allegedly were given weapons—and even official vehicles—to assist them in their rampages. The Gómez Palacio scandal was especially upsetting because the cartel soldiers who were allowed to use the prison as a base of operations were apparently responsible for the slaughter at the birthday party in Torreón earlier that month that resulted in the deaths of 17 innocent people (see chapter 3).[28]

The factor of pervasive, long-standing corruption makes it unlikely that Calderón's administration, or any future government, will make any more lasting progress than previous administrations against the drug trade. Several major scandals have surfaced in just the past few years. In April 2008, authorities arrested the police chief of Reynosa for allegedly protecting members of the Gulf cartel.[29] In October of that year, prosecutors charged that employees of the federal Attorney General's office were working for a subunit of the Sinaloa cartel. Two top employees of the organized crime unit and at least three federal police agents assigned to it allegedly were passing information to the cartel regarding surveillance targets and potential raids. They supposedly received payments of between $150,000 and $450,000 *per month* for their information.[30] Less than two weeks later, prosecutors announced that Rodolfo de la Guardia García, the number-two official in Mexico's Federal Bureau of Investigation from 2003 to 2005, had been placed under house arrest pending an investigation into allegations that he, too, had leaked information to the Sinaloa cartel.

The scandals continued. In late November, the government announced the arrest of Noé Ramírez, the chief of the Special Organized Crime Investigation Division until July 2008, for allegedly taking bribes from traffickers. Ramírez had been President Calderón's highly regarded drug policy czar and the chief liaison with U.S. anti-drug officials. The ensuing scandal cast a shadow over Ramírez's boss, Attorney General Eduardo Medina Mora, and was a factor in Medina Mora's resignation in September 2009.

The size of the alleged payoffs underscore why Mexican law enforcement personnel are so susceptible to corruption by the cartels. By cooperating with the drug trafficking syndicates, individuals can earn more—often far more—in a single month than they could ever hope to earn in their legal jobs in years—and in some cases, more than they could earn in decades. That is especially true for local police, many of whom make a mere $4,000 to $5,000 a year. The situation in Uruapan, a city of 280,000 that sits astride one of the major trafficking routes in the Sierra Madre Mountains, is typical. There, the average police officer receives a monthly salary of about $460, and some of the more junior officers get a paltry $300. Many times, they also have to pay for their own uniforms—and even their own bullets. Police Chief Adolfo Medina tried to improve the situation by tapping into the $1 billion dollars the Calderón government had made available to improve the quality of local police forces. Medina's goal was to boost the base salary to $615 a month.[31]

Given such low salaries, the financial temptations that the drug cartels create are hard to resist. According to a former mid-level Tijuana policeman, "there is barely a Mexican police officer along the U.S. border who isn't involved in the drug trade. Even if you try to resist, your superiors pressure you into it or sideline you."[32] He had resigned from the force after reportedly witnessing his commander receive a $5,000 bribe to ignore drug smuggling in his sector.

The Calderón government has made a major effort to purge federal and local police forces of corrupt personnel. In September 2009, Mexican federal authorities arrested 124 law enforcement officials in Hidalgo state on suspicion of being linked to the Zetas. According to a spokesman for the attorney general's office, most of those arrested were municipal police officers, but there were some high-level state and federal officials as well. Among them were Juan Antonio Franco Bustos, chief of coordination for Hidalgo state security; Julio César Sánchez Amador, head of public security in the city of Mineral de la Reforma; Mario Hernández Almonasi, director of the auto theft unit for the state ministerial police; Raúl Batres Campos, regional chief for the Federal Investigation Agency; and José Esteban Olvera Jiménez, a deputy director with the state security service.[33]

Despite those efforts, the corruption beat goes on. Mexican federal police arrested the mayor of Cancún, Gregorio Sánchez, in May 2010 on charges of drug trafficking and money laundering. At the time of his arrest, Sánchez had taken a leave of absence from his mayoral post to run for governor of Quintana Roo.

It was hardly the first time that Quintana Roo had been an arena for scandal. Mario Villanueva, who had served as governor in the mid-1990s, later became a notorious fugitive on drug-trafficking charges. He was ultimately captured and given a 36-year sentence following his conviction. And Quintana Roo was rocked again in the summer of 2009 by a scandal involving top police and prosecution officials. A judge ordered eight of them to stand trial for aiding the Beltrán Leyva and Gulf cartels. Those indicted included the two highest officials in the federal attorney general's office stationed in Quintana Roo, the former state public safety secretary, and two other former department heads.

The circumstances surrounding Sánchez's arrest remained murky and raised questions about just who might be corrupt. Sánchez, the candidate of the leftist Party of the Democratic Revolution, alleged that as soon he made his bid for governor, he was warned: "Resign from the race, we are going to put you in jail or kill you."[34] Perhaps that allegation was just a smokescreen to conceal his guilt, and he did ultimately withdraw from the race, but given the brass-knuckles nature of Mexican politics and the pervasive reach of the traffickers, no one could be certain.

In addition to the effort to root out corrupt political office holders, during the summer of 2009 Calderón's government embarked on a similar purge regarding customs agents in the Servicio de Administración Tributaria (SAT)—the tax administration service. The SAT ousted some 1,100 customs agents and replaced them with 1,470 new personnel who had undergone special training and background checks.[35] Customs agents were notorious for failing to inspect cargo and deliberately looking the other way as drug shipments passed through Mexico on their way to the United States or other markets. Given the enormous temptation that drug money poses, only the most incurable optimist would assume that the new agents will be more honest than their predecessors—or at least that they will remain honest, even if they start out that way. That is true of even the highest-level officials in charge of key Mexican ports.

Corrupt officials are frequently offered deals for reduced sentences. But those who try to turn on their drug lord patrons and aid the prosecution run a grave risk. It is clear that the Mexican authorities cannot really provide safety to such "protected witnesses." A graphic example of that inability occurred in December 2009 when former federal police official Edgar Bayardo was gunned down while drinking coffee at a Starbucks in Mexico City. Bayardo was detained and placed under house arrest in 2008 on suspicion of collaborating with the Sinaloa cartel. He had attracted suspicion with an upscale home and an assortment of high-priced cars, an extensive art collection, and other luxury items—things he could not possibly afford on a civil servant's modest salary. Faced with probable felony charges, Bayardo promptly decided to turn state's evidence and became a protected witness. Yet there appeared to be little or no protection provided on the day he was murdered. All he had with him was a lone bodyguard, who was himself seriously wounded in the attack.

The incident raised major questions both about Mexico's protected witness program and the extraordinary reach of the trafficking organizations. Javier Oliva, a political scientist at the National Autonomous University of Mexico, charged that the Bayardo killing and similar episodes "show that it is far too easy for criminal organizations to penetrate security arrangements." Furthermore, "the situation is getting worse all the time, and instead of improvement in security, we're seeing more problems."[36]

Certainly, the cartel assassins seemed to have no trouble locating Bayardo, and that information had to come from within the law enforcement bureaucracy. Some members undoubtedly had a motive to silence him, since he reportedly was implicating other top police officials in drug corruption. Former top anti-drug prosecutor Samuel González provided an appropriate epitaph, both for Bayardo's descent into corruption and his eventual murder, "The story of Edgar Bayardo is the story of the tragedy of police forces in Mexico."[37]

The Cartels as Major Economic Players

But it is not merely the financial power to corrupt or intimidate government officials that serves as the foundation of the cartels' power. The problem is broader. The traffickers have become major players in the overall economy. The value of illegal drug exports in 2010 and 2011 probably exceeded the value of the country's single biggest earner of foreign currency: oil. Extensive research by professor Buscaglia indicated that the involvement of organized crime in Mexico's economy accelerated dramatically between 2003 and 2009, and drug trafficking gangs are now involved in nearly every significant economic sector.[38]

The tentacles of the cartels reach into illegal activity not directly related to the drug trade, as well as into legal ventures. It is clear that the drug gangs are branching out into other criminal pursuits to gain revenue. That is most evident in communities, especially Tijuana and Ciudad Juárez, where the drug war has caused even the previously shaky degree of social order to break down. Underlings in the Juárez gangs have branched out into kidnapping, extortion, carjacking, and garden-variety robbery. There were some 1,900 carjackings in 2009 alone, and the pace has accelerated since then.

A less violent example of illegal cartel activities not related to the drug trade is the pirating of Mexico's most vital natural resource: oil. Over a two-year period between mid-2007 and mid-2009, traffickers siphoned more than $1 billion worth of oil from the country's network of pipelines, tapping into those lines with high-tech drills and then directing the oil flow through rubber tubing into stolen tanker trucks. It was likely not coincidental that a major upsurge in such theft took place soon after Calderón launched his military offensive against the cartels. True, the surge of siphoning incidents also coincided with a spike in global oil prices, which undoubtedly created a powerful incentive, but the traffickers also wanted to weaken Calderón's administration by reducing the amount of oil revenues the government could receive. That is not a trivial matter, since Mexico's federal government gets 40 percent of its revenues from taxes that Pemex (the national oil monopoly) pays into the treasury.

Cartel oil piracy became even worse during the 2009–2011 period. Pemex detected 712 illicit pipeline taps in 2010—a five-fold increase from 2005, the last full year of Vicente Fox's administration. Independent energy analysts believe that the black-market fuel was worth $2 billion to $4 billion annually. One measure of the depth of the corruption is that some of the thieves were municipal policemen. Another is that some of the oil was sold by middlemen to Pemex stations. Although the drug cartels are not the only organizations involved in the black-market diversion of oil, numerous cases have been traced back to the Zetas and other drug gangs.[39]

As in so many other instances involving worrisome developments, Mexican and U.S. authorities try to put the best face possible on the surging petroleum thefts. White House drug czar Gil Kerlikowske told reporters in January 2011 that the drug cartels have moved into such crimes because of the intense pressure from the anti-drug offensive. "They are spending more time robbing Pemex or stealing cars or kidnapping or extorting."[40] But skeptics could argue that such diversification indicates that the cartels are becoming more powerful and dangerous, contaminating ever more sectors of the Mexican economy and Mexican society.

A large amount of the theft has occurred in the oil-rich states of Veracruz and Tamaulipas, and the Zetas appear to be largely responsible. In addition to stealing the oil directly, the Zetas impose a "tax" on other groups involved in the siphoning. According to one federal lawmaker, the Zetas "are a parallel government" in that part of Mexico. "They practically own vast stretches of the pipelines, from the highways to the very door of the oil companies."[41] Much of the illicit oil is sold to relatively minor U.S. petroleum companies that are willing to look the other way and pocket a handsome profit.

And it's not just the diversion of oil. There are related menaces to Mexico's crucial petroleum industry. Zetas gunmen have confronted construction workers drilling natural gas wells in both Tamaulipas and Nuevo León, threatening to kill them unless their employers paid protection money. In one case, the cartel demanded 10 percent of what Pemex was paying the drilling firm. Such threats caused a drop of 13 percent in output from the Burgos basin, a large reservoir of natural gas under those two states. The sense of fatalism was apparent in the comments of one drilling-firm executive: "They say they're from the Zetas, and what are we to do?"[42] The most likely answer is: pay the protection money.

Some cartels are branching into other natural-resource ventures. When police arrested a key La Familia figure in 2010, they discovered that the organization had sold 1.1 million tons of illegally obtained iron ore to China. In addition to the direct profits from such sales, the cartels use mining and other natural resource firms to launder money. One silver-mine executive told Mexican authorities that the drug gangs were "buying up small- and medium-size mines to do all types of tricks to justify the income from their operations."[43]

Those maneuvers are examples of expanding "gray area" economic activities. For example, U.S. officials accused a pharmaceutical company, Grupo Collins, of branching out from its production of antibiotics and other medicines to provide chemicals that drug cartels used to manufacture methamphetamine. Grupo Collins executives denied the allegations, but there is little doubt that the leading drug-trafficking organizations maintain a variety of ties with ostensibly legitimate businesses. U.S. and Mexican authorities have dozens of enterprises under suspicion or active investigation for laundering money for the cartels. Such firms allegedly receive a cut of anywhere from 3 percent to 8 percent of the proceeds for their laundering services.

Reuters correspondent Jason Lange aptly describes the extensive economic reach of the traffickers. "From the white Caribbean beaches of Cancún to violent towns on the U.S. border and the beauty parlors of Mexico City's wealthy suburbs, drug cash is everywhere in Mexico. It has even propped up the country's banking system, helping it ride out the financial crisis and aiding the country's economy."[44]

The penetration first occurred with the greatest visibility in western Mexico, where the Sinaloa cartel made major commercial real estate investments, but the trend has spread to other areas of the country, especially fueling a real estate boom in Cancún and other resort cities. One U.S. law enforcement official stationed in Mexico City says that known traffickers have purchased large tracts of land in areas where any shrewd investor would buy. A leading Mexican economist estimates that the cartels have laundered more than $680 million through the banks of Sinaloa—which is by no means a leading money center—and that drug money accounts for nearly 20 percent of the state's economy.[45]

Perhaps most important, the cartels have become major employers, offering well-paying jobs to tens of thousands of people. "Today, the traffickers have big companies, education, careers," Sinaloa congresswoman Yudit del Rincón lamented. "They're businessmen of the year; they even head up social causes and charitable foundations."[46]

Most of the job opportunities are snapped up by young men who have few other employment prospects, and certainly none at the wages that the cartels offer. At the height of its power, La Familia employed several thousand people, mostly in the state of Michoacán, and claimed to pay wages of at least $2,000 per month.[47] That compensation was more than 10 times Mexico's minimum wage and roughly four times the average wage. An intelligence agent with the Michoacán state government noted the vast array of legitimate enterprises—ranging from bars and nightclubs to hotels and real estate firms—that La Familia controlled, observing "it is an infrastructure that provides lots of jobs."[48] At the same time, the organization ran a blatant protection racket that assessed "fees" on other businesses. Associated Press correspondent Mark Stevenson described how the arrangement worked in one small town, Ciudad Hidalgo:

> Shopkeepers in this pine-covered mountain region easily recite the list of "protection" fees they pay to La Familia drug cartel to stay in business: 100 pesos (about $7.50) a month for

a stall in a street market, 30,000 pesos (about $2,225) for an auto dealership or construction-supply firm. First offense for nonpayment: a severe beating. Those who keep ignoring the fees–or try to charge their own–may pay with their lives.[49]

Poverty-stricken young Mexicans probably regard such brutal tactics with indifference, since the victims are usually members of more prosperous classes. Well-paying employment offers make the cartels very appealing to job seekers. Even in good economic times, the drug-trafficking organizations are major employers. Given the devastating impact of the global recession, and especially given the dramatic decline in the construction industries in both the United States and Mexico, which had provided many jobs for young Mexican males, the cartels are now in an especially strong position. According to a study by the Pew Hispanic Center, the number of Mexicans immigrants entering the United States dropped by nearly 60 percent between 2005, the year before the housing construction bubble burst, and mid-2009. Although that decline has apparently bottomed out in the past two years, it is still a far cry from the pace during the boom years.[50]

While legitimate employers in Mexico may be reluctant to hire new workers, and in some cases may be trimming their work forces, the drug traffickers definitely are not. That means that their relative economic power within Mexico's economy is on the rise. Indeed, the growing prominence of the illegal drug trade is insidiously displacing honest economic activity. The violence, especially in the border cities, is causing legitimate businesses, both domestic and foreign firms, to hesitate about making additional investments and creating more jobs. Soledad Máynez, the leader of the local factory association in Ciudad Juárez, contended in January 2010 that at least a dozen foreign corporations had postponed investments in manufacturing facilities there because of the dangerous security environment.[51] That development magnifies the importance of trafficking organizations, which are less risk averse, as both investors and employers.

Damage to the overall economy, and especially the weakening of legal enterprises in areas hard hit by the drug violence, perversely strengthens the economic position of the cartels. The ugly employment situation in Ciudad Juárez, fueled in large part by the drug war chaos, has swollen the ranks of the unemployed. Carlos Chavira

Rodríguez, the local head of the Mexican Employers Conferation, confirmed in April 2010 that "Juárez has 70,000 young people between the ages of 15 and 29 who neither study nor have jobs." Stating the obvious, he concludes: "These people are easy pickings for the gangs."[52]

Using the Stick

The drug gangs have a huge quantity of financial carrots at their disposal, but they also are not shy about threatening to use the stick to get their way. That is the essence of the silver-or-lead alternative given to those people who are in a position to either assist or hinder the cartels. When rival trafficking outfits began to wage a turf war in Monterrey, they first targeted recalcitrant police. In the first quarter of 2007 alone, 16 law enforcement personnel were killed in and around the city. Another 50 apparently got the message and quit.

The situation in Tijuana is also worrisome. During the first 11 months of 2009, 28 police officers were killed—twice the number of the fairly bloody 2008. At least some of the murders appeared to be an attempt to intimidate the city's uncompromising police chief, Julián Leyzaola, into resigning. In late 2009, the cartels issued a new threat to kill five officers a week until Leyzaola left office. He flatly rejected that demand. "To even consider that would make me an accomplice of the cartels," he told CBS News. "I will never resign."[53]

Yet even Leyzaola has been sobered by his time on the job. When interviewed a year earlier, shortly after he took the post, he boasted: "If the cartels only understand the language of violence, then we are going to have to speak in their language and annihilate them."[54] That blunt approach perhaps reflected his military background as a former army lieutenant colonel. Leyzaola soon discovered that not only were the traffickers better armed and better organized than even he anticipated, but many of his own uniformed officers were fifth-columnists. He proceeded to investigate all 2,200 members of the force. By November 2009, he had fired 460 employees, mostly for suspected ties to the cartels, and jailed dozens of them where evidence of such links was strong enough to warrant prosecution. "We have prosecuted commanders, chiefs, officers, those who served as the eyes and ears of the drug cartels in the department," Leyzaola stated.[55]

His own story typifies the problems faced by law enforcement officials who apparently try to stay honest. Almost immediately after he became police chief, one of the cartels tried to bribe him. When that ploy failed, they made repeated attempts to assassinate him. On one occasion, using military uniforms and camouflaged vehicles, gang enforcers plotted to blow up police headquarters—with Leyzoala inside. Police narrowly foiled that scheme, which was the fourth major assassination attempt. Afterward, the chief traveled with no fewer than 15 bodyguards wherever he went.

Although the death toll among police personnel in Tijuana, Monterrey, and many other cities is alarmingly high, the reason for the killings is not always clear. Some victims may merely have been in the wrong place at the wrong time. Others were likely honest cops who resisted attempts at bribery and paid the ultimate price. But some were probably individuals who didn't resist the financial blandishments; they simply made the mistake of taking money from the "wrong" cartel. Nati González, the state governor of Nuevo León, and other officials discovered that hundreds of police were on the payrolls of competing drug lords. That was hardly unique to Monterrey or Nuevo León, but it added another motive for violence as the cartels vied for control in an area where no single organization was dominant. And sometimes rank-and-file police may have felt that no matter what they did, their actions would put themselves and their families in danger.

What happened to Julio Ledezma, the police chief of La Junta, a town of 8,700 not far from the Mexico-U.S. border, was all too typical of the silver-or-lead strategy.[56] He had held his post for barely three months when two strangers bearing gifts paid him a call. Those gifts were a new truck for his personal use and a briefcase containing several thousand dollars in cash. In return for that generosity, he was to distract federal police at security checkpoints by making fake calls for assistance. That distraction, the traffickers assumed, would enable them to send their shipments through the area without having to worry that they might be intercepted.

Ledezma was an honest man, and he did not want to be owned by the Juárez cartel. So, he attempted to rally support from leaders of the community to reject the attempt at bribery. That proved to be a big mistake. Word of his reluctance to accept the "silver" got back to the cartel. While he was out shopping for his 45th birthday dinner, six armed men surrounded his home and told his wife that they would find him and kill him no matter where he might go in

Mexico. After terrorizing her for 20 minutes, the gunmen left, just before Ledezma returned home. When she told him of the incident, he realized that trying to rebuff the cartel would be signing his death warrant, and perhaps those of his wife and 15-year-old daughter as well. It was probably too late even to accept the offer of a bribe, since it was clear to the traffickers that he could not be trusted to become part of their operation. Ledezma chose to flee to the United States with his family.

Politicians face the similar silver-or-lead choice given to law enforcement personnel. The months leading up to the July 2010 local elections were marked by a surge of threats and attacks, as well as offers of money. The "lead" component seemed especially dominant in the trafficking corridors near the border with the United States. In that region, one candidate (as well as his son) was gunned down in his place of business, another was missing after assailants torched her home. So many candidates had been threatened that in some jurisdictions, Calderón's National Action Party was unable to find anyone brave enough to run for office.

The risks that elected officeholders incur if they defy the cartels are enormous. That point was illustrated by the fate of Edelmiro Cavazos, the mayor of Santiago, a quaint tourist town a few hours from the U.S. border. Santiago has the misfortune of being located on a major cocaine trafficking route from South America. Cavazos, a dynamic 38-year-old politician, became mayor following the November 2009 election. His friends and family insist that he was an idealist who sought to clean up the town's corrupt police department. One investigative journalist noted sarcastically: "their uniform may have said 'Santiago Police Department,' but "in reality they worked for the cartels."[57]

It was Cavazos's bad fortune to take office at a time when the Gulf cartel's control of the drug trade through Santiago was under mounting challenge from the Zetas. That meant that two competing groups were offering the silver-or-lead option to law enforcement figures. Accepting silver from one would increase the likelihood that the other would resort to using lead against the recipient. On the night of August 15, Cavazos was abducted from his home while his wife and children were visiting relatives in Texas. Two days later, his corpse was found dumped by the side of a road. He had become one of 14 mayors killed in 2010, but his murder was not the only awful aspect of the episode.

The security surveillance system showed one of the police officers assigned to guard the mayor's house walking out to meet an approaching convoy of cars. Armed men emerged from those vehicles and walked up to the front door. When Cavazos answered the door, the gunmen threatened him with drawn weapons, forced him outside, and pushed him into the back seat of the lead vehicle. The guard would later claim that he was kidnapped with the mayor, but the video showed him getting into the next car with no sign that he was under duress.

The subsequent investigation implicated the guard and five other officers for involvement in Cavazos' kidnapping and assassination. Their subsequent confessions created an even greater stir. According to Alejandro Garza y Garza, Nuevo León State Attorney General, the officers said "they thought he was working for the other cartel. Mayor Cavazos was against them. So that's why they killed him."[58]

Such is the nature of Mexico today that no one can be certain whether that explanation was just a cynical excuse or whether Cavazos, despite his reputation as an idealistic reformer, may have been working with one of the cartels. Whatever the reason, the traffickers had sent a potent message. Garza y Garza admits that the message is: "We don't stop with anybody. We can kill policemen. We can kill mayors. We can kill everybody." He added ruefully: "How many people want to work at the police department in Santiago now? Nobody wants to be a police (sic) anymore here. Why? Because they know if they have to go, they have to go—silver or lead."[59]

Just how far the campaign of intimidation by the cartels has developed became apparent with the May 2010 abduction of Diego Fernández de Cevallos Gutiérrez (see the account in the Introduction).[60] The government immediately launched a massive search, but called it off a few days later upon the request of Fernández de Cevallos' family. That request, in turn, followed the appearance of a photo on social networking sites of a shirtless, blindfolded man with a grey beard who bore a striking resemblance to the missing man.[61] The kidnappers sent additional materials in July, including a letter that Fernández de Cevallos had apparently written to his son complaining about health problems while in captivity, which indicated the man was still alive.

111

What made Fernández de Cevallos abduction so jarring was the victim's prominence. As a former candidate for president, Fernández de Cevallos was not only a member of the country's political elite, he was in the highest echelon.

After months of tense negotiations, the abductors finally released him five days before Christmas, reportedly after his family and friends paid a $20 million ransom, although no one would confirm that figure.[62] He looked gaunt at a press conference outside his home in Mexico City, with a much fuller beard than his normal style—one that would have done Santa Claus proud. Ever the fighter, he insisted that he was strong and that his life would go on as it had before. One suspects, though, that his days of traveling without a security detail are at an end.

The Fernández de Cevallos abduction meant that the drug cartels were sending a message that even the highest members of the country's political elite were not safe. The implicit warning was that if someone with Fernández de Cevallos' pedigree was vulnerable to abduction or assassination, lesser political figures had better take heed and cooperate with the traffickers. Noting that the cartels seemed to operate with "impunity," José Antonio Ortega, the president of the Citizen's Council for Public Security and Criminal Justice in Mexico City, concluded that "we are all exposed."[63]

Given the seemingly inexhaustible financial resources of the drug gangs, combined with the ruthlessness that they're willing to employ, Mexican political and administrative officials are put in an impossible position. The monetary temptations alone are often irresistible to those who make, at best, modest incomes. And even if they are inclined to resist the tempting offer of a bribe, such ingrained honesty is usually overwhelmed by the realization that if they reject the blandishments of the traffickers, they put themselves—and possibly their loved ones—in mortal danger. Either way, the cartels win.

As long as the trafficking organizations remain as powerful as they are now, the corruption and violence in Mexico will not diminish. It is increasingly clear that the approach that the Calderón administration has adopted, and that Washington has backed so enthusiastically, is not working. The inevitable question then arises, how bad could the situation in our southern neighbor become? And there is an even more ominous question lurking in the background: Is there a danger that Mexico could become a "failed state"?

5. Mexico: A New Failed State?

The bloodletting in Mexico is now so bad that some respected analysts warn that the country is on the brink of becoming a failed state–something akin to a Latin American version of Somalia. Even the Pentagon has apparently factored that scenario into its planning, asserting in a fall 2008 document that Mexico, along with Pakistan and Sudan, were among the most worrisome arenas for possible failed-state status. A 2011 RAND study, commissioned by the Office of the Secretary of Defense, reached a conclusion that is only marginally less alarming. After studying 30 insurgencies that had occurred between 1978 and 2008, the analysts concluded that the threat posed by the drug cartels in Mexico would be "in the empirical gap" between those insurgencies that had succeeded and those that had failed.[1] In other words, the situation in Mexico was serious and the outcome could go either way. Independent experts are equally uneasy. Former U.S. drug czar Barry McCaffrey warns that Mexico is "fighting for its survival against narco-terrorism," and he worries that the Mexican government could lose control over major swaths of its territory near the border with the United States.[2]

Such allegations enrage Mexican officials. In a March 2009 speech, President Felipe Calderón denounced those who suggested that his country was in danger of becoming a failed state. "It is absolutely false," he fumed, to contend "that Mexico does not have control over one single part of its national territory. I challenge anyone who says that to tell me what part of the country they want to go to, and I will take that person there."[3]

Officials also contend that Mexico's overall homicide rate is actually a little lower now than it was in the early 1990s. But that statement is misleading for two reasons. First, much of the decline during the late 1990s was because of the fading of the Zapatista uprising—a rebellion concentrated in the southern state of Chiapas, which was fueled by virulent land disputes. When that conflict subsided, the homicide rate in Chiapas dropped by more than

80 percent, and the decline in Chiapas was a significant factor in the fall in the national homicide rate.

And although the death rate dropped steadily beginning in 1993, declining from nearly 20 killings per 100,000 people in 1992 to slightly under 13 per 100,000 in 2006, there is no denying the dramatic spike since then, which coincides with the onset of the Calderón administration's offensive against the drug traffickers. Indeed, the death rate in 2009 was nearly back to its 1992 levels.[4] And given the additional increase in drug-related murders in 2010, the national homicide rate is now well above the 1992 peak. According to Human Rights Watch, the overall homicide rate in Mexico increased some 260 percent from 2007 to the end of 2010.[5] Moreover, there has been a shift in the geographic focus of the violence from the exceedingly poor rural south in earlier periods to the more prosperous, more urbanized— and more economically crucial—northern states. Indeed, the spike in the homicide rate has been by far the most dramatic in those states where Calderón has sent in the army to challenge the drug cartels.

A second misleading aspect of the Mexican government's assertion that the current rates of violence are not all that ominous is that the earlier homicides were more amorphous, often involving juvenile crimes, family disputes, random criminal acts, and land disputes. The new wave of killings is much more organized and concentrated; it is largely attributable to powerful groups that pose a challenge to all levels of government—local, state, and federal—in Mexico. That is a worrisome shift in the nature as well as the extent of the violence.

Skeptical U.S. analysts are nearly as quick as Mexican leaders to dismiss the notion that Mexico might become a failed state. According to Council on Foreign Relations scholar Shannon O'Neil:

> The question is not whether the Mexican state will fail. It will not. The Mexican state does, and will continue to, collect taxes, run schools, repair roads, pay salaries, and manage large social programs throughout the country. The civilian-controlled military has already extinguished any real guerrilla threats. The government regularly holds free and fair elections, and its legitimacy, in the eyes of its citizens and of the world, is not questioned.[6]

Former DEA administrator Robert C. Bonner is equally categorical in dismissing the failed-state theory. He acknowledges that the upsurge in killings during Calderón's presidency "has led some to conclude that the violence in Mexico is out of control. Others have suggested that the country is on the verge of becoming a 'failed state' (or in the words of a 2008 U.S. military reports, at risk of 'rapid and sudden collapse'). The former is a gross exaggeration, and the latter is simply untrue."[7]

George W. Grayson, a prominent U.S. expert on Mexico, argues that "only a Cassandra in a deep funk could conclude that Mexico will implode as is possible in Afghanistan or Pakistan. There are too many factors . . . to let this happen." That statement is not all that comforting, though, since Cassandra's prophecies were invariably correct—they simply were never believed. Furthermore, in the next breath, Grayson emphasizes that "Felipe Calderón and his successors must act to prevent ungovernability in cities like Ciudad Juárez and Tijuana, and in states like Guerrero, Durango, Sinaloa, and Michoacán."[8]

And the problem of ungovernability is spreading. *Los Angeles Times* correspondent Richard Marosi wrote of his travels with a police convoy in October 2010, attempting to deliver government pensions to recipients in the northern portion of the state of Sonora. There, a turf fight between the Sinaloa cartel and a faction of the Beltran Leyva cartel led to "a siege of medieval proportions" that "cut off a region about the size of Rhode Island from government services, and severed a lifeline to thousands of ranch hands, storekeepers and retirees."[9]

Although the views of O'Neil, Bonner, and Grayson may be too complacent, fears that Mexico is on the brink of becoming a new Somalia or Afghanistan are somewhat overblown. The country still has a number of institutional strengths, including well-organized political parties; a sizable, influential business community; a significant military establishment; and an especially powerful moral force—the Roman Catholic Church. Such institutions are largely absent—or at least are far weaker—in countries that have become failed states or are on the brink of doing so. Mexico's major political, economic, and religious players are not about to implode and cede the field to the drug traffickers. Yet even Bonner admits that "Mexico is in the throes of a battle against powerful drug cartels, the outcome of which will determine who controls the country's law enforcement, judicial, and political institutions."[10] The prospect of violent criminal organizations controlling the principal institutions of the state is not all that far removed from a failed-state scenario.

There are also troubling developments that suggest that Mexico's societal cohesion is weakening. President Calderón is technically correct that there is no sizable area of the country where the federal government's writ has been obliterated. That is in marked contrast to the situation in Colombia during the 1980s, 1990s, and the early years of this century, when Marxist groups allied with drug-trafficking organizations controlled vast swaths of territory. Indeed, at one point the Bogotá government tacitly ceded control of an area the size of Switzerland to the Revolutionary Armed Forces of Colombia (FARC). Nothing on that scale has occurred yet in Mexico.

No Region Is Truly Safe

But as noted above, there are significant portions of Mexico where the government's control is tenuous, at best. The Archdiocese of Mexico warned, in June 2010, that the drug gangs thoroughly intimidate state and local governments in several states, and "control entire neighborhoods in some cities."[11] That assessment is all too accurate. In such places as Tijuana, areas of Michoacán, Ciudad Juárez and its environs, and major chunks of Tamaulipas, government personnel dare not venture without a sizable military or police escort. And the number of those precarious locations is growing, including some locales that Mexico's political and economic heavy hitters had considered their own safe recreational playgrounds.

One of those places is Cuernavaca, nicknamed the City of Eternal Spring because of its mild climate, located just 40 miles south of Mexico City. In early April 2010, a faction fighting for control of the Beltrán Leyva cartel circulated an e-mail warning Cuernavaca residents to stay off the streets after 8:00 p.m. "We recommend you not go out to restaurants, bars, etc. because we might confuse you with our enemies," the e-mail read.[12] In other words, the cartel imposed a curfew on the city. And it worked. For several evenings, the city's normally crowded central plaza was virtually empty—a major blow to the businesses there. Offices, and even schools, closed early, well before the curfew deadline. Restaurants and bars shut their doors—some for as long as two days.

Residents had reason to fear that the warnings were not idle threats. The armed struggles between rival drug gangs had already come to Cuernavaca. As in other cities, bodies were dumped outside police stations or hung from overpasses. In at least one case, the body of a victim who had his face skinned was left on a busy street.[13] By April 2010, more than 50 people had died in gang battles, and by early July, the total had risen to 120.

Such situations are typical in the urban areas along the U.S. border that have become the main battle zones in the drug war. But this threat was in a city that is a popular weekend retreat and vacation destination for Mexico's leading political and economic players. That the drug traffickers were so bold as to target Cuernavaca came as a shock to those elites. It should not have been a shock, though, because an increasing number of the rich and powerful in the city were the newly minted, multimillionaire drug lords. For a time, affluent residents tended to ignore the nature of their new neighbors, probably hoping that the traffickers would treat Cuernavaca as neutral territory—a sanctuary for themselves and their families. Instead, the city became yet another battleground.

In addition to the border cities and a growing number of other metropolitan areas, the authority of the Mexican government is not much in evidence in some of the main, and largely rural, trafficking corridors leading to the United States. In the Juárez valley, a region of small towns largely devoted to serving cotton-farming activities located about 50 miles east of Ciudad Juárez, the Sinaloa cartel warned families to leave the area or suffer the consequences. The motive appeared to be to depopulate the corridor to minimize the prospect of witnesses or other interference with drug shipments headed to the United States.

Associated Press correspondents Mark Stevenson and Alicia A. Caldwell reported that hundreds of families were fleeing the area. Cartel enforcers "have burned down homes in Esperanza (Hope) and torched a church on Good Friday in El Porvenir (The Future). Wherever they plan to strike, they leave notes ordering residents to leave." Typewritten notes circulated in one town told people: "You have just a few hours to get out."[14] About a week after the arson incident in El Porvenir, a group of nearly 100 armed men in a convoy of trucks took over the town of Maycoba, located southwest of Ciudad Juárez and just over the border between Chihuahua and Sonora. They killed four people and forced most of the remaining townspeople to leave. In El Porvenir, a town of about 3,000 residents, only a mere 200 or so remained, according to Stevenson and Caldwell. "During Easter Week, when schools were closed and the

117

plaza would normally bustle, the only things moving in the center of town were a few stray dogs."[15]

But such cartel "cleansing operations" are not unique to the Juárez valley. Hundreds of miles away in a remote region of Durango, a similar depopulation incident took place in December 2010, just three days after Christmas. A column of 50–60 armed men, some in military-style uniforms, filed down a steep mountain road and attacked the small village of Tierras Coloradas. Before they left about a half hour later, they torched some three dozen homes—approximately half the village—along with two schools, the community store, and numerous vehicles. The only reason there were few fatalities is that most residents had already fled because of a smaller raid two days earlier that had left one villager dead. Residents were living in caves or sleeping out in the open under trees. The second raid made their exile permanent, leaving some 150 people homeless in the bitter mountain winter.[16]

This appeared to be a classic turf fight with civilians caught in the middle. Tierras Coloradas is in the marijuana and poppy-growing heartland, Mexico's so-called Golden Triangle. The perpetrators of the December 2010 incidents appeared to be enforcers for the Sinaloa cartel, which is battling the Zetas for control of that portion of the Golden Triangle. The Sinaloa gunmen either thought the villagers were siding with the Zetas or concluded that they were merely in the way of efforts to secure the territory. In any case, the episode was only one incident in a broader campaign. Other drug war ghost towns are beginning to appear throughout Durango. By the time that Tierras Coloradas was attacked, the Durango state government was already grappling with the task of settling some 1,400 refugees from nearby municipalities, such as Pueblo Nuevo, who had fled their homes because of threats and violence from the warring cartels.

As in the case of the cartel sweeps through the villages of the Juárez valley, there was little evidence of a government police or military presence until long after the terrified populations had left. At the very least, such an inability to protect the citizenry raises doubts about the president's bold assertion that there is no portion of the country that is not under government control.

Inhabitants in Texas across the border from the Juárez valley report a steady exodus of frightened refugees from Mexico. Between October 2009 and April 2010, some 47 of those refugees officially asked the U.S. government for asylum, but that is certainly just a small fraction of the numbers in the ongoing exodus. Most people fleeing Mexico do not ask for asylum; they merely blend into Mexican-American communities where there is already an abundance of undocumented aliens who came to the United States for economic reasons. One unlucky woman, captured by the U.S. Border Patrol near El Paso with her four children (an eight-year-old boy and three younger girls), explained why she had left Mexico. "All the children, the only thing they know how to play is *sicarios*" (hired killers).[17] A society where that sort of play is becoming normal is a society in trouble.[18]

The cartels are also increasingly professional and powerful in their challenge to the authority of the Mexican government. Since late 2009 and early 2010, cartel forces have become dramatically more adept at ambushing police and military units. Those are well-planned attacks, luring adversaries into traps, cutting off escape routes, and launching commando-style assaults. "These are war-fighting tactics they're using," concludes Javier Cruz Angulo, an expert on crime at a Mexican research institute. "It's gone way beyond the normal strategies of organized crime."[19]

That trend became apparent throughout 2010 in such cities as Nuevo Laredo and Monterrey. Numerous incidents took place in which cartel fighters commandeered buses and tractor-trailers to create blockades. Residents soon coined a new term, *narcobloqueos* (narco blockades) to describe the growing phenomenon. At a minimum, the tactic creates massive travel snarls and impedes the movement of police (which often appears to be the primary motive), thereby allowing drug shipments to proceed without interference. But in several cases, the blockades were followed by firefights with police or rival gangs, raising the level of anxiety among worried civilians to new heights.

In an August 2011 report given to the U.S. Congress, Texas Department of Public Safety Director Steven C. McCraw echoed warnings that the cartels are adopting full-blown military tactics. "They incorporate reconnaissance networks, techniques and capabilities normally associated with military organizations," he emphasized. Those tactics include "communications intercepts, interrogations, trend analysis, secure communications, coordinated military-style tactical operations, GPS, thermal imagery and military armaments, including fully automatic weapons, rocket-propelled grenades and hand grenades."[20]

It's not just in a few major cities that the traffickers are engaging in setting up roadblocks and engaging in other military tactics. In Creole, Mexico, a police security camera recorded a cartel enforcement squad shutting down a major highway with a checkpoint, threatening drivers and extorting money, and killing those people who resisted. Before the enforcers withdrew, they killed nine people.[21] Such incidents are typical in countries where insurgencies or terrorism is rampant, and the authorities exhibit an inability to securely control territory. But until a few years ago, that was not common in Mexico.

If the strategic and tactical sophistication of cartel attacks gets any better, it will be an extremely worrisome development for the health, perhaps even the viability, of the Mexican state. In most instances, the weaponry the drug gangs use is already superior to that of Mexican police forces and at least comparable to that of the Mexican military. If the cartels now have the competence to routinely use military tactics to utilize their superior firepower, they move from being mere criminal organizations to being a serious insurgency. That would be a dramatic escalation of the threat they pose to the Mexican state.

So, too, is another tactic that first emerged in July 2010. On July 15, security forces in Juárez responded to an anonymous emergency call that reported a wounded policeman lying in the street at a major intersection. (It was actually a civilian the cartels had shot and left bound as bait.) When police, medical personnel, and other first responders reached the scene, a car bomb containing 10 kilos (about 22 pounds) of Tovex, an industrial explosive, blew up, killing three people and wounding a dozen others.[22]

Such bombings are commonplace events in such places as Iraq, Afghanistan, and Pakistan–as well as in Colombia during the 1980s and 1990s, during the peak of that country's drug violence. But this was something new in Mexico. Authorities quickly placed blame on La Línea, an enforcement unit of the beleaguered Juárez cartel. The attack apparently was in retaliation for the arrest earlier that same day of Jesús Armando Acosta Guerrero, a senior member of that gang. Both the nature of the weapon (a car bomb detonated by a cell phone) and the ploy used to lure victims into the trap suggested that the violence in those other terrorist arenas had come to Mexico, and that this episode might not be the last.

Arturo Chávez, at the time Mexico's attorney general, put up a brave front, asserting the following day that there was no evidence in Mexico of the kind of "narcoterrorism" that had afflicted other countries. But Chávez showed a remarkable ability to miss the point. "The implications of this [attack] are not to destabilize the state, but to frighten society," he intoned.[23] Yet that is a distinction without a difference. One of the time-honored tactics that terrorist groups use to destabilize a state is to frighten the population and expose the state's inability to provide security on a consistent basis. Car bombs in major urban areas are an ideal way to achieve that goal.

U.S. officials adopted a decidedly less complacent attitude about the car bombing than did Chávez. Dan Kumar, chief of international affairs for the Bureau of Alcohol, Tobacco, Firearms and Explosives, conceded that the cartels "absolutely have the capacity" to conduct similar attacks, and that authorities should "expect more of this type of violence."[24] Kumar noted that in their battles with each other and with Mexican authorities, the drug gangs had already increased their use of grenades and other explosive devices. Although those weapons are on a smaller scale than a car bomb, it would be a relatively small step to move up to that level.

Concerns rose that future bombings might occur when authorities apprehended a number of gunmen following a skirmish in Chihuahua a little more than a week after the Juárez bombing. Those cartel foot soldiers had with them 50 large tubes, containing 26 kilograms (57 pounds) of Tovex, the same industrial explosive that the Juárez attackers had used.

News reports indicating that the cartels may have begun to work with Hezbollah and other experienced terrorist organizations added to the jitters in both Mexico City and Washington.[25] The Juárez bomb was a relatively small-scale affair—a modest, minor-league effort. But Hezbollah is a major-league terrorist outfit. Indeed, some terrorism experts in the West describe Hezbollah as the "A" team, and al Qaeda as the "B" team, of terrorism—even after the latter's spectacular attack on 9/11. If the Mexican drug cartels begin to collude with Hezbollah and tap into that group's expertise, the threat to Mexico's stability will take a significant jump in severity.

Even if they're merely operating on their own, the use of car bombs by the cartels would be an alarming escalation. Worries that the Juárez episode was a prelude to a new phase in the drug wars seemed to be confirmed in August 2010, when a similar bomb exploded in Ciudad Victoria, the capital city of Tamaulipas. Later that same month, two more two car bombs exploded, one in front of a transit police station and the other in front of the Televisa station in Ciudad Victoria. The Televisa explosion—the larger of the two on that day—was felt several blocks away, and when the smoke cleared, all that was left of the vehicle that had contained the bomb was the engine and a portion of the chassis. Miraculously, no one was killed or seriously injured in either bombing (probably because the explosive devices were detonated late at night), but the Ciudad Victoria attack did knock Televisa off the air in Tamaulipas for several hours.[26] Just a day later, two other bombs exploded in the city of Reynosa, injuring at least one person who was unlucky enough to be in the downtown area at the time.

The timing of the bombings in late August heightened the sense of alarm, since they came just days after police discovered the bodies of 72 executed migrants from Central and South America just north of San Fernando (see chapter 3). Indeed, the two bombs in Reynosa were set off near a morgue in which the bodies of those victims were being stored. All of those bombing incidents also occurred just a few weeks after the assassination of Rodolfo Torre Cantú during the closing days of his candidacy for governor, and they coincided with the assassination of city of Hidalgo mayor Marco Antonio Leal García and the wounding of his four-year-old daughter, who was in Leal García's SUV when gunmen launched their attack.[27]

The combination of so many high-profile incidents in such a short time period suggested that the Zetas might be engaged in a broad strategy of terrorism in Tamaulipas. That explanation gained additional evidence in early September 2010, when police discovered two decomposing bodies in a field about 30 miles northeast of San Fernando. Identification documents found on the corpses matched those of a state detective and the San Fernando police chief. Both men had disappeared several days earlier while they were investigating the massacre of the migrants. It seemed a calculated and very effective way to demonstrate the utter impotence of the authorities in Tamaulipas.

At the least, the group responsible for those attacks was trying to make an especially aggressive power play at the expense both of trafficking rivals and the Mexican government. And that development was making Tamaulipas a very dangerous place.

There has not been the feared proliferation of bombing incidents following the flurry in the late summer and early autumn of 2010. Nevertheless, the worry has not gone away. The cartels have demonstrated that they are both willing and capable of launching such attacks. And perhaps that was the main point—to intimidate Mexican authorities by conveying a stark message that further assaults could be made whenever and wherever the drug gangs decided.

Rising Fear and Its Economic Impact

The atmosphere of intimidation and fear now gripping more and more portions of Mexico is only the most visible sign of trouble for the health of the Mexican state. Larry Birns, director of the Council on Hemispheric Affairs, based in Washington, D.C., notes the subtle but dangerous corrosion that the drug violence appears to be having on Mexico, including on the country's overall economic future. "The [casualty] figures in Mexico are so scary that it has produced a subliminal sense that Mexico is a dangerous place and you'd better keep away."[28] If Birns is correct, and that attitude takes hold among potential investors in Mexico's economy, the effects for the country could be quite negative.

Such effects are already evident in the hardest-hit area, Ciudad Juárez. As many as 200,000 people left the city between mid-2008 and mid-2010—partly in response to the economic recession, but much more so because of the soaring violence. That is more than 10 percent of the city's population. Indeed, the exodus has reached the point that city leaders are beginning to detect a shortage of skilled workers— even in the current, relatively weak economy. Reuters correspondent Julian Cardona describes the extent of the economic havoc:

> Once one of Mexico's fastest growing cities, Ciudad Juárez is now blighted with shuttered restaurants and shops. Garbage and unopened mail gathers around the doorways of empty office buildings, and once upscale suburbs are devoid of cars. About a quarter of homes in the city lie empty as residents escape or new houses are left vacant.[29]

The experience that the head of a cross-border trucking firm described to Cardona illustrates why the legal economy in Ciudad Juárez is in such distress. "I fled to El Paso when a gang tried to kidnap me last year," the man stated. "They came for me, but I had a change in my schedule, so I wasn't home and they kidnapped my neighbor instead."[30]

Now, the same problem is beginning to impact other large population centers. Caterpillar, a major employer in Mexico, ordered its executives with children to leave Monterrey in September 2010, following a similar move by the State Department regarding diplomatic personnel. Jim Dugan, Caterpillar's chief spokesman, explained the reasons in an e-mail to the *Wall Street Journal*. "Based on recent guidance from the State Department," the e-mail read, "Caterpillar has informed expat employees in some regions of Mexico (including Monterrey) that they and their families should repatriate as soon as possible."[31] Other U.S. firms have not gone quite that far, but they are urging their American employees to consider leaving the area.

Some Mexican business leaders are following suit. An executive at leading cement producer, Cemex SAB, headquartered in Monterrey, stated that at least 20 families from his circle of friends and acquaintances had left. "It's a rush for the exits," he said.[32] That development is disturbingly similar to what occurred in Ciudad Juárez and Tijuana two or three years earlier. But the economic impact of such an exodus from Monterrey would be vastly greater than the meltdown of those two cities. Monterrey is Mexico's industrial heart, and in many respects, its economic heart. "Mexico can't afford to lose Monterrey" to the cartels, one expert warned.[33]

But the internal refugee problem is becoming increasingly worrisome as people who have the necessary financial resources seek to relocate to less volatile portions of the country. And then there is the growing number of people who are simply driven from their homes, or who are so terrified of the threats and violence that they flee— often with little more than the clothes they're wearing. Although no official figures exist for the number of internal refugees in Mexico, the Geneva-based Internal Displacement monitoring center estimates that at least 115,000 people have been displaced by the drug violence.[34]

Refugees Fleeing the Chaos

Prominent business leaders fleeing dangerous regions of the country because of kidnapping threats is another sign of the cracks in Mexico's political and social stability. So, too, is the increasing number of cases in which police officers, and even some elected officials, resign their posts. In December 2009, eight public officeholders in Tancitaro, a city in Michoacán, resigned, saying that they were being threatened by traffickers. They had reason to take such threats seriously, since a prominent city councilor, Gonzalo Paz, had been kidnapped, tortured, and murdered earlier that year. Among those who resigned in December was the city's mayor. In August 2011, the entire 20-person police force of Ascension in Chihuahua quit after a series of attacks over the previous three months that had killed five officers and the police chief. Their departure left the city of 13,000 without any local police services. The state and federal governments had to scramble to fill that vacuum.[35]

Perhaps even more worrisome, some officials are seeking refuge in the United States for themselves or their families. Police personnel especially feel under siege. In May 2008, three Mexican police chiefs requested political asylum in the United States because of drug cartel threats to them and their families. Other prominent cases of asylum-seekers have included several journalists who have fled Chihuahua after repeated threats. So far, the number of law enforcement and political refugees are relatively small, but that total may be misleading.

U.S. immigration authorities have generally refused to grant asylum to such applicants, especially police officers, ruling that the dangers they face, while very real, are inherent in police work. Given the mounting threats against law enforcement personnel and political figures who defy the drug cartels, there would likely be far more individuals seeking refuge in the United States if the U.S. immigration bureaucracy adopted a different attitude. George Grayson concludes that if immigration judges began to grant asylum liberally to people fleeing the cartels, "we'd have literally tens of thousands of police officers coming to the United States, not to mention some mayors too."[36]

U.S. officials probably have reached a similar conclusion. Admitting law enforcement and political personnel as political refugees—hereby treating the cartels as the equivalent of brutal

125

governments that persecute or murder opponents—would run counter to Washington's policy. First, it would be a tacit recognition of just how powerful the drug organizations have become, and that they are now credible competitors to the Mexican state. Second, a liberal asylum policy would implicitly concede that Calderón's much-vaunted offensive against the cartels is not only failing but is also producing a very nasty blowback. A flood of Mexican police officers and local elected officials fleeing to the United States would underscore just how badly the U.S.-backed anti-drug strategy is faring. Understandably, the Drug Enforcement Administration, the State Department, the Department of Homeland Security, and the White House itself are not eager to admit such a policy failure. Maintaining a tight rein on asylum applications from Mexico is imperative to keeping up a good front.

But the pressure is growing. The case of Marisol Valles García illustrates the dilemma for the United States. She made international headlines in October 2010, when as a 20-year-old college student and mother of a toddler, she became the police chief of the violence-plagued town of Praxedis Guadalupe Guerrero, near Juárez. That municipality had become a battleground between the Juárez and Sinaloa cartels, and the population of the town had plummeted from 8,500 in 2005 to fewer than 4,500 in 2010. She got the job of supervising the 13-person department primarily because no one else was willing to take it.[37]

Valles García sought to avoid directly challenging the cartels, asserting that her approach to police work was to focus on rehabilitating public spaces and strengthening relationships among neighbors as a means to improve general security. Her idealism was apparent in her comment that the town "was different in the time of its oldest residents—people walked the streets at night, they knew each other, they talked and met up."[38]

Such a mild, inoffensive approach mattered little to the drug gangs. Death threats against the young police chief mounted over the next few months, and residents said that there had been at least one kidnapping attempt. By early March 2011, she had enough. Marisol Valles García fled Mexico and applied for asylum in the United States. When asked by journalists, U.S. authorities would not even reveal where she was staying while her asylum application was considered.[39]

Aside from asylum requests, there is the issue of prominent Mexican family members who live quite legally on a "temporary" basis in the United States. A case that received considerable attention in Mexico in late 2009 was the admission by Mauricio Fernández, the controversial and flamboyant mayor of the Monterrey suburb of San Pedro Garza García, that he had sent his family to live in the United States.[40]

Fernández is hardly alone. Rumors swirled that then–Ciudad Juárez mayor José Reyes Ferriz maintained a home across the river in El Paso, where he allegedly spent most nights, and where his family resided on a constant basis. Reyes Ferriz refused to comment on those rumors, but others had no such hesitation. The notion that the mayor actually lives in the violent maelstrom that Juárez has become is "a joke," scoffed Miguel Fernández, a former Coca Cola executive who heads up a nonprofit organization, Strategic Plan for Juárez, which is trying to stem the chaos. "The law says he has to live in Juárez, but everyone knows he lives over there [in El Paso]."[41] Gustavo de la Rosa, a prominent human-rights lawyer, openly admits that he now lives in El Paso and commutes daily for his work in Ciudad Juárez. And there are credible rumors that the mayor of Monterrey sent his family to Dallas for safety.[42]

Alejandro Junco de la Vega runs *Grupo Reforma*, the largest print-media company, not only in Mexico but in all of Latin America. Yet this media mogul despairs of protecting his journalists or even himself. Junco moved his family to Texas in 2008 because of growing personal threats from drug cartel operatives.[43] He still commutes to work daily, although he is careful to vary his routes and take other precautions.

Even small business owners in Mexico seem to be emulating the actions of the elite by sending their families to the United States for safety. Gustavo Pérez, who is merely the owner of a convenience store in Juárez, expresses a determination to keep operating his business, although it is directly across the street from the site of a January 2010 massacre. But while trying to keep his business operating, he also had the prudence to send his 11-year-old daughter to live with relatives in El Paso.[44]

An early warning signal that a country has at least the potential to become a failed state is when members of the business and political elites are so worried about the security environment that they send their loved ones out of the country. Mexico may have entered that stage. Indeed, in the worst centers of violence, such as Ciudad Juárez and Tijuana, there are unmistakable signs of an even more worrisome precursor of a failed state: large numbers of upper-class and middle-class families exiting the country. Since late 2008, the number of abandoned homes in Juárez, many in previously affluent neighborhoods, has skyrocketed. The number is growing so fast that officials have trouble keeping track of the growth. "The exodus is dramatic," admitted Gustavo de la Rosa. Yet even he is not certain just how bad the situation has become. "There are at least 20,000 abandoned homes," de la Rosa stated, but he conceded that the total might be as high as 30,000.[45] Municipal leaders in El Paso estimate that at least 30,000 Mexicans, primarily middle-class people, have moved across the border in the past three years to find a safe haven from the violence.

Signs of Vigilantes

Another ominous development is the emergence of armed vigilante groups to counter the drug gangs. Although vigilantism is not entirely a new phenomenon in Mexico, there does appear to be a modest upward trend. About a dozen self-defense organizations had gone public by late 2009. In all likelihood, others are operating, but have decided to adopt a lower profile and so have not made any public announcement. That would seem to be the more prudent strategy, reducing the danger that the drug gangs would be able to snuff out such opponents before they grew large enough to gain traction with the Mexican people.

There are clear indications, though, that vigilante organizations are already active. One group in Ciudad Juárez, styling itself the "Citizen Command of Juárez," (CCJ), issued a missive to news organizations pledging to "clean our city of these criminals." The CCJ claimed that it was organized and funded by local businesspeople who were fed up with the murders, extortion, and intimidation plaguing their city. *El Universal*, one of Mexico's top newspapers, reported receiving a CCJ message that it would kill one criminal every 24 hours until the drug gang outrages subsided. The message added that, "if criminals are identified, information can be sent electronically about the 'bad person' who deserves to die."[46] Another shadowy group, "Businessmen United: The Death Squad," put a video on YouTube, in which they threatened to kill drug traffickers, kidnappers, and other criminals in Ciudad Juárez.[47] Two other self-styled vigilante organizations, one in Sonora and one in Guerrero, have also sent threatening statements to the news media.

It is possible that such organizations are nothing more than some-one with a hero fantasy and an e-mail "send" button, but there are signs that serious vigilantism may be for real—and not just with the drug traffickers as targets. On a quiet August evening on a seaside boulevard in Navolato (a coastal community near Culiacán), gun-men in a white SUV fired on a group of young revelers, killing eight people, including a 15-year-old girl. Two members of that group, men in their twenties, had long records of car thefts.[48] A self-described vigilante group, the Death Squad, had repeatedly threatened to exe-cute car thieves if they did not desist, and was suspected in some previous, though less spectacular, killings. In the town of Cuijingo, police had to rescue four suspected kidnappers from a town hall after hundreds of angry residents surrounded the building and demanded the right to punish the men, at one point attempting to set the build-ing on fire. The men, suspected of working for one of the cartels, had allegedly tried to kidnap a leading local businessman for ransom.[49]

Other episodes suggest that vigilantes may be specifically target-ing drug gang members, especially in the vicinity of Juárez. In one case, a body found outside the city had a note attached: "This is for those who extort." In another incident, the bodies of six men were dumped in Ciudad Juárez in what appeared to be a vigilante slaying of drug gang members. Similar killings have occurred in other loca-tions. Police in Guerrero found the bodies of 10 men in October 2009, with an attached sign: "This is what is going to happen to all thieves and extortionists. You know what you're getting into."[50] Another episode occurred in Morelia in January 2010, when police found the bodies of five men scattered throughout the city. Each of the bodies had a note with an identical message attached to it, warning that a similar fate awaited other thieves and extortionists.[51]

Such slayings, of course, could be the work of rival traffickers, but many of the incidents have different characteristics from typical drug gang hits. In the Morelia killings, for example, the victims had been strangled. Although cartel enforcers were known to sometimes asphyxiate victims with tape, they almost never just manually stran-gled them. Also, none of the bodies had been mutilated, in marked contrast to most drug gang killings. And, finally, in a majority of cases, the trafficking organizations like to take credit for their handiwork. The Morelia killers clearly did not.

The proliferation of killings that do not fit the pattern of cartel hits raises the possibility that some Mexican citizens have lost all confidence in the government and have decided to fight back on their own against the cartels for the damage they are inflicting on the country. That is what happened in Colombia during the 1990s and early 2000s, when conservative factions formed right-wing paramilitary organizations (as well as outright death squads) to attack the Revolutionary Armed Forces of Colombia (FARC) and other radical left-wing insurgent groups and selected trafficking organizations.[52] A similar development in Mexico would be worrisome. The Colombian vigilantes sparked an additional surge in violence that convulsed the country and intensified an already simmering civil war. It took a monumental effort by the administration of President Álvaro Uribe to both weaken the FARC and disarm the paramilitary militias. A significant vigilante movement in Mexico would certainly not enhance that country's stability. As yet, incidents of vigilantism appear to be relatively rare, but that could change if government authorities are unable to stem the spiraling violence and the growing power of the cartels.

The possible vigilante episodes are not the only signs that the Mexican people may be losing confidence in their own government's ability to maintain order. That discontent boiled over in November 2009, when business groups in Ciudad Juárez called for the introduction of United Nations peacekeepers to quell the violence. Daniel Murguía, president of the local Chamber of Commerce, observed sarcastically: "We have seen UN peacekeepers enter other countries that have a lot fewer problems than we have."[53] Granted, Juárez has been harder hit by the drug violence than other areas of Mexico, but it is hardly a vote of confidence in the stability of the state when leading citizens in a major city conclude that the national government is incapable of fulfilling one of its most basic functions—maintaining internal order. Frustrations are clearly surfacing in a variety of settings. A heckler encountered then–Interior Secretary Fernando Gómez Mont during an official visit to Juárez, and matters escalated from angry, derisive words to physical action when the man contemptuously slapped Gómez Mont on the back of the head.

If the request for UN peacekeepers was not humiliating enough for the Mexican government, a few weeks later more than 5,000 people surged through the streets of Juárez carrying signs demanding that the military leave the city. One 53-year-old businessman, who refused to give his name to reporters, summarized the attitude of the demonstrators. "We are living in hell. Things have only worsened since the army arrived." Another participant was even more caustic and cynical. "There's evidence that soldiers and federal troops are behind some of the extortions and kidnappings, and they are protecting the drug gangs, not the population."[54] That allegation is especially serious. If true, it means that the Mexican military may be going down the same path of drug-related corruption that had already widely infected the police and other governmental institutions. And the military was considered the last bastion against that plague.

The Military and Human-Rights Abuses

A more probable danger than the chance that Mexico could become a failed state is that Calderón's use of the military for law enforcement purposes could transform the country in undesirable, authoritarian ways. Such unintended consequences already seem to be occurring. Mexico is one of the few countries in Latin America in which civilian rule has been the norm since the 1920s, with the military staying out of the political process. The military's record on respect for civil liberties is more mixed, especially given the evidence that has emerged about abuses committed against students during the volatile anti-government demonstrations in 1968. Yet even in the arena of civil liberties, Mexico's military has a decidedly better reputation than most of its counterparts in the hemisphere.

But President Calderón has given the military far more power than it has enjoyed in many decades, and there are already signs that such power is being abused. Some incidents merely reflect the reality that military forces in any country are trained—as one analyst famously put it—to "break things and kill people." Their entire training and orientation is not well suited to domestic law enforcement missions in which many, if not most, of the people they encounter are law-abiding civilians. Nasty incidents are bound to occur, even though many of them are just tragic accidents.

Typical of the tragedies that can take place when soldiers are expected to play the role of cops was an incident in December 2008, when soldiers fatally shot a 35-year-old pregnant woman who reportedly failed to stop at a highway checkpoint in Chihuahua. Military personnel in combat zones are trained to regard an attempt to run a checkpoint as an extremely dangerous and probably hostile act. They tend to shoot quickly, lest they become victims of an enemy ambush. In a domestic setting, though, such a rapid, lethal response is all too likely to victimize an innocent, although clueless, civilian. In fact, sometimes the hapless target is someone other than a civilian. In November 2009, soldiers shot to death a federal police agent who made the same kind of mistake as the pregnant woman.

Beyond such tragic accidents, human-rights organizations accuse the Mexican army of illegal searches, kidnapping, torture, rape, and even murder in the campaign against the cartels. More than 2,000 complaints had been filed with the government's National Human Rights Commission between the start of Calderón's administration and 2009, and the pace was increasing. During 2009, they were coming in at a rate of more than 140 per month. According to the *Wall Street Journal*, in July 2010 that total had climbed to nearly 4,000, and the human rights office in Chihuahua was investigating 465 complaints in that state alone.[55]

Mexican officials typically dismiss such allegations as part of a propaganda offensive by the traffickers to erode public support for the anti-drug military offensive. The comments of Brigadier General Jesús Hernández Peréz are typical, "Many times they make human-rights complaints because they want to limit our capacity for action and besmirch the institution."[56]

But some cases cannot be so easily dismissed. Investigators with the National Human Rights Commission concluded that the army ran amok in Michoacán, committing abuses against 65 individuals. Those abuses included several instances of torture, as well as the rape of two girls. The Commission was also busy investigating cases in Tijuana and several other cities. By early July 2009, investigators ruled that at least 26 of the cases had merit, including episodes that involved blatant use of torture, such as asphyxiation and applying electrical shocks to the genitals of drug suspects.[57]

It would be surprising if such abuses were not taking place, especially once the cartels began to capture, torture, and kill soldiers. It was probably not a coincidence that the incidents of apparent human-rights violations in Michoacán took place shortly after five soldiers were killed in that state in May 2007. As *Washington Post* correspondents Steve Fainaru and William Booth point out, most of the violations have taken place "in regions where the sight of dismembered bodies of soldiers and police is remarkably common."[58] It is a pattern that has taken place in counterinsurgency campaigns around the world (including the U.S. operations in Vietnam, Iraq, and Afghanistan), as the brutality of insurgents and government forces creates a vicious cycle. By exposing the military to that process, Calderón may have caused a long-term problem for the relationship between the military and Mexico's civilian population.

The U.S. Congress was concerned enough about the allegations of human-rights abuses that it held up approval for $110 million of Mérida Initiative funding in the summer of 2009. That was an indication of the extent of U.S. uneasiness, since the Merida Initiative was the principal symbol of bilateral collaboration against the drug cartels. Only intense lobbying by the Obama administration, and escalating threats from Mexico City to back away from cooperation on drug cases Washington deemed crucial, caused Congress to relent. Eventually the funding was released after congressional fact-finders concluded that while the Mexican military had committed some violations of civil liberties, the violations were not so serious or pervasive as to justify cutting off funds.

But concerns about human-rights abuses are not about to go away. A scathing December 2009 report by Amnesty International created another public-relations black eye for Mexico's military. Not only did the Amnesty report document extremely serious cases of unlawful detention, torture, and murder, but it also indicated that Mexican authorities were covering up such violations:

> A comprehensive or detailed analysis of human rights violations committed by members of the military is not available for two significant reasons. First, deficiencies and unnecessary restrictions in the gathering and publishing of data on human rights related complaints received by both military and civilian authorities against military personnel prevent reasonable scrutiny. And second, intimidation and threats against some victims and their relatives mean that an unknown number of abuses are never officially recorded.[59]

As an example of the latter problem, the report noted that a human-rights organization in Nuevo Laredo indicated that it had received 70 complaints of torture and other incidents of ill-treatment by military personnel between January 2008 and June 2009. Yet only 21 individuals filed legal complaints, "as the rest feared threats against them would be carried out." Amnesty's bottom-line conclusion was damning, "Despite the restrictions and deficiencies in official information, the little data available suggests a sharp rise in military abuses over the last two years."[60]

The incidents that Amnesty International was able to document were certainly disturbing. In one case in October 2008, men in military uniforms and vehicles arrested 31-year-old Saúl Becerra Reyes along with five other men. "After being tortured and held illegally for five days by the military at the barracks of 20th Motorized Cavalry Regiment," five of the detainees were transferred and charged with drug and firearms offenses.[61] But Becerra Reyes was not among them. One of the other detainees reported that Becerra Reyes had told him that he had been badly beaten. Despite repeated efforts by his relatives, Mexican authorities refused to divulge any information about his whereabouts. The reason for that became apparent a few months later. At the beginning of March, "Saul Becerra's body was found on the road between Nuevo Casas Grandes and Ciudad Juárez. The one-page death certificate issued by local authorities states that he died on 22 October 2008 (one day after his detention) of a cerebral hemorrhage from head trauma."[62]

Other incidents are equally chilling. On March 17, 2009, the Mexican military detained three men in Nuevo Laredo. That same night, 50 soldiers arrived at the home of Dulce María López Duarte, the wife of one of the men. Despite having no search warrant, they proceeded to search her home and remove a variety of articles, including credit cards and computers. In the following days, López Duarte and other relatives sought information about the status of the men and then filed complaints when no information was forthcoming. They also protested in the streets outside a building believed to be a secret military detention facility. Still, the military denied any knowledge of the arrest of the men. Then, on April 29, 2009, "three burnt bodies were located in the municipality of Vallecillo, Nuevo León state."[63] On May 5, the bodies were identified as the missing men. The overwhelming evidence of military involvement finally forced the military commander of the region to launch an investigation. On May 8, the Ministry of Defense announced that 12 military personnel had been detained and charged regarding the disappearance and murder of the men. Astonishingly, the military refused in the subsequent months to give any further information to the families, human-rights organizations, or the news media about what punishment, if any, the soldiers had received or were likely to receive.

The ongoing tensions between the Mexican military and local police forces became the occasion for one of the more flagrant and extensive cases of human-rights abuses. Over a period of seven days in late March 2009, the military detained 25 members of the Tijuana police force. The Amnesty report describes what apparently happened next:

> According to all 25 police officers, during their initial deten-tion at the military base they were subject to continuous torture and other ill-treatment by military officials trying to obtain false confessions and information implicating other police officers in criminal offenses, or signatures for unseen statements. According to the testimony of the detained police officers, they were bound with tape around their head, hands, knees and feet for days, denied food for three days, beaten repeatedly, asphyxiated with plastic bags over their heads and given electric shocks to their feet and geni-talia. A military doctor was present to resuscitate those who collapsed or lost consciousness.[64]

An investigative report by *Wall Street Journal* correspondent Nicholas Casey in July 2010 regarding the arrest and incarceration of two Americans, Shohn Huckabee and Carlos Quijas, on drug trafficking charges, was chillingly similar to the Amnesty report and other accounts of human-rights abuses.[65] As the Americans were driving back to El Paso from an afternoon in Ciudad Juárez, Mexican army trucks surrounded their vehicle. According to the Mexican military, they found two suitcases full of marijuana, where-upon they arrested Huckabee and Quijas, questioned them briefly, and then turned them over to civilian authorities.

The accused defendants told a very different story. They alleged that the army not only planted the suitcases but took both men to a military base where they were tortured for several hours. The

135

alleged mistreatment included being bound, blindfolded, struck with rifle butts, and given electric shocks. Quijas contended that interrogators soaked him with water and then used an electrified metal rod to administer shocks to his neck, legs, back, testicles, and anus. Huckabee stated that he was similarly given electric shocks, some so severe that he was unable to speak for several minutes, and was told that if he didn't tell the truth, he could be electrocuted.

Mexican authorities denied the accusations and dismissed allegations of evidence planting and torture as a desperate attempt of two drug traffickers to discredit the military and get the charges thrown out of court. But there were troubling features that strongly suggested that Huckabee and Quijas might be telling the truth. Neither man had ever been charged with drug offenses, even minor possession charges, in the United States. Quijas had no criminal record at all, and Huckabee's sole run-ins with the justice system consisted of speeding tickets and a charge of illegal dumping, involving the small construction firm that he owned. Those are odd profiles for drug traffickers.

Records from Huckabee's cell phone were much more consistent with his account than with the military's version. The Americans contended that they were arrested at about 6:40 p.m., and not taken before a civilian magistrate to be charged until after midnight. The military's account contended that they were apprehended more than three hours later and, after brief questioning, were promptly turned over to civilian authorities for formal charges—as Mexican law requires. Yet Huckabee's phone records showed a series of calls throughout the day, then ending abruptly around 6:30—just before the Americans said they were arrested. The three-hour difference is significant, because those extra hours would have provided ample time for the alleged extended interrogations and torture.

Even more troubling, though, three witnesses testified that they saw the military put suitcases into the Americans' Dodge Ram truck at the time of their arrest. Window washer José Antonio Bujanda said that "two soldiers went to their own truck. I saw them take out two suitcases and put them in the gray truck." Another window washer, Fernando Monsivais, confirmed that account. So did a 19-year-old candy seller, Abraham Antero Torres. There was no indication that the Americans had a prior connection to any of those witnesses, nor did it appear that the three men were involved in the drug trade. In what was, at the very least, a gruesome coincidence, Bujanda was shot and killed by an unknown assailant a few months after his testimony. Equally troubling, the other two witnesses subsequently disappeared from Juárez. Whether they fled or met foul play is unknown, but the incidents cast even further doubt on the prosecution's case. Yet despite the mysterious disappearance of the defense's three key witnesses and other disturbing aspects of the case, a Mexican judge convicted Huckabee and Quijas in early September 2010.[66]

A lengthy, 212-page November 2011 report by Human Rights Watch documented many more cases along the lines described in the earlier Amnesty International report.[67] Although Human Rights Watch conducted its investigation in only five states—Chihuahua, Baja California, Nuevo León, Guerrero, and Tabasco—the organization was able to document 170 cases of torture, 39 "disappearances," and 24 extrajudicial killings involving the security forces—most often, the army. The report also confirmed a systematic cover-up of such abuses by the military hierarchy.

As chilling and repulsive as the mounting allegations of arbitrary arrests, torture, and other misconduct by the Mexican military might be, they are not the chief danger to Mexico's democratic system and viability as a state. More insidious, and ultimately more worrisome than the flagrant human-rights abuses, is the undeniable reality that Mexico's military is playing a far more visible and activist role in the country's affairs than at any point in nearly a century. Other populations in Latin America may be accustomed to military patrols in major cities and having troops involved in domestic law enforcement raids, but the Mexican people—until now—have been largely spared that sight. Calderón may have unleashed a force in his country that has been destructive of political stability, civilian supremacy, and the rule of law in all too many other countries.

The Corroding Mexican State

Despite the country's many troubles, it is still an exaggeration to describe Mexico as an emerging failed state. The drug violence, bad as it is, has not yet reached that dire level. However, the cohesion and competence of Mexico's governmental institutions are already under severe strain, and the problem is getting worse. The cartels are becoming bolder and stronger, and they now control significant portions of the country—or at least they have made the environment so dangerous that Mexican authorities no longer control those areas. The situation is worst in Ciudad Juárez, Tijuana, and much of Tamaulipas, but portions of Michoacán, Guerrero, Durango, and swaths of rural areas along the Rio Grande also have become virtual "no go" zones for police and military personnel. And that plague of disorder is spreading to other areas of the country.

The apparent impotence of the authorities to contain, much less destroy, the cartels is fast eroding public confidence in the ability of the government to maintain order and provide basic security. The exodus of affluent Mexicans is an emphatic vote of no confidence, as is the presence of vigilante groups.

A growing number of Mexicans are losing confidence in the government for another reason: episodes of human-rights abuses suggest that the Mexican military may be out of control. Such conduct alienates the civilian population and undermines the legitimacy of the state in the view of the public. That has long been a problem in other Latin American countries, but until now, that defect has not generally characterized Mexico. At a minimum, the growing power and swagger—and resulting unpopularity—of the Mexican military is a troubling development.

And the Calderón government's hostile, defensive reaction to criticism of the military is not helping matters. Interior Minister Gómez Mont enraged critics when he accused human-rights activists of being "unwitting accomplices" of organized crime.[68] Such a crude smear was not likely to boost public support for the Calderón administration or its war on drugs.

Mexico may not be a failed state, but it is a corroding state. Both the strength and the legitimacy of key institutions are showing serious cracks. Furthermore, the warfare between the cartels themselves appears to be spiraling out of control. In such cities as Acapulco, Monterrey, and Cuernavaca, there used to be an implicit code that gangs did not attack the neighborhood sanctuaries where rival kingpins maintained their multimillion dollar residences. But in the past three years or so, the truce involving such sanctuaries appears to have broken down, and attacks in those posh neighborhoods have multiplied. That development leads some observers to wonder whether the violence has now reached the point that it is totally out of control—that not even the capos themselves can contain it. If so, that would create a deadly dual threat to the stability of Mexico: the weakening of the country's institutions and the emergence of a chaotic conflict, bordering on anarchy, among the drug gangs.

It is possible that Mexico's turmoil is a process that can still be reversed. But if it is not reversed—and relatively soon—even the full-blown failed-state scenario would no longer be a far-fetched notion. And that would be a huge problem for the United States.

6. Calderón's Strategy: A Failing Grade

Mexico's drug war body count is steadily rising. But it's a problem that has been building for several years, and some of the roots involve changes that have taken place in Mexico's political system, beginning in the late 1980s and accelerating dramatically since the start of the new century. For nearly seven decades, since the 1920s, Mexico was, for all practical purposes, a one-party state. Although opposition parties were permitted to exist, most notably the relatively conservative National Action Party (PAN), the Institutional Revolutionary Party (PRI) dominated at the national, state, and local levels, using a vast patronage machine and engaging in rather unsubtle vote rigging. That political stability, combined with pervasive corruption, created the environment for an implicit arrangement between Mexican authorities and drug trafficking organizations. Shannon O'Neil, the Douglas Dillon Fellow in Latin American Studies at the Council on Foreign Relations, aptly describes the nature of that arrangement:

> Through the Mexican Ministry of the Interior and the federal police, as well as governorships and other political offices, the government established patron-client relationships with drug traffickers (just as it did with other sectors of the economy and society). This arrangement limited violence against public officials, top traffickers, and civilians; made sure that court investigations never reached the upper ranks of the cartels; and defined the rules of the game for traffickers. This compact held even as drug production and transit accelerated in the 1970s and 1980s.[1]

But the erosion of the PRI's dominance began to destabilize the relationship between the drug cartels and the government. O'Neil catalogues the emergence of a competitive political system in Mexico and its correlation with the rise in drug-related violence:

As the PRI's political monopoly ended, so, too, did its control over the drug trade. Electoral competition nullified the unwritten understandings, requiring drug lords to negotiate with the new political establishment and encouraging rival traffickers to bid for new market opportunities. Accordingly, Mexico's drug-related violence rose first in opposition-led states. After the PRI lost its first governorship, in Baja California in 1989, for example, drug-related violence there surged. In Chihuahua, violence followed an opposition takeover in 1992. When the PRI won back the Chihuahua governorship in 1998, the violence moved to Ciudad Juárez–a city governed by the National Action Party. With the election of Vicente Fox, the PAN candidate as president in 2000, the old model–dependent on PRI dominance–was truly broken.[2]

O'Neil's analysis oversimplifies matters slightly—but only slightly. One key factor that accompanied the end of the one-party system and the stability that it provided was the growing commerce in illegal drugs and the prominence of Mexico's cartels within that trade. When the main Colombian cartels, Cali and Medellín, were disrupted during the 1990s—and ultimately fragmented—Mexican traffickers moved in to fill the resulting vacuum. That competition for control of a huge, financially rewarding industry helped fuel the violence—and it probably would have done so even if the PRI had been able to maintain its political monopoly, but the increased political volatility and unpredictability played a role as well.

The result was a steady, troubling rise in violence. In 2005, more than 1,300 people perished in drug-related killings. But that was just a prelude to what would occur when newly elected PAN President Felipe Calderón opted to confront the cartels head on. His decision immediately ratcheted-up the carnage another notch. By 2007, the yearly total of fatalities had soared to 2,673. And it continues to get worse; according to the U.S. government's annual *International Narcotics Control Strategy Report*, there were 11,583 drug-related killings in 2010 alone. The Mexican government estimated in August of that year that more than 28,000 people had died in drug-related incidents since the start of the Calderón administration, a tally that was revised upward to 35,000 by year's end. By mid 2011, the cumulative toll had reached nearly 43,000, and by late 2011, it reached 47,000.

The centerpiece of Calderón's strategy has been to wage a full-blown offensive against the cartels, using the Mexican military as the point of the spear.[3] That decision was less a sign of admiration for the military than it was a no-confidence vote in Mexico's police forces. In fact, at the time he made the military the lead agency in the new anti-drug offensive, Calderón initiated a less-publicized step to reform the country's notoriously corrupt and incompetent law enforcement agencies. He appointed the energetic, if not frenetic, Genaro García Luna as Public Security Minister to direct that effort, with a mandate to rebuild the police from scratch.

A key element of the rebuilding program was to convince the sons and daughters (even the college-educated sons and daughters) of the middle class to become members of a new, professional police force. García Luna barely concealed his contempt for the force he inherited. "We've had a corrupt, uneducated police force, without a budget, driving stolen vehicles and basically decomposing for 40 years," he sneered.[4] He worked to model the new Federal Police Force after America's FBI and similar agencies, and to provide it with modern equipment and training. Both Calderón and García Luna stressed that the decision to use the military so extensively in the anti-drug fight is a stop-gap measure. The ultimate goal was to bring the Federal Police up to full strength at 40,000 personnel and gradually replace the military on the front lines, allowing the soldiers to return to their barracks.

Whatever the hopes of García Luna and other officials, though, the Mexican army is still taking the lead in the anti-drug campaign. During the initial phase of the military operation in late 2006 and throughout much of 2007, those forces were concentrated in the states of Nuevo León, Guerrero, and Michoacán, and the city of Tijuana. Ultimately, the military presence expanded into other areas, most notably the state of Tamaulipas, where the Zetas are especially active, and the original deployment of about 25,000 troops has ballooned to more than 45,000.[5]

But the military deployment has sometimes played into the hands of the drug trade at least as much as it has caused problems for it. For example, as the violence has skyrocketed in such states as Tamaulipas, Nuevo León, northern Chihuahua, and Michoacán, military commanders have pulled units out of other locales to send to those hot spots. That redeployment has been a bonanza for drug crop farmers and traffickers in some regions. Army eradication squads used to conduct numerous raids to hack down marijuana and opium poppy crops in the western Sierra Madre Mountains. But most of those squads have now departed to try to stem the killings in Ciudad Juárez, Monterrey, Tamaulipas, and other fronts in the drug war. As a result, marijuana cultivation is soaring in the Sierra Madre. Aerial surveys showed pot plants flourishing in valley after valley in the rugged mountains.[6]

Calderón's strategy is encountering the "push-down, pop-up" effect that has bedeviled counternarcotics campaigns in the Andean region, and elsewhere, for decades. When intensified efforts to eradicate drugs take place in one sector or region, production declines, but it simply increases in another sector or region where pressure is less severe at the moment. When authorities divert their attention to the new problem spot, production shifts to yet another area, and so on, in an endless chain. And the people involved in the drug trade in the Sierra Madre are not likely to submit tamely if the military returns to their region and tries to stamp out their livelihood. Virtually all of the farmers, even the poorest ones, now tote weapons—very likely supplied by the cartels.

Calderón: Elliot Ness or Ambrose Burnside?

President Obama praised Felipe Calderón as Mexico's Elliot Ness— the "Untouchable" federal law enforcement official in the 1920s who took on Al Capone, Frank Nitti, and other bootleggers and organized-crime figures. Even political adversaries generally concede that Calderón seems to be personally incorruptible, much as Ness was. Nor is there much doubt about his personal and political courage. It would have been easier—and certainly safer—for him to emulate the phony anti-drug campaigns that his predecessors waged, doing just enough to placate Washington without antagonizing those powerful cartels that were willing to keep the violence in bounds and continue to provide generous bribes to elected and appointed officials. It took both boldness and integrity to abandon that model so dramatically.

But while Calderón's courage and honesty may receive at least grudging admiration, his judgment does not win the same degree of approval. Critics in both Mexico and the United States are appalled at the rising tide of violence since the December 2006 decision, and at the mounting allegations of human-rights abuses by the Mexican military. There is also uneasiness, if not dismay, at Calderón's stubborn determination to stay the course in spite of the troubling developments to date. Observers might ponder whether the model for Felipe Calderón's behavior is not Elliott Ness, but another figure from U.S. history, General Ambrose Burnside, who was commander of Union forces during a brief period in the Civil War.

Burnside is best known for the Battle of Fredericksburg in December 1862. His command decisions during that battle have become legendary for a combination of poor judgment and pit-bull stubbornness. Burnside ordered wave after wave of Union troops to mount frontal assaults uphill across an open field against Confederate infantry and cannon entrenched on the bluffs above the Virginia town. The result was an appalling slaughter that left nearly 13,000 Northern soldiers dead (compared with just 5,000 Confederate fatalities).

And it was not as though he wasn't warned. Several of his division commanders were openly skeptical of the strategy even before the first attempt. And with each failure, they urged Burnside again and again to retreat and attempt to engage Robert E. Lee's Confederate army at another location at another time. Day after bloody day, the commanding general rejected their advice. In the end, his campaign failed utterly and President Lincoln removed him from command.

Of course, there is no one who can remove Felipe Calderón in that fashion. But given the public discontent about his policies, including his strategy toward the cartels—as evidenced in the PAN's poor performance at all levels in elections held since he took office—his political party might wish that there was someone with that authority. There certainly seemed to be an echo of General Burnside's frustrating stubbornness in the president's annual state-of-the-nation address in September 2010. "I am well aware that over the past year, violence has worsened," Calderón told his audience. "But we must battle on."[7]

The Decapitation Strategy

Both U.S. and Mexican leaders insist that Calderón's robust campaign against the cartels is working. Their favorite piece of evidence is the rise in the number of arrests, including the snaring of several

145

high-profile traffickers, since the offensive commenced in December 2006. By the autumn of 2009, Calderón boasted that more than 50,000 people had been arrested on drug offenses. But independent observers remained skeptical, noting that the Mexican government refused to provide statistics on how many of those arrests resulted in convictions. *New York Times* correspondent Marc Lacey concludes that many of the suspects "are quietly released after they have been paraded before the news media."[8] Wags in both the United States and Mexico have begun to compare the strategy regarding drug arrests with a technique common in fishing: "catch and release."

An investigation by Associated Press correspondents Julie Watson and Alexandra Olson in 2010 confirms that sarcastic judgment. "It's practically a daily ritual: Accused drug traffickers and assassins, shackled and bruised from beatings, are paraded before the news media to show that Mexico is winning its drug war. Once the television lights dim, however, about three-quarters of them are let go." Indeed, the farcical nature of the process goes deeper. "Sometimes, the drug cartels decide who gets arrested."[9] The records that Watson and Olson obtained from the Mexican government back up their assertions. Of the more than 226, 000 drug suspects arrested between December 2006 and September 2009, less than 25 percent were even charged with a crime, and only 15 percent of the cases resulted in a verdict. And the Mexican government wouldn't even say how many of those outcomes were guilty verdicts.

Some of the most spectacular announcements about the apprehension of cartel enforcers produce no substantive results. In one case, Chihuahua authorities accused a captured hit man of having killed 15 people. A few weeks after that announcement, he simply disappeared. State police said that they delivered him to federal authorities, but federal officials say that he never arrived. Another cartel enforcer, accused of being involved in 23 killings, was quietly freed from prison a year later without having been charged with murder.

In addition to the general effort to apprehend individuals involved in drug trafficking, the Mexican government has offered rewards of up to $2.2 million apiece for some two dozen leading cartel figures. That is a core feature of a "decapitation" strategy—capturing or killing drug kingpins and thereby disrupting and weakening the organizations. To some extent, the offer of large financial rewards, along with devoting more military and law enforcement manpower to the hunt for such prominent fugitives, has paid off. In just a three-week period in March and early April 2009, authorities apprehended four major traffickers. A huge reward, some $2.2 million, may also have played a role in the August 2010 arrest of Edgar Valdéz Villarreal "La Barbie."

One of the traffickers apprehended in the March-April period was Vicente Carrillo Leyva, the son of Amado Carrillo Fuentes, the "Lord of the Skies," who died while undergoing plastic surgery in 1997. Carrillo Leyva was one of the leaders of a faction of the Juárez cartel, and was arrested as he exercised in a park in Mexico City, where he had been living under an alias. A week earlier, authorities nabbed Héctor Huerta Ríos, a top lieutenant of the Beltrán Leyva cartel. The previous week, they arrested Sigifredo Nájera Talamantes, a prominent hit man. Nájera Talamantes was suspected of being responsible for an attack on a U.S. consulate and for killing several Mexican soldiers. He was also a prime suspect in the rifle and grenade assault on the Televisa station in Monterrey (see chapter 3).

But the most celebrated victory for the Calderón government's decapitation strategy came in December 2009 when Mexican naval marines killed Arturo Beltrán Leyva during a raid in Cuernavaca, the posh resort community outside Mexico City. There is no doubt that Beltrán Leyva was a hugely important figure in Mexico's drug trade. He wasn't known as the "boss of bosses" for nothing. Along with his several brothers, including Alfredo (who was arrested in 2008), he ran the Beltrán Leyva cartel after it broke away from the Sinaloa organization. The new cartel also maintained a de facto alliance with the Zetas. At the time of his death, Arturo Beltrán Leyva was Mexico's third-most-wanted fugitive, with a $1.5 million reward offered for his capture. Anthony Placido, chief of intelligence for the U.S. Drug Enforcement Administration, was gleeful: "Arturo Beltrán Leyva wasn't a big fish. He was a whale."[10]

Nevertheless, the notion that eliminating him would weaken Mexico's drug syndicates was naive. Skeptics predicted that his death would simply cause instability in the Beltrán Leyva organization, and perhaps even more important, create an opportunity for rival cartels to move in on the business and territory of the weakened group. That was not a good development, especially for those who want to see drug-related bloodshed decline in Mexico.

Just as the weakening of the Tijuana and Juárez cartels earlier in the decade fueled brutal turf battles and an orgy of violence (see chapter 2), the decline of the Beltrán Leyva cartel promptly produced a surge of fighting, especially in western Mexico. Even Mexico Attorney General Arturo Chávez Chávez conceded that danger right after Arturo's Beltrán Leyva's death: "Without a doubt, when a cartel leader is taken down it's a big blow and surely this will force a restructuring. I don't dismiss the possibility that this could bring about violence."[11]

His prediction soon proved depressingly accurate. The months following the elimination of Arturo Beltrán Leyva became the most violent period of Calderón's presidency, with more than 2,800 drug murders by the spring of 2010. Most ominous, there was a surge of killings of teenagers and other civilians who appeared to have no connection to the drug trade. That development raised the possibility that the cartels were now waging a broader campaign of terrorism to discredit the Calderón government by demonstrating its impotence in being able to protect the Mexican population. In any case, the celebrations in Mexico City and Washington following the takedown of one drug lord were both premature and wildly excessive.

Yet the same celebratory atmosphere took place following the subsequent capture of La Barbie. President Calderón even boasted of the arrest on Twitter.[12] After police paraded Valdéz in front of the media, federal police official Facundo Rosas told them, "This operation closes a major chapter in drug trafficking in Mexico."[13] A similar glow of satisfaction occurred less than two weeks later, when Mexican marines apprehended yet another Beltrán-Leyva capo, Sergio "El Grande" Villarreal (no relation to La Barbie), after their convoy of armored vehicles cornered him at a safe house in the central Mexican city of Puebla. Government spokesman Alejandro Poiré gloated that "this is a new and resounding blow by the federal government" against the Beltrán-Leyva organization, which "is today badly weakened."[14]

Even before the arrests of La Barbie and El Grande, some analysts expressed cautious hope that the Beltrán Leyva gang might have been so weakened by the take-downs of top leaders and the growing struggle for power among competing factions that it could no longer effectively wage a war to defend its turf. David Shirk, the director of the University of San Diego's Trans-Border Institute, noted that the Mexican government had delivered significant blows over the past few years to seven of the country's eight most prominent drug cartels. Shirk speculated that the eighth, largely unscathed group, the Sinaloa cartel, might now become dominant, especially in western and northwestern Mexico. If that occurred, he believed that it would reduce the bloody power struggles that have so convulsed the country.

From the beginning of 2009 through the end of 2010, the Beltrán-Leyva cartel seemed to be the government's primary target—by a wide margin. But we've seen that pattern before: in the late 1990s and the early 2000s, federal authorities seemed to direct most of their efforts against the Arellano-Félix organization in Tijuana. The interesting question is why officials seem to zero in on one gang of traffickers, while devoting less attention—sometimes much less attention—to certain competitors. In the late 1990s, it was because Mexico's drug czar was on the payroll of a competing cartel. It is uncertain whether similar corrupt motives were in play on this occasion. But whatever the reason, Shirk is correct—the damage to other cartels, and especially the recent devastation of the Beltrán-Leyva faction, worked to the definite advantage of the Sinaloa cartel. That also was true of the earlier offensive against the Tijuana cartel.

Edgardo Buscaglia, a scholar with the Instituto Tecnológico Autónomo de México (ITAM) in Mexico City, estimated in January 2010 that the Sinaloa cartel was responsible for approximately 45 percent of Mexico's illegal drug trade. But after studying statistics from Mexico's own security agencies, he concluded that only 941 of the 53,174 people arrested for organized-crime offenses in the previous six years were affiliated with the Sinaloa organization.[15] A National Public Radio (NPR) report in May 2010 found a similar pattern, which raised serious questions about the relationship between the Mexican government and that trafficking operation. The team, headed by veteran correspondent John Burnett, stated that their investigation "had found strong evidence of collusion between elements of the Mexican army and the Sinaloa cartel" in Juárez.[16] That conclusion was based on dozens of interviews with current and former law enforcement officials, elected representatives, victims of violence, and outside experts.

149

The arrest statistics that NPR compiled reinforced suspicions about a government bias in favor of El Chapo Guzmán and his organization. Between December 2006 and early 2010, authorities arrested 2,600 mid- and high-level cartel members. Of that number, the greatest percentage (44 percent) came from the Gulf-Zeta operation, both when those factions were united and after their split. La Familia came in second with 15 percent, followed by the Beltrán-Leyva group with 13 percent. The Sinaloa and Tijuana cartels followed with 12 percent each, and the damaged and fading Juárez cartel brought up the rear with a mere 5 percent.

The Sinaloa total stood out as strikingly low. Virtually every credible expert considered the Gulf and Sinaloa organizations to be the most powerful trafficking operations during that period. Yet, the number of arrests of Sinaloa operatives was just a little more than one-fourth of the Gulf-Zeta total. More members of the smaller Beltrán-Leyva gang were arrested, and the much smaller and weaker Tijuana remnant was in a virtual tie with the Sinaloa cartel. The disparity involving the Beltrán-Leyva cartel undoubtedly grew in the months following the May 2010 NPR report, given the number of arrests of that group's leaders.

It was a little unsettling that the Beltrán-Leyva faction had split off from the Sinaloa cartel, and that defection—and resulting competition—was especially threatening to Guzmán and his henchmen. By focusing so intently on taking down the Beltrán-Leyva gang, the Mexican government benefitted the Sinaloa leadership and the cartel's overall position in the drug trade.

Statistics involving arrests in Chihuahua, a key front-line state in the drug war given the massive violence in Ciudad Juárez, produced an even greater cloud of suspicion. NPR studied police and military press releases announcing the apprehension of drug gang members between March 2008 and May 2010. Since the Juárez and Sinaloa cartels were the primary combatants in the war to control the drug trade through Juárez, it would be reasonable to expect a similar number of arrests involving each faction. Yet nothing of the sort occurred. Eighty-eight Juárez cartel members were taken into custody. The Sinaloa cartel? A paltry 16.[17] That massive disparity fairly reeked of government favoritism.

Given that track record, one must wonder about the reasons for the government's recent intense focus on battling the Zetas, especially in Tamaulipas.[18] True, that cartel's prominence has soared since late 2008, and it is an especially violent organization. But it is also true that the Zetas have emerged as the Sinaloa cartel's principal rival, and a campaign by government security forces that concentrated on weakening the Zetas in Tamaulipas and elsewhere would greatly benefit El Chapo Guzmán's somewhat beleaguered operation.

The Calderón government, of course, vehemently denies any softness toward the Sinaloa cartel, much less any willingness to admit that Guzmán has been more skillful in bribing federal police and military officials. But the most benign interpretation of the huge disparity in arrests, both nationally and in Chihuahua, was that Calderón and his advisers decided to go after either the most violent or the most vulnerable organizations, and that the Sinaloa cartel does not stand out in either category. The Zetas and La Familia were more appealing targets at the time, given the first standard. The Tijuana, Juárez, and Beltrán-Leyva groups might have been better targets based on the second standard. A less benign interpretation is that the Sinaloa cartel has the authorities in its pocket, just as some of its predecessors did in the 1980s and 1990s with previous administrations in Mexico City.

Despite being in the cross hairs of the Mexican government's anti-drug offensive, the Beltrán Leyva cartel showed few signs of going away quietly. In fact, the organization immediately struck back in response to the loss of Arturo, and did so in an especially nasty fashion. One of the special-forces sailors killed in the gun battle that took Beltrán Leyva's life was Petty Officer Melquisedet Angulo Córdova. The military and the Calderón government immediately hailed Angulo Córdova as a hero and a martyr in the war against the traffickers, and gave him a burial ceremony with a full military honor guard. The secretary of the navy personally presented the flag that had draped Angulo Córdova's casket to his mother.

That prominence and publicity proved to be a tragedy for his family. Just hours later, more than a dozen gunmen armed with AK-47s and other weapons burst into a home in the Gulf Coast state of Tabasco and murdered several of Angulo Córdova's relatives, including his mother, aunt, sister, and brother. Another sister was critically wounded in the attack.[19] Needless to say, the Mexican government's victory celebration seemed a bit hollow after that incident.

The decapitation strategy symbolized by Arturo Beltrán Leyva's death and the arrests of La Barbie, El Grande, and other key figures is fundamentally flawed. Numerous cartel leaders have been killed or captured over the past three decades. One of the most notorious early cases involved the torture and murder in 1985 of U.S. Drug Enforcement Administration agent Enrique "Kiki" Camarena Salazar, who worked as a liaison with Mexican law enforcement personnel. Predictably, Washington put excruciating pressure on Mexico's government to go after the people responsible for the brutal killing of a U.S. agent. And the Mexican government responded. Before the end of the year, the hit man, Rafael Caro Quintero, and the cartel leader who had ordered the hit, Ernesto Fonseca Carillo, were in custody, and would shortly be sentenced to lengthy prison terms.

Four years later, authorities captured Miguel Ángel Félix Gallardo, a founder of the Guadalajara cartel, a predecessor to the Sinaloa organization. In 1995, Héctor Palma, a partner of El Chapo Guzmán, was arrested and sentenced to 33 years in prison. Juan García Abrego, at the time the head of the Gulf cartel, was arrested in 1995 and later extradited to the United States, where he is now serving 11 life terms.

A dual decapitation victory occurred against the Arellano Félix brothers in 2002. Ramón, once Mexico's most-wanted drug trafficker, was gunned down in Mazatlán in February. A month later, police captured his brother, Benjamín, in a town east of Mexico City. The following year, Mexican authorities arrested Osiel Cárdenas, who ran the Gulf cartel, after a shootout in Matamoros.

But all of those highly touted victories proved ephemeral, and both the flow of drugs and the accompanying power struggles have continued unabated. Indeed, some of the episodes seemed to be catalysts for intensified turf wars. The removal of Félix Gallardo, for example, caused the Guadalajara organization to split, with one of the new factions becoming the Sinaloa cartel under El Chapo Guzmán's control. And as described in chapter 2, the demise of the Arellano Félix brothers caused fragmentation of the Tijuana cartel and the subsequent extremely bloody maneuvering to fill that power vacuum. Decapitation is not—and never has been—a solution to Mexico's problems of drug trafficking and its attendant violence.

Yet neither Mexican nor U.S. leaders seem to have lost their enthusiasm for the strategy, as evidenced by their reaction to the downfall of the Beltrán Leyva brothers. That enthusiasm even intensified a few weeks later when Mexican federal police captured Teodoro García "El Teo" Simental just before dawn at his vacation home near the southern tip of the Baja California peninsula. Once again, there was rejoicing in both Mexico City and Washington.

The same enthusiasm surfaced again in July 2010 when the Mexican army conducted one of its few high-profile attacks on the Sinaloa cartel, cornering and killing Ignacio "Nacho" Coronel, the organization's number-three leader, in a shootout near Guadalajara. Coronel was called the "king of ice," because he was the principal founder of Mexico's vast methamphetamine trade, and his organization came to dominate trafficking in that drug. At the time of his death, the Mexican government was offering a $2 million reward for his apprehension, and the United States was offering $5 million for information leading to his capture. Coronel did not depart this world without a struggle, though, waging a running gun battle that killed one soldier and wounded others. Some of his shots found their mark even as he was dying from his own wounds.[20]

Government proclamations of a definitive victory have become a routine occurrence every time a drug kingpin is taken down. A typical example took place in June 2011 when Mexican federal police arrested José de Jesús Mendez, alias "El Chango" (The monkey), who had been the number-two leader of La Familia and had later led a splinter faction. According to Alejandro Poiré, the government's national security spokesman, that capture, combined with the killing of La Familia founder and top leader Nazario Moreno González the previous December, meant that "what was left of the command structure of this criminal enterprise is destroyed."[21]

Ordinary Mexicans seem much more skeptical—and realistic—than U.S. and Mexican officials about the potential benefits flowing from high-profile arrests or killings of drug kingpins. Dulce González Armendez, a resident of Tijuana, summed up the prevailing attitude in response to the capture of García Simental. "I know that politicians are making a big deal about this arrest, but honestly, there is a line of ill-intentioned people waiting to take the place of that man."

Some outside experts agree with her assessment. University of Arizona professor Oscar J. Martínez, who studies the cartels, predicted that the arrest would "just create more violence, mayhem and suffering for ordinary people, as his associates retaliate and rival gangs take advantage of perceived weaknesses in the camps of competitors."[22] Erubiel Tirado, a security expert at Mexico City's Iberoamerican University, reached a similar conclusion. The record over the past decade, he contended, showed that each time a capo is removed, violence spikes because lower-ranked members of a cartel then vie for control. "It tends to multiply criminal networks," he added, because the contenders for the leadership succession are often those "who can be more violent and less strategic."[23]

It is even more unrealistic to believe that the decapitation strategy will have any beneficial impact on the drug-trafficking business itself. Jorge Chabat, one of Mexico's top experts on the drug trade, paints a depressing but totally realistic picture. "The arrest of these drug lords does not have any significant effects in terms of the flow of drugs to the U.S. It did not happen in Colombia, where the government has dismantled the big cartels but they are producing more cocaine." Chabat believed that in the long term "the dismantling of these cartels would in principle produce a reduction in the levels of violence," but in the short term, there would be no decline.[24] In fact, he worried that it could be a catalyst for even more ferocious turmoil.

Drug lord Ismael "El Mayo" Zambada openly ridiculed the decapitation strategy. In an interview with the investigative magazine *Proceso* in early 2010, Zambada was fairly dripping with sarcasm about the government's strategy. "One day I will decide to turn myself in to the government so they can shoot me," he joked. "They will shoot me and euphoria will break out. But at the end of [a few] days we'll all know that nothing has changed." Zambada pointed out the obvious reason why that was the case. "Millions of people are wrapped up in the narco problem. How can they be overcome? For all the bosses jailed, dead or extradited, their replacements are already here."[25]

War Weariness

As the violence grows more intense and spreads to more and more areas in Mexico, Calderón is gradually losing public support for his military offensive against the drug lords. War weariness is setting in. One subtle sign is the change that has taken place in nature of the celebration of Mexico's famous Day of the Dead, an annual festival popular with U.S. tourists. Despite its name, the event had always had an upbeat tone. The tradition blends Catholic rituals with the pre-Columbian belief that the dead return from the underworld once a year. People parade to cemeteries to heap flowers (usually marigolds), candy skulls, and candles at the tombs of ancestors. There is typically a party atmosphere and an undercurrent of joy, not mourning. The 2009 celebration, though, was markedly different in Juárez and other cities that have been hard hit by the drug violence. The tone was much more somber, as relatives and friends marked the mounting toll of victims.

There is also the phenomenon of the "narco widows" (along with mothers, sisters, and children) of actual or accused drug gang members, whose lives have been disrupted—and in some cases, wrecked—by the multisided fighting in Mexico's drug war. Reuters correspondent Catherine Bremer noted that "for every gruesome photo of a hacked-up corpse or severed human head, there is at least one woman, often several, left with her life in pieces."[26] And it's not just the relatives of the dead who are suffering. Calderón's crackdown has put more than 80,000 alleged drug gang members behind bars. Their female relatives and children are often collateral damage in that law enforcement dragnet, and many of them direct their rage at the Calderón government for putting them in such dire financial and emotional straits.

When Calderón launched his military campaign at the end of 2006, most Mexicans seemed to support the strategy. But they did so because they believed the president's confident predictions that confronting the cartels would weaken them and reduce their ability to intimidate and terrorize. In other words, the assumption was that the overall security environment would improve.

That clearly has not happened. A father grieving over his son's grave in Ciudad Juárez epitomized the growing pessimism about the decision to call in the military. "The only thing that the military presence has provoked here . . . is more death," he lamented.[27] Public opinion, while still generally hostile toward the cartels, has become increasingly skeptical toward the drug strategy and toward Calderón's leadership in general. His National Action Party fared poorly in the July 2009 elections, which chose members of the Chamber of Deputies (the lower house of Mexico's Congress) and numerous governors, mayors, and other local officials. True, disappointment at the results of his war against the cartels was not the only factor that led to PAN's electoral defeats. Several corruption scandals tarnished the party's carefully cultivated reputation for honesty—in marked contrast to the notoriously corrupt PRI. "Yes, I admit the PRI is corrupt," said one voter in Mexico City. "So we voted for the PAN, and they turned out to be just as corrupt."[28]

There was also widespread dissatisfaction with the overall state of the economy, which was suffering at the time from the global recession. Although Calderón correctly pointed out that factors outside of Mexico were largely responsible for the recession, and that even internal factors had been building for decades when the PRI ran the country, his arguments did not seem to resonate with voters. That's not surprising. Voters rarely reward incumbent parties in any country when economic times are tough.

But discontent about the alarming blowback from the war against the drug traffickers certainly played a role as well. Even some of Calderón's political allies began to have second thoughts. As early as 2008, Rubén Aguilar, the president's former director of communications, proposed opening negotiations with the cartels, essentially allowing them to conduct their business in exchange for a commitment to halt the kidnappings, torture, and gruesome murders. Aguilar was even willing to go so far as to consider wholesale legalization of drugs. "We are not going to eliminate narco trafficking," he stated in an interview with a Mexican newspaper, but "we can diminish the violence with which it seeks to enhance its operating spaces." At a minimum, negotiations would likely lead to less destructive "rules of the game" among the competing cartels.[29]

Other advocates of change are speaking out as well. "The people of Mexico are losing hope, and it is urgent that Congress, the political parties and the president reconsider this strategy," said Senator Ramón Galindo, a Calderón supporter, several months after Aguilar's interview.[30] Galindo may have a special vantage point to be alarmed, since he is a former mayor of Ciudad Juárez. The Chihuahua state legislature conducted a debate in July 2009 about whether Calderón's strategy was "a total failure."

PAN's performance in the July 2010 elections provided little evidence of strong support for the anti-trafficking campaign. The party did not fare as badly as some pre-election polls indicated, but the results were hardly gratifying to Calderón or other leaders, either.

The bright spot was that the rival PRI lost three governorships that it had held for decades, including Sinaloa. But that occurred only because of an alliance of convenience between the conservative PAN and the left-wing Party of the Democratic Revolution (PRD)—a coalition of odd ideological bedfellows that is inherently unstable—and because of unusual circumstances in each of those states. The PRI candidate for governor of Sinaloa, Jesús Viscarra, for example, was constantly dogged by allegations (and more than a little evidence) that he was cozy with drug traffickers. Vizcarra, the mayor of Culiacán, was not only a relative of slain drug lord Inés Calderón, but he repeatedly dodged media questions about whether Ismael Zambada, the number-two man in the Sinaloa cartel, was the godfather to one of Vizcarra's children. Shortly before the election, the influential newspaper *Reforma* published a photo of Vizcarra attending a party with Zambada.[31]

If PAN couldn't defeat a candidate with that baggage, it would have been a pathetic hulk incapable of winning much of anything. And yet, despite the controversy surrounding Viscarra, PRI would still have carried Sinaloa were it not for the PAN-PRD alliance. On its own, PAN would have lost that state.

Indeed, the party was not able to carry a single state on its own, and it lost the governorships of two states it previously held. Even more telling, PAN's showing was especially weak in two front-line states in the drug war: Chihuahua and Tamaulipas. Threats and violence from the drug gangs clearly had an effect. Party leaders in Tamaulipas told the Associated Press that they couldn't even find candidates willing to run in many of the towns where the cartels were powerful. And voter turnout, already low in many parts of the country, was even worse in those two states. In Tamaulipas, less than 40 percent of eligible voters cast ballots—well below the norm of 65 to 75 percent in previous elections. The turnout in Chihuahua was even worse than in Tamaulipas, with a mere third of the voters casting ballots. The depressed turnout there was understandable after cartel enforcers hung four bodies from traffic bridges early on the morning of the election.[32]

The main outcome of the balloting seemed to be a widespread political malaise. Voters were unhappy with Calderón and his party, but they gave no mandate to the PRI either. The weak voter turnout appeared to be a combination of cartel intimidation and general disillusionment with all three major parties and their policies.

Calderón: No Surrender!

The president and his advisers show no sign of backing down, despite the rising discontent in the country about the drug war. As the casualties mount, they have become even more adamant about defending the strategy. Minister of the Interior Fernando Gómez Mont was both blunt and fatalistic, asserting that to ease up on the offensive would be appeasement of criminal behavior and the pervasive corrupting influence that cartels have on Mexico's society. "We have to do this while we are strong enough to do it," Gómez Mont stated. "We are committed to enduring this wave of violence."[33] His attitude signaled that the body count would rise even beyond the previous awful levels—a point that was confirmed the following year. As it turned out, though, Gómez Mont would no longer be a leader of the campaign against the cartels. Calderón replaced him in July 2010 with José Francisco Blake Mora, who had served as the point man in anti-drug efforts in the state of Baja California. Blake Mora remained in that post for less than 17 months before he died in a mysterious helicopter crash on the outskirts of Mexico City—the latest in a series of air mishaps over the past five years that have claimed the lives of prominent security personnel.

Despite the alarming and often bloody setbacks, Mexican officials insist that the current strategy, while risky, is working, and they point to the surge in the number of arrests. Between December 2006 and July 2011, authorities have arrested more than 100,000 drug suspects. Although the vast majority consists of low-level gang members, some are definitely more significant players. Yet despite the impressive total of arrests, there is no evidence that the cartels have been significantly weakened in the process. Indeed, the cartels that have faded in power in the past two or three years—especially the Gulf cartel—have done so primarily because of the rise of more powerful rivals, not because of the wave of arrests. And the incarceration of drug gang members certainly has not had a beneficial impact on the bloodshed taking place throughout the country.

The Calderón administration, and most of its political allies, summarily reject suggestions about trying to reach an accommodation with the cartels to reduce the violence. One prominent deputy in the Mexico's congress dismissed Aguilar's proposal for negotiations as "crazy." Another stated: "You cannot cut deals with crooks, least of all with [powerful] criminal organizations."[34] Calderón himself denounced the suggestion. "My government," he thundered, "does not negotiate nor will it ever negotiate with criminal organizations." Instead, he pledged "not only to confront them but defeat them with all the force of the state."[35]

When a spokesman for La Familia called a television station talk show in Michoacán following the cartel's assault on police and military personnel in July 2009 and indicated that his organization was "open to dialogue," Gómez Mont summarily rejected the proposal. Even negotiations, to say nothing of accepting a de facto truce with La Familia and the other drug organizations, Gómez Mont stressed, would be sanctioning criminal behavior and its corrosive influence. "Do I have to accept corruption as a way of stabilizing our society?" he asked. "No, I have to act."[36] During 2009 and early 2010, the administration actually escalated its use of the military, first sending some 5,500 troops (in several stages) into Ciudad Juárez to bolster beleaguered local authorities, and then dispatching 860 troops to Tijuana.

Even as evidence accumulates that the government's confrontational strategy is not working and is, in fact, leading to greater turmoil, Calderón and his advisers seem determined to press on. Following the unprecedented surge of killings in early June 2010, which claimed hundreds of lives in less than a week, Calderón issued a 5,000-word manifesto warning that the campaign against the cartels must continue, "or we will always live in fear."[37] Two months later, he admitted that there might be more bouts of violence as the struggle against the traffickers continued. In fact, "the victory we are seeking and will gain is unthinkable without more violence." But along the same line of reasoning that his one-time attorney general used, Calderón argued that the prospect of greater violence was actually a good thing. "This is a process of self-destruction for the criminals."[38]

For all the hard-line rhetoric and highly publicized initiatives on both sides of the border, a "devil's bargain" with the cartels may be the only politically feasible strategy at the moment to reverse Mexico's slide toward chaos. Former President Vicente Fox is the latest prominent political figure to suggest that such an approach be considered. Speaking at an anti-crime conference in August 2011, Fox stated that he wanted to "start a public debate" on two related ideas: first, that the Mexican government should "call on the violent groups for a truce," and second, that the government should "evaluate the advisability of an amnesty law."[39]

No Real Change in Strategy

Is there a possibility that Calderón could reverse course and embrace an appeasement policy toward the cartels? As noted in chapter two, he is under growing pressure even from some close political allies to back away from his current strategy of unrelenting confrontation. Speculation about a possible policy change intensified following his decision to sign drug reform legislation in August 2009. That measure decriminalized small-scale drug possession for personal use. Speculation deepened a few weeks later when he accepted (and probably had asked for) the resignation of Attorney General Eduardo Medina Mora. Calderón's choice for a replacement, little-known federal prosecutor Arturo Chávez Chávez, puzzled many observers. Prior to his roles in the federal government in both the justice and interior departments, Chávez had served as state attorney general in Chihuahua. Given the orgy of drug-related violence in that state, having held that post would hardly seem to be a point in his favor. Victoria Caraveo, a long-time human-rights activist in Ciudad Juárez, expressed the view of other critics of the appointment. "He was in charge of solving a local problem, and he did nothing about it. What makes President Calderón think he will be able to solve a national problem?" It was a "terrible decision," she said.[40]

Medina Mora's departure may have had more to do with a mundane bureaucratic power struggle than with signaling a dramatic change in policy, though. Throughout his tenure, Medina Mora had feuded with Public Security Minister García Luna. The main source of friction was García Luna's attempt to create a single national police force under his personal command. Medina Mora regarded that move as an undesirable centralization of power that could someday undermine Mexico's democratic system. Although the Mexican Congress killed the original plan, García Luna went ahead with the creation of another organization, the Federal Police Force, that would have most of the same characteristics. And Calderón did nothing to stop him. The departure of Medina Mora, and his replacement by a less prominent figure, strengthened García Luna's relative position in the administration. Since his approach to the drug war was, if anything, even more hard-line than

Medina Mora's, his rise in status did not suggest the onset of an appeasement or even an accommodation strategy.

Moreover, Chávez Chávez came from the same faction of the PAN as García Luna, and the two men had been long-time political allies. George W. Grayson, a professor of government at the College of William and Mary and the author of *Mexico: Narco-Violence and a Failed State?* concluded that Chávez's appointment not only was a victory for García Luna in a bureaucratic power struggle, it "backs the muscular approach as they try to ramp up their capabilities to fight the cartels."[41]

There was a similar lack of policy significance in Calderón's appointment of Blake Mora to replace Gómez Mont. Blake Mora, a former congressman, was at least as hard-line as his predecessor regarding the drug traffickers. However, he seemed to be more effective in minimizing feuds between the police and military in his home state of Baja California. It was no coincidence that Calderón singled out "the good relations he has managed to build between the police and army" as a major quality that would make his appointment a good one. Conversely, the army had let it be known on several occasions that it was upset with Gómez Mont and his strategy to build a more powerful federal police force that would eventually give that agency the lead role in the offensive against the drug cartels. It should be noted that Blake Mora's successor, Alejandro Poire, was Calderón's appointed head of the national security agency and had previously served as the president's spokesman on security issues. The appointment of such a long-time, trusted aide suggested that there would be no change in policy.

Gómez Mont also had annoyed Calderón by opposing the political alliance with the leftist PRD—an alliance that may have diluted the ideological brand of the PAN but was the main factor that prevented the July 2010 local and state elections from being a total debacle for the party. Especially annoying to Calderón was that Gómez Mont had vented his displeasure publicly and engaged in grandstanding for the media by resigning his PAN membership. So, perhaps even more than was the case with the president's decision to replace Medina Mora, the ouster of Gómez Mont reflected mundane politics rather than policy considerations. The same factor seemed to be the main reason why Calderón replaced Chávez Chávez in March 2011 when legislators (especially PRI members)

161

became relentless in their criticism of the attorney general's unimpressive job performance.

The official justification for Calderón's signing of the drug law reform also indicated that the hard-line policy toward the cartels was still in place. In reality, the reform measure did little more than formalize and expand a long-standing informal system whereby small-time drug users would often bribe an arresting police officer to avoid going to jail and being prosecuted in the courts. But government officials hailed the reform as a significant measure that would aid the campaign against the drug lords. Commenting on the legislation, Bernardo Espino del Castillo, an official with the attorney general's office who helped write the new law, stated: "This frees us from a flood of small crimes that have saturated our federal government and allows the authorities to go after big criminals."[42]

Personnel shifts, and even the modest drug reform law, do little to repair the disarray in Mexico City's strategy. It does not alter the fundamental economics of the black-market drug trade and the enormous revenues that the trade generates. Nor does it alter the potential for corruption, including corruption at the highest political and administrative levels, that such vast revenues create. The latter point has produced some tension between the Calderón administration and the military hierarchy.

Military leaders have been grumbling for some time that more needs to be done about elected officials and other prominent officeholders who are on the take from the cartels. Grayson notes: "It's one thing to go after capos, but behind the capos are those who are benefiting from the drug dealing—the governors, senators, deputies, mayors and thousands of civilian public officials. The military is furious that there are governors who live high on the hog while they are putting troops in harm's way. That is the buzz among the brass."[43]

But taking on such powerful players would be even riskier than the strategy has been to this point. It could also prove more than a little politically embarrassing, if not damaging, to Calderón's administration. Not all of the elected officials who are in bed financially with drug traffickers are members of the PRI or the PRD—some of them are PAN members.

That is one aspect of the larger political and economic context in which Calderón's war against illegal drugs must operate. And it is becoming an ever more difficult context. The Mexican public's widespread discontent regarding government corruption and ineptitude, which was a key factor in the PAN's electoral defeat in the 2009 mid-term elections, has grown worse. Calderón's first major speech in 2010 seemed to recognize the public restlessness and anger about the economy, corruption, and other issues. The drug war and other anti-crime initiatives that had dominated the first half of his term now placed third on his list of priorities, after creating jobs and reducing overall poverty.[44] That shift caused speculation about a possible de-emphasis of the military campaign against drug trafficking, but Calderón's subsequent actions indicated that the change was merely rhetorical and cosmetic, not substantive.

The domestic criticism of his strategy, though, continues to mount—and it is coming from ever more prominent sources. Perhaps the biggest blow occurred in early August 2010, when former president Vicente Fox posted an essay on his blog calling for the legalization of drugs. If those comments were not enough to signal Fox's break with the policies of his successor, the former president also called for a rapid withdrawal of the military from internal security missions. But the use of the military against the cartels has been the centerpiece of Felipe Calderón's strategy. And in a final barb directed at Calderón, Fox asserted that the rampant violence was damaging the country's reputation internationally and undermining the government's legitimacy domestically. He stressed that "the first responsibility of a government is to provide security for the people and their possessions." But "today, we find that, unfortunately, the Mexican government is not complying with that responsibility."[45]

When he read that blog post, Calderón could be forgiven if he had responded "Et tu, Brute?" And the president's feelings about his predecessor undoubtedly did not improve the following year when Fox suggested that the government consider a truce with the cartels. But Fox seems to better reflect the trend in public opinion than does Calderón.

Wall Street Journal columnist Mary Anastasia O'Grady provides an accurate summary of the results of Calderón's approach to the issue of illegal drugs since his inauguration—a strategy that has received such enthusiastic backing from the United States:

> Having staked his presidency on restoring Mexico's rule of law, Mr. Calderón has an incentive to claim that his blitz is working. And there is no doubt that it has had an effect.

Wherever the army has moved in, extreme lawlessness has subsided. Thousands of criminals have been killed, either by law enforcement or by rival gangs who now fight over shrinking turf. Drug shipments have been confiscated, traditional supply lines . . . have been disrupted, and corrupt officials have been ousted.

Yet the war rages on. Dead capos are replaced, new supply lines . . . crop up, and corruption persists. The racketeers kidnap, rob and trade in weapons."[46]

In other words, Calderón's strategy has done little to alter the fundamental conditions in Mexico–except perhaps, to stoke even more violence. Both O'Grady's and Vicente Fox's harsh assessments are on the mark.

Spreading the Problem to Mexico's Neighbors

The only other significant effect has been to divert some of the trafficking routes to areas outside of Mexico.[47] Already, there has been an upsurge of drug seizures in the Caribbean as shipments through that region have increased in response to the crackdown in Mexico. Using commercial airline flights that originate in Puerto Rico for smuggling drugs has become especially popular because flights from that U.S. territory are not subject to inspection by U.S. Customs authorities—as are flights from foreign countries.

If that change in trafficking patterns intensifies, it would reverse the shift that occurred in the 1990s. We will have come full circle. Previously, most illegal drugs from the Andean source countries flowed through Caribbean transit points. When the United States both pressured and bribed the governments of Caribbean countries to do more to disrupt that trade, the primary trafficking routes moved westward to Mexico. As Shannon O'Neil points out, "in 1991, 50 percent of U.S.-bound cocaine came through Mexico; by 2004, 90 percent of U.S.-bound cocaine (and large percentages of other drugs) did."[48]

The ongoing shift back to Carribean routes raises the interesting question of whether that is an unintended or intended consequence of Calderón's crackdown on the cartels. Mary O'Grady and other experts suspect that such an outcome may be the real motive—or at least one of the motives—underlying his strategy. According to O'Grady, "Mexico seeks to raise the cost of trafficking so that the flows go elsewhere."[49] And, one might add, so that much of the violence accompanying the drug trade also goes elsewhere.

There is little question that, whether intended or not, Calderón's anti-drug offensive is causing the cartels to become much more active in places outside of Mexico. That development is most evident in Mexico's neighbors in Central America. Indeed, the marked deterioration of the security environment in the region seemed to begin in 2008, when the Zetas began to penetrate those countries. Local traffickers in Guatemala, Honduras, and El Salvador invited the Zetas in to provide both protection and to help professionalize their operations. It was not long, though, before the Zetas displaced the locals and took over. And once that occurred, other Mexican cartels—especially La Familia, the Sinaloa cartel, and the Gulf cartel—also moved in, lest their ruthless competitor gain control of all of the lucrative trafficking routes through Central America.

In a *Time* magazine interview shortly before his assassination in December 2009, Honduras' anti-drug czar Julián Aristides González said that in the years he had held the post, he had seen the presence of the Mexican cartels explode. According to Aristides González, authorities "found one huge hacienda bought by Mexicans with landing strips for major aircraft." He made a glum assessment: "Almost all of the big Mexican organizations are carving out territory here. And when they run into each other, they will fight over it."[50] The principal combatants, he said, were the Sinaloa cartel, La Familia, and the Zetas.

The subsequent fragmentation of La Familia has left the field dominated by the Sinaloa cartel and the Zetas. Both organizations now sub-contract Honduran groups to ship drugs for them. And the violence that has afflicted the drug trade in Mexico is taking hold in Honduras, where the homicide rate reached 53 per 100,000 in 2009. The Mexican traffickers are also penetrating the Honduran economy in a variety of ways, especially by buying real estate and scooping up legitimate businesses to launder drug money.

After investigating developments in Mexico's southern neighbors, *Washington Post* reporters William Booth and Nick Miroff concluded that "drug cartel violence is quickly spilling south into Central America, threatening to destabilize fragile countries already rife with crime and corruption."[51] Other experts reach similar conclusions. David Gaddis, chief of operations for the Drug Enforcement

Administration, contends that the Mexican organizations are moving into countries "where they feel, quite frankly, more comfortable" than they do in Mexico.[52]

There is ample evidence to back up such pessimistic assessments. El Salvador's murder rate, already one of the higher ones in the world, jumped another 37 percent in 2009. That rise was due almost entirely to intensified fighting among drug trafficking organizations. El Salvador's defense minister, David Munguía Payés, stated bluntly: "The more pressure there is in Mexico, the more the drug cartels will come to Central America looking for a safe haven."[53]

That situation certainly seems to be playing out in Guatemala.[54] Then-president Álvaro Colom declared a "state of siege" in Alta Verapaz, an especially violent province near the border with Mexico, in December 2010. Colom alleged that the Zetas had overrun that province. The following month, he extended that state of siege, giving the government additional powers to combat the heavily armed cartel.[55]

Colom's worries were not excessive. The area in and around Alta Verapaz had become a major corridor for the transportation of drugs from South America through Honduras and eventually into Mexico. The Zetas operated with such impunity that before the siege declaration and the deployment of several thousand troops, the cartel's heavily armed gunmen effectively controlled the streets of several towns in Alta Verapaz and even imposed curfews on the inhabitants.

The troubling security environment in Alta Varapaz was symptomatic of a much larger problem. According to Leonel Ruíz, Guatemala's federal prosecutor for narcotics offenses, the Zetas had gained control of three other states and nearly half of Guatemala's territory.[56] Kevin Casas-Zamora, a former vice president of Costa Rica and now a fellow at the Brookings Institution, puts the figure at 40 percent, which includes a large northern region known as the Petén. "The Zetas have roadblocks there," he notes. "You can only enter the Petén if the Zetas allow you to."[57]

The cartel penetration of Honduras and El Salvador has also reached the point where significant portions of those countries' governmental control is precarious, at best. El Salvador's president, Mauricio Funes, admits that the Zetas are bribing elite police units with $5,000 monthly payments to cooperate with the cartel and to steal high-powered weapons and grenades from the military. In the spring of 2011, nearly a dozen El Salvadoran soldiers were arrested trying to sell 2,000 grenades to traffickers.

Honduran President Profirio Lobo contends that in his country, drug gang members now outnumber police officers and soldiers.[58] An Al Jazeera interview with "Victor," a former major trafficker, confirms how bad the situation in Honduras has become, "I had a godfather," Victor told reporters. "I just needed to call him up if the police stopped me at a checkpoint." The Al Jazeera correspondents saw with their own eyes how the traffickers dominated the rural portions of Honduras, including the province of Colon. "Everyone is armed: we saw drug dealers with AK-47s . . . and gunmen in trenches within the perimeters of the palm oil plantations."[59] Those plantations often serve as cover for drug trafficking operations. The reputed local drug kingpin, Leonel Rivera, travels the area freely, but honest farmers are fleeing the province in droves, and the local press has become as wary as their colleagues in the most violent portions of Mexico about reporting on cartel activities.

Even Costa Rica, long an enclave of democracy and stability in the region, has come under growing pressure. The drug trade there is more prominent than ever before, and the Obama administration, for the first time, put that country on the official list of "major drug transit or major drug producing countries."[60] Costa Rica's security ministry contends that trafficking organizations are now storing large quantities of drugs in the country, converting Costa Rica from a "bridge" to a "warehouse," a change that automatically entails a much larger ongoing presence of cartel operatives.[61] Costa Rican authorities are sufficiently worried about the cartel menace that they implemented a "Strategic Association Accord" with Mexico, an agreement initially signed in 2009, to share intelligence and coordinate other measures to counteract the trafficking organizations.[62]

Central American leaders are clearly agitated about the impact of the Mexican cartels on the security and stability of their countries. Even the leftist government of Nicaragua, led by the Sandinistas, Washington's arch-nemesis during the 1980s, seems not only receptive to aid from the United States to combat the traffickers, but eager for such assistance. Francisco Campbell, Nicaragua's ambassador to Washington, stated that "unlike the imaginary threats of the past, this one is real. This is the first time we can talk about an honest hemispheric threat."[63]

A more moderate leader like Guatemala's Álvaro Colom expressed a similar view shortly before leaving office. "Fundamentally, I think we made a mistake, a miscalculation, of the scale of the problem," he conceded. "We are witnessing a very serious aggression, which is part of a regional phenomenon."[64] He attributed 42 percent of the crimes in his small country, which included 6,000 murders in 2010, to the drug gangs. Highlighting the financial resources of those organizations, Colom noted that Guatemalan authorities had seized almost $12 billion in property, drugs, and cash during his three-and-a-half years in office. The comparable figure for the previous eight years was approximately $1.1 billion. Twelve billion dollars, he emphasized, was equal to almost two years of Guatemala's state budget.[65]

What is so worrisome about the malignant presence of the drug cartels in Central America is the vulnerability and overall weakness of those countries. There has been speculation that the violence in Mexico could ultimately cause that country to become a "failed state." But for all of its problems, Mexico has powerful institutions that serve as a formidable barrier to the drug gangs. Mexico faces a serious threat from the drug cartels—and there are some areas of the country in which the government's writ has become precariously weak—but Mexico is still a long way from becoming a failed state.

The situation is considerably more dire in Central America. Associated Press correspondent Katherine Corcoran observes: "Mexican drug cartels now operate virtually uninhibited in their Central American backyard. U.S.-supported crackdowns in Mexico and Colombia have only pushed traffickers into a region where corruption is rampant, borders lack even minimal immigration control, and local gangs provide a ready-made infrastructure for organized crime."[66]

Worries about the threat that the Mexican cartels seem to pose are even causing Central American governments to mute their traditional—and often quite strident—nationalist rivalries. President Colom, for example, called for a unified regional counter-narcotics force that would combine troops from Guatemala, El Salvador, and Honduras. The specific mission of that combined force was to retake territory that the traffickers had seized.

The drug gang turf fights that have so plagued Mexico are now being played out with increasing frequency and ferocity in Central America. And the same gruesome trophies, especially severed

168

heads, are now showing up with greater frequency as well. Rival cartels are establishing a strong presence in several Central American countries. The Zetas have set up several training camps in Guatemala, and other trafficking organizations have established bases of operation in both Guatemala and Honduras to facilitate drug shipments northward by sea and air.

Corruption, a long-standing problem in Central American states (as it is in Mexico), is reaching new heights as the cartels consolidate their beachheads. Since late 2008, four high-level figures, including two national police chiefs and former Honduran president Alfonso Portillo, have been sent to prison on drug-related corruption charges.

The potential destabilizing impact that the cartels could have in Central America is even stronger than the potential effect in Mexico. One major reason for worry about the power of the cartels is the political fragility of the Central American countries. Mexico had eight decades of political stability, from the 1920s to the early years of the 21st century, under the domination of the Institutional Revolutionary Party. Even though the country now has a multiparty system, and the PRI has lost the last two presidential elections to the National Action Party, Mexico is still a bastion of political stability compared with its Central American neighbors.

With the exception of Costa Rica, those countries have been characterized by decades of turmoil, including violent peasant rebellions, military coups, bloody civil wars, and ideologically driven societal upheavals. Mexico's weaknesses, especially the pervasively corrupt police forces and prison system and dysfunctional court system, are not only replicated but greatly magnified in most Central American countries.

It was only a little more than two decades ago that the Reagan administration feared that the entire region could be aflame with revolutionary convulsions. Indeed, that fear was the driving force that caused Washington to support a series of brutal dictatorships in Guatemala, undermine the left-wing Sandinista government in Nicaragua, and strongly back El Salvador's beleaguered government against a radical insurgency. Central America was at or near the top of Washington's national security agenda. The relative calm in the region since the early 1990s has caused that memory of earlier turmoil to fade. But if the Mexican cartels deepen their presence in Central America, that precarious equilibrium could come to an end—and do so with stunning speed.

In addition to the much weaker political institutions in Central America compared with Mexico, those smaller countries lack Mexico's other institutional bulwarks. Both the overall economies and the business communities are not nearly as strong. Other nongovernmental organizations, which are the foundation of vibrant civil societies, are far less numerous and influential. The cartels have a much greater ability to produce a failed-state scenario—or at least create a full-blown narcostate—in one or more Central American countries.

There is growing alarm among both Central American and U.S. leaders about the penetration of the region by the trafficking organizations. At a regional summit meeting in June 2011, Secretary of State Hillary Clinton assured nervous officials: "The United States will back you." She also underscored how seriously the Obama administration took the ominous trend. "We know the statistics—the murder rates surpassing civil war levels," she said, referring to the Cold War–era conflicts between left-wing and right-wing forces that plagued El Salvador, Nicaragua, and Guatemala from the 1970s to the early 1990s, and added that "we know the wave of violence also threatens our own country."[67]

Clinton's comments were accompanied by a pledge of $300 million in aid. But that pledge was less impressive than it might seem, since some of the funds were simply repackaged under the new Central America Security Initiative approved by Congress and diverted from the Mérida Initiative, the centerpiece of the U.S.-sponsored multiyear anti-drug program for Mexico and its neighbors that was signed in October 2007. The Secretary's commitment of $300 million, however, was in addition to the $200 million that President Obama promised during a visit to El Salvador in March 2011 to assist Central American governments confront the drug gangs.

Leaders in the region seemed unimpressed with Washington's offers. Instead, the seven countries proposed 22 economic and security initiatives to combat the cartels. Those projects would cost at least $900 million, which political leaders stressed that their countries could not afford on their own. "For us, it is the difference between life and death," Álvaro Colom asserted.[68]

The dissatisfaction with Washington's aid offers is nothing new. In late 2010, Costa Rican president Laura Chinchilla prodded the

United States to offer an anti-drug aid program specifically for Central America. "We don't want to be seen as an appendix of the Mérida Initiative," Chinchilla stated. "We want a plan for Central America."[69] Her irritation on that point is not surprising. In 2010, for example, Congress appropriated $1.3 billion for Mexico, but only $248 million for all of Central America.

Chinchilla clearly expected that a plan geared to Central America's problems with the drug cartels should be much larger than $248 million. That view was equally evident among her fellow leaders in Central America. President Colom asserted that the United States and other drug consumer countries owed significant financial support to "transit countries" in the battle against the cartels. He contended that Central American governments spent $4 billion on security measures in 2010, but that Washington and other international donors promised only $1 billion and delivered a paltry $140 million.

Colom implied that the consumer countries ought to at least cover the region's $4 billion in security expenditures. But his goal was modest compared with the comments of Mexico's Felipe Calderón. Describing the trafficking route from South America through Central America and Mexico as "a highway of death," Calderón argued that the consumer countries (primarily the United States) should give the same amount to the governments of the transit countries as the drug cartels make from their illegal commerce—at least $35 billion a year.[70]

The U.S. government is caught in a bind. Clearly, Washington does not want to see Central America become a region of narco-states, in which the drug cartels are the political players that really matter. And Central American leaders have a point when they argue that their countries are at risk largely because of their geographic location along the route between drug source countries and the insatiable consumer market for illegal drugs in the United States.

At the same time, U.S leaders need to guard against letting excessive guilt feelings make them receptive to what could become a financial shakedown from Central American regimes. Murder rates in those countries were among the highest in the world before the Mexican cartels moved in. The drug gangs have certainly exacerbated security problems in Central America, but they did not create them.

Moreover, pouring U.S. tax dollars into the police and militaries of Central American countries would have only a modest beneficial effect on the security situation. As in the case of Mexico, the root of the problem lies deeper than the need to strengthen the forces of law and order, or even to help bolster the legal economies of those countries. The fundamental problem is the great financial resources of the drug gangs, and that is a result of the basic economics of the illegal drug trade caused by prohibition and the black-market premium it creates.

It is not certain whether Felipe Calderón anticipated the growing cartel menace in Central America as a probable consequence of his own war against the traffickers. But he certainly should have recognized that danger. At best, Calderón's strategy inadvertently created alarming problems for Mexico's small neighbors. At worst, he did anticipate that development, but chose to adopt a cynical "beggar thy neighbor" strategy in the hope of deflecting at least a portion of Mexico's drug war problems southward. Either way, the spreading corruption and violence is producing a worrisome situation. Central America is beginning to reappear on Washington's security radar.

Mexico's Drug War after Calderón

Given the failure of Calderón's confrontational strategy to achieve its objective of weakening the drug cartels, combined with the hideous rise in the number of casualties, the question arises whether his approach will persist beyond his presidency. A new president will take office in Mexico City at the end of 2012, and that new chief executive will face a crucial decision within the first few weeks in office about whether to stay the course or try a new strategy. At the time this book was written, it was uncertain who that new president would be or what views on the drug war that leader might hold.

Much may depend on which party the winning candidate represents. If the PRI wins the presidential election, the likelihood increases that the Mexican government would at least dampen the military offensive and determine if there were other options for dealing with the cartels. That would not necessarily mean a policy of accommodation or appeasement, but PRI leaders have tended to be less enthusiastic about the all-out war that has marked the Calderón years. Part of that may reflect partisan politics, but some of the ambivalence may represent honest misgivings about the strategy.

A PRD president would probably be even more likely to make a significant course change in the direction of a less-militant approach.

Members of that party have openly expressed criticism, not only of Calderón's military offensive, but of entire the war on drugs. The PRD as a whole had signaled at least some receptivity to outright legalization. Given the political realities in Mexico, though, a PRD presidency is the least likely scenario.

The most interesting situation is if the PAN retains the presidency. Given Calderón's waning popularity, the odds seem against a PAN victory, but the Mexican economy is slowly recovering from the global recession, and the party does have the allegiance of much of the business community and a major segment of the Mexican public. As noted, though, the PAN seems sharply divided regarding the wisdom of Calderón's drug war policies. The defection of Vicente Fox underscores the division, but there have been other vocal dissenters as well. It might be difficult politically for a PAN president to explicitly repudiate Calderón's military offensive against the cartels, but a quiet, gradual movement to a less-militant strategy might be another matter.

Finally, there is the key variable of the probable U.S. posture in the post-Calderón era. It is unclear whether Washington would tolerate a retreat from the confrontational approach pursued in recent years by Mexico City. That could well depend on the political outcome in the United States. A second Obama administration might be at least reasonably accepting if Mexico adopted a new, more accommodating strategy, although there is no certainty of such tolerance. The victory of a Republican candidate, on the other hand, would increase the likelihood that Washington would take a very hard-line position about any drug policy apostasy coming out of Mexico City. 2012 could prove to be a very crucial year politically for both countries in terms of the drug war. Policies that the administrations in Mexico and the United States adopt following the 2012 elections will go far in determining whether the drug violence in Mexico—and in its Central American neighbors—diminishes or becomes even worse in the coming years.

7. Mexico's Corruption and Violence: A Threat to Americans?

Mexico's drug-related corruption and violence are no longer a tragedy just for that country. Increasingly, those developments are posing worries for the United States. The extent of the problem at this point is the subject of debate, but there is no doubt that U.S. officials are deeply concerned about the danger of a "spillover" effect. Following a major nationwide anti-drug raid in June 2010, Kevin L. Perkins, assistant director of the FBI's Criminal Investigation Division, told reporters that "drug trafficking across the U.S. southwest border" was not only leading to a "surge of drugs in our neighborhoods across the country," but was leading to "increased border violence, kidnapping, extortion and human smuggling."[1]

The Growing Mexican Cartel Presence in the United States

The cartels are clearly expanding their operations north of the border, either directly or by forging ties with American affiliates. Some of that expansion is commercial in nature. For example, authorities have noticed that both the number and size of marijuana farms—mostly on public land in the national forests of California and other western states—have increased dramatically in the past few years.[2] Indeed, some of the operations are now so large and sophisticated that police have begun to refer to them as "plantations" rather than farms, and there are indications that the Mexican cartels provide the financial resources and expertise for their development. Such enterprises often have a menacing quality about them. The plantations are continually guarded by armed personnel equipped with assault weapons, night-vision goggles, and sophisticated communications gear. Ominously, nearly half of the 487 pot farms that DEA and other authorities raided during one 12-month period were tended by foreign nationals, many of whom appeared to have ties to Mexican traffickers.[3]

Some of the raided plantations contained as may 75,000 plants, each with a potential yield of a pound of marijuana—more than 35 tons for the entire operation.[4] From a business standpoint, setting up such vast operations makes sense. By growing the marijuana in the United States, traffickers are able to bypass a crucial component of the counter-drug strategy that the U.S. and Mexican governments use: intercepting drug shipments at the border. Instead, the crops are harvested on-site and then broken up into relatively small shipments to be distributed to cities around the United States. In essence, the drug gangs have emulated a model that foreign automobile manufacturers began to use more than a decade ago—setting up assembly plants in the United States instead of shipping cars from Japan or Europe, thereby being closer to the consumer market.

In addition to expanding their drug production operations, the cartels are enlarging their distribution networks in the United States.[5] According to law enforcement authorities, Mexican drug organizations now have ties to criminal gangs in at least 230 American cities, including all of the 50 largest cities. The cartel presence now even extends to relatively small cities and, in some cases, to rural counties—and not just in the southwestern states, but portions of the South, the Midwest, and other regions.[6] The gradual displacement of the Colombian trafficking operations, which has occurred throughout the Western Hemisphere and in the global illegal drug market generally, is also evident in the U.S. market. The DEA estimates that Mexican traffickers now control at least 70 percent of the drug trade in the United States. Their penetration of American society is also likely to be more pervasive than their Colombian predecessors. *Wall Street Journal* correspondents Evan Pérez and David Luhnow highlight a key difference, "Unlike Colombian cartels of the past, which transported cocaine from Colombia to the U.S. but didn't dominate the retail end of the business, Mexican cartels are more vertically integrated—from growing their own marijuana [and other drugs] to selling it on U.S. streets."[7]

The increasing Mexican domination of all phases of the drug trade in the United States carries with it the obvious risk that the turf battles in Mexico between rival cartels could become proxy wars in U.S. communities. There is some evidence that such struggles have already taken place on a few occasions. In at least three cases, members of La Familia kidnapped competing drug dealers in Houston and held them for ransom. Similar events have occurred in Phoenix, Las Vegas, and other U.S. cities.

Atlanta has become an especially prominent hub for all of the leading Mexican cartels. That's not surprising, since several major interstate highways and other thoroughfares converge in the Atlanta metropolitan area, making it convenient for traffickers to distribute to destinations throughout the South, Midwest, and Northeast. Rodney D. Benson, Special Agent in Charge of the DEA's Atlanta office, stated that his city was now "a strategic operations center for Mexican organized crime." Mexican traffickers were "able to blend right in and establish metro Atlanta as that strategic trans-shipment point."[8]

Corruption Migrating North of the Border

Not only is Mexican drug trafficking becoming more entrenched in the United States, corruption is also migrating north of the border. For decades, the cartels have bribed political leaders and law enforcement personnel in Mexico as part of the cost of doing business (see chapter 4). People in the United States have always regarded the widespread corruption in Mexico with a mixture of amusement and contempt. There was also an element of smug moral superiority, with more than a tinge of ethnic bigotry. U.S. officials would not succumb to the temptation of bribery like their Mexican counterparts, the conventional wisdom assumed. Whether that was ever as true as Americans wanted to believe is debatable. What is not debatable is that whatever validity the assumption might have had at one time, the times are changing.

A graphic example of how law enforcement officials in the United States are not immune to the financial blandishments of Mexican drug traffickers came to light in late 2008 with the arrest of Reymundo "Rey" Guerra, the sheriff of Starr County, Texas, on the border with Mexico. Guerra confessed to his role in an extensive marijuana and cocaine smuggling operation in south Texas. He apparently assigned police patrols in such a way as to facilitate the movement of drug shipments through his county. The ring in charge of those shipments was headed by José Carlos Hinojosa, who himself had worked at one time in law enforcement in Mexico before defecting to the Zetas.

Interestingly, the Zetas did not have to pay Guerra a tremendous amount of money for his assistance. The sheriff reportedly received several payments of a mere $3,000 to $5,000. Upon sentencing Guerra to 64 months in prison, federal district judge Randy Crane observed: "For really pennies, nickels, you were influenced by these people."[9] But he is hardly the only official in the southwestern United States to have accepted money from the Mexican cartels. According to an Associated Press tally in August 2009, more than 80 law enforcement officers at the local, state, and federal levels working along the border had already been convicted of drug-related corruption charges since late 2006. A report from U.S. Customs and Border Protection (CBP) in June 2011 conceded that 127 employees of that agency, mostly in the southwestern states, had been arrested, charged, or convicted of corruption charges since October 2004, with the pace accelerating since 2006.[10]

Worries about the rising tide of corruption allegations became apparent again in September 2009 when a former high-ranking Immigration and Customs Enforcement agent, Richard P. Cramer, was arrested on suspicion of conspiracy to smuggle cocaine into the United States. Cramer was once the resident agent in charge of the Customs and Immigration Office in Nogales, Arizona, and had been stationed in Mexico before retiring in 2007. According to the federal indictment, he provided a leading Mexican cartel with information from law enforcement databases that one of its members was actually a government informer. In addition, federal authorities charged that Cramer had invested $400,000 in a cocaine shipment from Panama that transited Mexico and the United States on way to its final destination in Spain. Finally, prosecutors stated that a cartel leader convinced Cramer to retire from the customs agency and work full time in smuggling and money laundering operations.

Not surprisingly, the CBP agency is a high-priority target for corruption efforts by trafficking organizations. And they have achieved a considerable amount of success. The case of Luis F. Alarid is typical. A veteran both of the U.S. Army and the Marine Corps, Alarid became a customs inspector at a major border crossing between San Diego and Tijuana in October 2007. By February 2008, he was waving in trucks carrying cargoes of marijuana. For looking the other way, he received at least $200,000. Federal authorities eventually busted Alarid, and he received a seven-year prison sentence.

The main area of doubt was whether Alarid started out as an honest employee and was simply corrupted by bribes, or whether he was a cartel infiltrator from the beginning. Authorities suspected the latter, since several members of Alarid's extended family, on both sides of the border, appeared to be members of a drug smuggling crew.

James Tomsheck, the assistant commissioner for internal affairs at Customs and Border Protection, confirmed that investigators "had seen many signs that drug organizations were making a concerted effort" to infiltrate the agency's ranks. "There have been verifiable instances," Tomsheck stated, "where people were directed to CBP to apply for positions only for the purpose of enhancing the goals of criminal organizations."[11] Most of those individuals were selected because they had no criminal records, which meant that they could pass a background check with little problem.

The cartels are engaged in active recruiting efforts and skillfully exploit family and friendship ties with U.S. citizens who might be able to become moles in the customs bureaucracy. One smuggler described how he enticed a close friend from high school in Del Rio, Texas, who was about to enter the CBP training academy, to work covertly for him. That agent, Raquel Esquivel, received a 15-year prison sentence in December 2009 for tipping off traffickers about where Border Patrol agents would be located, enabling drug shipments to enter the United States unmolested.

Perhaps the most notorious example was that of Martha Garnica, an attractive, if somewhat brassy, law enforcement veteran who served seven years on the El Paso police department before joining the U.S. Customs Service (a portion of which became the CBP in 2003) in the mid-1990s.[12] Fellow employees became suspicious of her early on, among other reasons because she frequented bars that were known hangouts for suspected drug dealers. Suspicions deepened in November 1997 when authorities intercepted a shipment of 100 pounds of marijuana coming into El Paso across the Bridge of the Americas from Juárez. An informant contended that Garnica was one of the conspirators involved in that smuggling operation. The FBI opened an investigation, but it soon faded as agents could not come up with any additional evidence.

The suspicions were well-founded, though, as Garnica had a succession of boyfriends, as well as relatives and other associates with multiple ties to trafficking organizations. And as a CBP agent at the busy Juárez-El Paso crossing, she was perfectly positioned to help them. Garnica would routinely wave-off drug sniffing dogs from her inspection lane at the border when a shipment was coming through. In March 2005, though, she became a target for investigation again after a van carrying more than 500 pounds of marijuana started to go through the crossing in the lane she was staffing. A drug-sniffing dog in another lane alerted border agents, causing them to stop and search the van. Witnesses later testified that Garnica looked shaken and then left for the day, pleading illness. To add to the suspicions, it became clear that the staffing roster had been tampered with; Garnica was not supposed to be working that lane on that evening.

From then on, she was under much greater scrutiny. But it was not until 2009 that she made a fatal error, when she flirted with and tried to recruit another CBP agent to work for the La Línea, the heavily-armed associates of the Juárez cartel. That agent, a recently divorced father who had money troubles, seemed to be the perfect candidate to work for the traffickers, which is probably why Garnica approached him. But instead of succumbing to her enticements, he became a covert operative, code-named Angel, as part of the ongoing investigation of Garnica. During the succeeding months, Garnica and her trafficking associates conducted a series of tests to see whether Angel was truly a potential recruit. "We were able to see the entire recruitment process play out through Angel," said a CBP official James Smith. "It starts with small probes. If you're willing to do that, it escalates."[13]

Angel wore a wire at several encounters, and what the investigation uncovered was the breathtaking extent to which Garnica was leading a double life. To the traffickers, she was known as Estrella (the Star). And she was a key coordinator for smuggling operations through the Juárez-El Paso corridor, often devising codes, instructions, and routes for directing shipments safely through the border. And she was well compensated for her services. The money she obtained was well into the six figures, funding lavish overseas vacations, fancy cars, and other luxuries for herself and her extended family.

It all came to an end in November 2009, when, with the information that Angel had helped gather, authorities moved to arrest Garnica. Ultimately she pled guilty to six counts of drug smuggling and bribery and in August 2010 received a 20-year sentence for helping to smuggle thousands of pounds of marijuana over at least a three-year period. A disturbing feature of the case, though, was that there were indications that Garnica had successfully recruited several other CBP agents over the years. Investigators do not yet know who those cartel operatives might be, much less how many others were recruited by people other than Garnica are on the payrolls of the cartels

The surge in hiring in the post–9/11 years has made it easier for cartels to infiltrate the CBP, and arrests of CBP agents on drug-related corruption charges surged more than 40 percent just between October 2006 and October 2009—before the spectacular arrest of La Estrella and her associates. As one internal investigator put it: "There's so much hiring; if you have a warm body and a pulse, you have a job."[14] Only about 15 percent of CBP applicants were asked to undergo polygraph exams. Tomsheck conceded that several recent hires are under investigation for possible ties to the cartels, and other applicants were rejected because investigators strongly suspected that traffickers had directed them to CBP. In one instance, while an agent was awaiting trial on smuggling charges, the woman's daughter applied for a job with the Border Patrol. Needless to say, CBP investigators took a rather jaundiced view of her application. But agency officials wonder, with good reason, how many infiltrators that do not have such obvious disqualifying features are getting through the screening process. Some certainly are. In addition to the increase in arrests, the number of corruption investigations opened by the agency's inspector general soared from 245 in 2006 to 770 in 2010.

Although most CBP employees appear to remain honest, the financial temptation to stray is enormous. As *New York Times* correspondent Randal Archibold notes: "The average officer makes $70,000 a year, a sum that can be dwarfed by what smugglers pay to get just a few trucks full of drugs into the United States."[15] Mexican authorities are all too familiar about the temptations that the cartels place in the path of low-paid government employees. The financial gap may not be as great in the United States, where federal, state, and local law enforcement personnel receive attractive salaries and generous benefit packages, but the gap—and the resulting temptation—is still substantial. And more American agents seem to be succumbing to the lure of easy drug money. In prepared testimony before a subcommittee of the Senate Homeland Security Committee in June 2011, Charles Edwards, acting Inspector General for the Department of Homeland Security, noted that his office had 267 active investigations of possible corruption by CBP employees.[16]

With a considerable degree of understatement, Senator David Pryor (D-AR), who chaired a Senate subcommittee on homeland security, conceded: "We have in our country today a big presence of the Mexican cartels. With about 50 percent of the nation's methamphetamine and marijuana coming through Mexico and about 90 percent of the cocaine, there is a huge financial incentive for cartels to try to corrupt our people."[17] Try—and succeed.

Dangers to Americans in Mexico

The spread of illegal drug trafficking and of drug-related corruption into the United States is bad enough, but the widening impact of Mexico's violence is an even more worrisome prospect. Americans who work or travel in Mexico are increasingly at risk, and even communities in the United States itself are no longer immune from the turbulence south of the border.

The U.S. State Department issued an updated travel alert in February 2010 adding both Durango and Coahuila to the list of states with areas that Americans should avoid visiting because violence had reached the point of posing an acute danger. This alert repeated the comment from warnings involving other Mexican states—that much of the fighting resembled small-unit combat operations. A travel alert issued in April 2011 mentioned additional regions of Mexico where there were "security concerns." The alert noted that "large firefights between rival TCOs [transnational criminal organizations] or TCOs and Mexican authorities have taken place in many parts of Mexico, especially in the border region. . . . During some of these incidents, U.S. citizens have been trapped and prevented from leaving the area. . . . You are urged to defer travel to those areas mentioned in this Travel Warning and to exercise extreme caution when traveling throughout the northern border region."[18] Those areas specifically mentioned were the states of Tamaulipas and Michoacán, and portions of the states of Sonora, Chihuahua, Coahuila, Sinaloa, Durango, Zacatecas, San Luis Potosi, and Jalisco. That list made up a sizable chunk of Mexico's territory.

A State Department report released in August 2008 noted that 131 U.S. citizens were victims of homicides or "executions" in Mexico between July 1, 2005, and June 30, 2008.[19] A similar report issued in early 2010 documented a worrisome trend. While 35 U.S. citizens were killed in Mexico in 2007, the toll for 2009 was 79. In Juárez, the epicenter of the killings, 23 Americans were killed in 2009, up from a mere two in 2007.[20] The April 2011 State Department Travel Warning confirmed that the number of Americans murdered in Mexico in 2010 had reached 111.[21]

Chad Foster, the mayor of Eagle Pass, Texas, nearly became one of those victims. In December 2009, Foster was dining with Mexican officials at a restaurant in Eagle Pass's sister city across the border, Piedras Negras. As they were toasting one another, gunmen began spraying the establishment with bullets. Fortunately, none of the officials was injured, but the troubling reality is that even a few years ago, such a scary incident in peaceful Piedras Negras would have virtually unthinkable.

Most of the American victims perished in cities along the U.S.-Mexico border where drug-related fighting is the most intense. Some of those individuals were undoubtedly involved in the drug trade, but others were not. Indeed, even coming from a prominent family does not seem to guarantee immunity from the violence; in June 2008, a female relative of Representative Silvestre Reyes (D-TX) was kidnapped in Ciudad Juárez. In November 2009, Mexican police in Tijuana rescued a 21-year-old U.S. citizen who had been kidnapped a week earlier near the border. Kidnappers had snatched the woman from her car and threatened to kill her unless they were paid $200,000. At the time she was rescued, police found her bound and beaten.[22] Another American woman was not so fortunate: authorities in Baja California discovered her bruised and battered body in a house near Tijuana.

FBI agent Keith Slotter noted in late 2008 that at least 40 San Diego residents had been kidnapped that year, more than double the number just three years earlier. The actual total was probably much higher, since many of those incidents go unreported out of fear of more lethal retaliation by the cartels. Slotter reported a typical example of that reluctance. One woman's husband, an American citizen who operates businesses across the border in Tijuana, was abducted, apparently by cartel members, who demanded $2 million.

Not only did the woman pay that ransom, even though she had to sell properties to raise the money, but she was afraid to reveal her identity after the incident.[23]

A more horrific case occurred in Ciudad Juárez, where a seven-year old Texas boy, Raúl Ramírez, was killed while visiting his father. Gunmen attacked the vehicle his father was driving, firing at least 18 rounds from 9mm weapons. The elder Ramírez died in the vehicle. Raúl escaped the car and tried to flee, but was shot in the back.[24] Police were uncertain whether the attackers thought that his father was involved in the drug trade, but the incident had all the characteristics of a cartel hit, and Raúl was an innocent victim in any case.

An enclave of Mormons, Colonia LeBaron, in the state of Chihuahua about three hours south of Ciudad Juárez, discovered that attempting to maintain a low profile will not necessarily shield people from attacks by the drug trafficking gangs. The founder of that enclave brought his polygamist followers, many of whom hold dual U.S. and Mexican citizenship, to Mexico some six decades ago in search of both peace and economic prosperity. Until recently, they enjoyed both. But they have now become victims of the turmoil afflicting Mexico. In July 2009, the leader of the colony, Benjamin LeBaron, was killed after he refused to pay a $1 million ransom for his kidnapped younger brother and instead publicly denounced the drug gangs. Shortly after his statement, 15 to 20 heavily armed men, dressed in police uniforms—complete with blue helmets and bullet-proof vests—abducted LeBaron and his brother-in-law. They were found a few miles outside of the compound, beaten, tortured, and shot execution style. LaBaron's killers posted a sign, "This is for the leaders of LeBaron who didn't believe and still don't believe." One college-age member of the enclave lamented: "All we want to do is live in peace. We want nothing to do with the drug cartels. They can't be stopped. What we want is just to protect ourselves from being kidnapped and killed."[25] After the murder of Benjamin LeBaron, the colony secured permission from the Mexican government to arm themselves and create a special rural police force. Whether that will help keep them secure over the long term remains to be seen.

Americans are becoming increasingly uneasy about traveling or doing business in portions of Mexico. U.S. tourism has noticeably declined in the turbulent Mexican border cities, especially Tijuana, Nuevo Laredo, and Ciudad Juárez. Occupancy rates at hotels in

184

Tijuana had plunged to an extraordinarily depressed 30 percent by the first quarter of 2010. Understandably, visitors were not too eager to go to a combat zone and risk getting caught in a hail of bullets during a fight between rival gangs or between one of those gangs and Mexican authorities.

Prominent American organizations are nervous about the violence in Mexico and the dangers it could pose to their personnel. In early 2010, the University of Texas at Austin recalled its students who had been studying in Monterrey. Even the U.S. military is taking precautions. In 2009, the Marine commander at Camp Pendleton, outside San Diego, issued an order barring his troops from spending leave time in Tijuana because that city had become too dangerous. A few weeks later, the 12th U.S. Air Force prohibited its personnel from traveling anywhere in Chihuahua, and the Army also barred its soldiers at Fort Bliss, near El Paso, from going to Chihuahua.

Such caution soon proved to be warranted. On November 4, 2009, gunmen armed with automatic weapons burst into the Amadeus bar in Ciudad Juárez as strippers were performing for customers. The gunmen sought out six men and shot them multiple times. Police noted that the attack bore the typical signs of a drug cartel hit. Enrique Torres, a U.S. military spokesman, stated that "it appears drugs were being sold out of the place. The hit men went directly for their victims and no one else."[26] One of those victims was an off-duty U.S. airman, Staff Sgt. David Booher, who worked in the medical unit of the 49th Fighter Wing at Holloman Air Force Base, near Alamogordo, New Mexico, about 90 miles north of Juárez. Why he was in the strip club, apparently in violation of Air Force policy, was unknown.

Even Americans who have no connection with the drug trade seem to be at increased risk of getting caught up in Mexico's violence. In November 2009, Lisabeth Marín, a U.S. citizen visiting the Mexican border city of Matamoros, died from a stray bullet while inside a friend's home. Authorities later determined that a soldier participating in a drug raid had accidentally discharged his weapon.

Affluent Americans living in Monterrey worried that they were in danger after a gun battle erupted in front of the American School foundation, which many children of American, as well as Mexican, business executives attend. The firefight took place between bodyguards working for the Mexican beverage company Femsa S.A.B.

185

de CV and cartel attackers, who were apparently attempting to kidnap the young relatives of a high-level company employee. In the course of the ensuing battle, two bodyguards were killed. The gunmen captured two other guards, although they released them a few hours later. The flying bullets caused students in the school to scramble for shelter in the school cafeteria.

U.S. Ambassador Carlos Pascual cautioned employees of the Monterrey consulate to keep their children home, "while we assess the risks and what measures can be taken to reduce it (sic)." Pascual gave that recommendation even though there was no hard evidence that the children of consular personnel had been targeted. Following the incident, the U.S. consulate in Monterrey posted an advisory on its website directed to Americans living in the area. "The sharp increase in kidnapping incidents in the Monterrey area, and this event in particular, present a very high risk to the families of U.S. citizens," the message read.[27]

Three days later, the State Department escalated its warnings and issued a stunning edict. "U.S. government personnel from the consulate general are not permitted to keep their minor dependents in Monterrey," a U.S. Embassy spokesman stated. "As of September 10, no minor dependents, no children of U.S. government employees will be permitted in Monterrey."[28] That was the kind of restriction, designating the Monterrey consulate a "partially unaccompanied post" for U.S. diplomats, which is normally imposed only in war zones and other extremely high-risk areas. It underscored just how seriously the Obama administration took the surge in fighting and the extent of the kidnapping danger. And this was in Monterrey, once considered an extremely safe Mexican city—in fact, the safest large city in Latin America.

Perhaps the most worrisome incident, though, occurred in March 2010, when an American citizen, Lesley Enriquez Redelfs, an employee of the U.S. consulate in Ciudad Juárez, was shot to death in her car along with her husband, Arthur, also an American citizen, in broad daylight after leaving a children's party sponsored by the U.S. Consul. The couple's infant daughter was in the car with them, but luckily was not hit by the barrage of bullets. The husband of another consular employee was killed and their two children seriously wounded on the same day in a separate drive-by shooting. His horrified wife, following in another car, saw the bloody incident unfold. Two killings of individuals connected with the U.S. consulate in such a brief period suggested that the incidents were not random killings or cases of mistaken identity.

The reasons for the assassinations were not entirely clear, though. One possible motive for the murder of Lesley Enriquez Redelfs emerged when Mexican authorities arrested the alleged mastermind of the hit, Jesús Ernesto Chávez, in early July. Chávez, a leader of Barrio Azteca, a gang that originated in the Texas prison system and now apparently does enforcement work for the Juárez cartel, told them that he ordered her killed because she had illegally supplied U.S. visas to members of a rival gang. U.S. officials immediately discounted Chávez's allegation, and there was no evidence that she had even been in a position to approve such visas.[29] But if the Barrio Azteca leaders *believed* that she had done so, however erroneously, that could easily have been a sufficient motive to order her assassination.

One of the alleged trigger men arrested a few days after the hit, though, reportedly told Mexican authorities that Arthur Redelfs, not his wife, was the primary target in that attack. Cartel enforcers were supposedly angry at Redelfs, a deputy sheriff in El Paso, for alleged mistreatment of drug gang members in the El Paso county jail.[30]

However, evidence also surfaced during the investigations of the killing that indicated the attacks may have been intended to send a warning to the U.S. consulate in response to Washington's push to place U.S. drug intelligence officers within the Juárez police department. If that interpretation was true, and the drug gangs have begun to attack U.S. diplomatic personnel in Mexico, it would be a dramatic escalation, making the collateral damage of drug war in that country a much greater concern to Washington.

The Obama administration's worries about that possibility concerning the Juárez consulate seemed to rise in July 2010, when the U.S. Embassy ordered the consulate closed temporarily pending a review of security protocols.[31] Although State Department officials gave no details about the reasons for that decision, developments on the security front during 2010 were clearly alarming. In addition to the March attack on the Redelfs, there was the first use of a car bomb in Mexico's drug wars—an attack on police in Juárez less than two weeks before the decision to close the consulate. That timing may not have been a coincidence. And the closure was no minor matter, since the Juárez consulate was the only place Mexican nationals could go to apply for permanent residency in the United States. A willingness to create such an annoyance and inconvenience, even for a few days, indicated that there were strong security fears behind the decision to shut the consulate's doors.

Further indications that a strategy of attacking U.S. government personnel and installations might be underway occurred in early April 2010 when assailants tossed an explosive device at the U.S. consulate in Nuevo Laredo.[32] The bomb merely blew out windows and caused some other minor property damage, but the issue is not the effectiveness of the attack but rather its intent. Given the upsurge in fighting between the Gulf cartel and its former armed wing, the Zetas, in Nuevo Laredo and the surrounding state of Tamaulipas, combined with Washington's increasingly visible support for the Calderón's government's offensive against the cartels, it was hardly a stretch to conclude that one of those factions was trying to send a message to the U.S. government. One has to put a lot of stock in coincidence to dismiss the significance of the Nuevo Laredo attack coming barely three weeks after the consulate killings in Ciudad Juárez.

The State Department's decision in August 2010 compelling U.S. diplomatic personnel in Monterrey from keeping their children in the area certainly suggested that Washington believes the cartels might be attacking U.S. government employees. That point was confirmed with a less prominent, but still significant, policy shift involving other diplomatic posts. U.S. consulates in all other northern Mexican cities, including Tijuana, Nogales, Ciudad Juárez, Nuevo Laredo, and Matamoros, were "authorized" (diplomat-speak for "encouraged") to send their children out of the country. Worries that the cartels might now be targeting U.S. government personnel were reinforced following the February 2011 killing of Immigration and Customs Enforcement agent Jaime Zapata and the wounding of another agent in an ambush.

One other aspect of the Juárez incident was extremely troubling. It appeared that the hit might have been part of a cross-border partnership between the Juárez cartel and Barrio Azteca, the increasingly powerful Mexican-American drug distribution gang on the U.S. side of the border. FBI agents, along with state and local police, raided suspected Barrio Azteca hideouts in New Mexico and Texas, detaining more than 200 gang members and making felony arrests of more than two dozen individuals. The explicit motive for the raids was the belief that the group had been involved in the consulate murders.[33]

Further investigation indicated that Barrio Azteca is not only a major distribution network for the Juárez cartel in the southwestern United States but has become the major contract killing arm of that cartel. In other words, Barrio Azteca performs the same function for the Juárez organization that the Zetas used to perform for the Gulf cartel. FBI officials believe that Barrio Azteca may have been involved in as many as half of the drug-related killings in Ciudad Juárez over a 12-month period in 2009 and 2010.

Violence Spilling Over the Border: Myth or Reality?

Former and current U.S. officials, and a number of independent experts, contend that the drug-related violence in Mexico frequently crosses the border. Jerry Langton, a Canadian journalist who has written a major book on the Mexican cartels, presents that case bluntly. "Mainstream media in North America pose questions asking when the Mexican cartels will bring their war north of the Rio Grande. The simple answer is that they already have."[34]

That is not a new allegation. As early as summer 2005, John Walters, director of the Office of National Drug Control Policy during the Bush administration, noted: "The killing of rival traffickers is already spilling across the border. Witnesses are being killed. We do not think the border is a shield."[35] Walters again emphasized the spillover feature in June 2008: "The shocking character of some of this violence, the viciousness of these groups, is not going to respect borders. It already doesn't." Not only was the violence already spilling across the border, according to Walters, "it will come more aggressively to wherever it feels it can survive and brutally take money and power."[36]

A Dallas narcotics officer also cited evidence of a spillover effect several years ago: "We're seeing an alarming number of incidents involving the same type of violence that's become all too common in Mexico, right here in Dallas. We're seeing execution-style murders, burned bodies, and outright mayhem. . . . It's like the battles being waged in Mexico for turf have reached Dallas."[37]

189

But other analysts and pundits argue that there is little evidence that Mexico's violence is seeping over the border into the United States. Ioan Grillo, who has reported on developments in Mexico and elsewhere in Latin America for more than a decade, concedes that Mexican cartels operate throughout the United States, but he insists "there has been no major spillover of violence from Mexico to its northern neighbor. As of 2011, after five years of cartel devastation south of the Rio Grande, the war simply hasn't crossed the border."[38]

Cornell University scholar Gabriel Arana, writing in the *Nation*, contends that "if media reports are to be believed, an Armageddon-like rash of drug-related violence" has "crossed from Mexico into the United States." He responds that "the numbers tell a different story."[39] A key piece of evidence Arana cites is that overall violent crime rates in such cities as Tucson and El Paso have not spiked, despite the orgy of killings on the other side of the border. He has a point, and it underscores the need to keep the cross-border impact of Mexico's drug conflicts in perspective.

Subsequent information and analyses tend to strengthen Arana's thesis.[40] FBI statistics have consistently shown low homicide rates in El Paso, Tucson, and most other cities near the border with Mexico. *New York Times* writer Andrew Rice, who spent weeks in early 2011 studying the effect of the drug violence in Juárez on El Paso, concludes that "spillover was notable for its scarcity." He notes further that while Juárez suffered more than 3,000 homicides in 2010, El Paso—a city of some 600,000 people—had an astonishingly low total of five.[41]

Mexico's killing spree has not—at least not yet—engulfed U.S. communities. But any sense of relief needs to be restrained. The modest rate of homicides in southwestern cities is merely consistent with an overall nationwide drop of some 10 percent in recent years (reflecting, in part, an aging American population—a demographic sector less prone to violence). We must be wary of other manifestations of smug complacency. An El Paso police sergeant boasts: "We haven't seen that brazen type of violence going on in Mexico, because they just wouldn't get away with it here. Our people are better trained, better equipped, and you don't have the kind of corruption that exists in Mexico."[42] Those observations have some validity, but as we've seen, drug-related corruption on the U.S. side of the border is on the rise, and better training and equipment, while important, go only so far in combating the equally well-equipped cartels with their deep financial pockets.

Moreover, homicides are only one manifestation of a spillover effect, although they are the most important one. There is a troubling admission buried in the middle of Gabriel Arana's article: even he had to concede that while homicide rates remained constrained, there had been an increase in drug-related kidnappings in border cities, especially in Phoenix, although he asserted that the increase was "not as dramatic" as some media reports suggested. Interestingly, a FoxNews report in August 2010 suggested that Phoenix authorities may have inflated the kidnapping statistics as a ploy to get more federal aid."[43]

Arana and other skeptics are correct that there has yet to be a surge of cartel-generated violence in the United States, and they are correct that some media outlets have hyped the danger. But there are enough incidents to suggest that the problem is not fanciful, and is, in fact, building. Moreover, some of the examples of relative calm in southwestern cities ignore the likelihood that special factors are involved. One prominent piece of evidence Arana and Rice both cite is that while Ciudad Juárez may be chaotic and deadly, its sister city across the border, El Paso, is one of the quieter cities in the United States in terms of homicides and other violent crimes.

But there appears to be an important, and not especially comforting, reason for that relative calm. El Paso has become a mecca for middle-class and upper-class refugees fleeing the violence in Mexico, especially the convulsions just across the river in Ciudad Juárez. In fact, that influx has fueled a mini real estate boom. Many of the new residents are honest people just trying to find a safer environment for themselves and their families, but others are not so benign. El Paso police and other officials acknowledge that some high-level cartel personnel and their families also reside in the city. "Without a doubt, there are a lot of cartel members among us," Robert Almonte, executive director of the Texas Narcotics Officers Association and a retired El Paso deputy police chief says. "They've been here for a long time. They come here for the same reasons as you or me. It's safer here. And if they have wives and kids, this is the place to be."[44]

Almonte's remarks imply that there is an implicit truce under which cartel operatives consider El Paso a safe haven for their families.

That would not be an improbable development. But while such an arrangement would make sense, it would be inherently fragile. Even a few violations could lead to retaliation and a rapid escalation of violence. The comments of Tony Payan, a professor at the University of Texas at El Paso and an expert on drug trafficking, suggest just how fragile the situation might be: "We live in a city of don't ask, don't tell. The city is filled with stash houses, money laundering, shipments. Trucks come. Trucks go. Garage doors open and close."[45] Yet city officials largely pretend that none of that is going on.

Even Joseph Arabit, the special agent in charge of the DEA's office in El Paso, concedes that the city serves as a crucial distribution point for drug trafficking. He attributes the lack of violence to cartel members not wanting to face justice in the United States. That wariness may play a role, but it is more likely that the traffickers do not want to engage in actions that would disrupt the distribution of their product throughout the United States and endanger the safety of their families living in El Paso.

That sense of having a sanctuary, though, is precarious at best. Indeed, officials and residents in El Paso were badly shaken in late June 2010 when seven bullets struck the upper floors of city hall. Fortunately, no one was killed or injured, but if the incident had occurred earlier in the day when more people were in the building conducting business, the outcome might have been different. Apparently, the shots came from an altercation in Juárez, and it was possible that Mexican federal agents may have fired the stray bullets. But whatever the details, the incident was a graphic reminder that Mexico's violence was not confined to Mexican territory. And it caused Texas attorney general Greg Abbott to send a blistering letter to President Barack Obama complaining about the growing sense of insecurity along the border and demanding that the federal government do something about it.[46]

Cartel hit men have not only killed victims—including Americans—in Mexico, but they have apparently struck at people inside the United States.[47] During 2008 and 2009, seven individuals were killed execution style in Laredo, Texas, across the Rio Grande from Nuevo Laredo. The victims included a person who was stalked and killed near his place of work and another man who was gunned down in the parking lot of a popular restaurant. Authorities arrested and convicted two Gulf cartel enforcers for the string of executions.[48]

In October 2008, a Las Vegas child was kidnapped, apparently because a relative owed money to one of the Mexican drug gangs.[49]

In September 2009, three armed men dragged Sergio Saucedo, a resident of Horizon City, Texas, out of his home and shoved him into an SUV. Saucedo's wife, as well as school children in a packed bus, witnessed the abduction. His body was found several days later in Ciudad Juárez, with its arms chopped off and placed on the chest. The following February, U.S. Border Patrol agents arrested four men, including two who were U.S. citizens, in connection with the crime. El Paso County Sheriff's Commander Paul Cross stated that "we know it had something to do with the drug trade," noting that Saucedo had a criminal record for drug trafficking and money laundering, and that two of the accused kidnappers were affiliated with a Mexican cartel, although Cross would not disclose which one.[50]

The drug lords now appear to be bold enough to put Americans living in the United States on target lists for execution. In June 2008, U.S. Immigration and Customs Enforcement officials obtained what was apparently a hit list from one of the cartels. The list named nearly 20 people, primarily individuals living in southern New Mexico, Albuquerque, and El Paso, and it included a sheriff's captain in Luna County, New Mexico.[51] It has become commonplace for the cartels to create, and sometimes publish, such lists of Mexican nationals, including police officers, but this was a new level of brazenness.

Cartel threats against U.S. law enforcement personnel are escalating. Police in Nogales, Arizona, went on heightened alert in June 2010 after receiving a threat, relayed through an informant, that officers would be targeted if they continued to carry out off-duty drug busts. Apparently traffickers considered it within the rules of the game for police to engage in such raids as part of their job when they were on duty, but that it was a gratuitous affront to do so on other occasions. When off duty, the cartel warned, police were to look the other way and ignore any drug shipments that came across the border—if they valued their lives. The warning occurred just days after two off-duty police officers seized 400 pounds of marijuana while horseback riding outside the city.[52] What was especially chilling about the cartel warning was that it specifically named the officers who were off duty in the area of the drug bust that day.

The Nogales police chief instructed his officers to keep weapons with them at all times and to frequently communicate their whereabouts to the department. He also encouraged them to wear body armor even when they were off duty. One officer, Mario Morales, follows the chief's instructions diligently. Morales told a reporter that, although he has relatives in Mexico, he hasn't attended family gatherings there in years. He sees such a trip as simply too dangerous, since the drug gangs assume that if they could kidnap an American police officer, he would fetch a sizable ransom. Stating "I never underestimate the cartels," Morales affirmed that he is careful to "keep a low profile."[53]

Perhaps the most jarring incident occurred in early August 2010, when reports surfaced that a Mexican cartel had put a $1 million bounty on the life of Arizona sheriff Joe Arpaio, the chief lawman in Maricopa County, which includes Phoenix and many of its suburbs. The threat originated in Mexico and was conveyed via a disposable cell phone—standard operating procedure for all of the drug gangs.

Arpaio is an extremely colorful and polarizing figure, both in Arizona and nationally. To his admirers, he is a folk hero. To his detractors, he is a publicity-seeking bigot. Arpaio is renowned for numerous controversial law enforcement measures over the years, including his decision to put male prisoners in pink prison jump suits, complete with pink underwear, and allowing them to watch only "G"-rated movies. In response to a lawsuit attempting to ban the use of chain gangs, primarily on the grounds that only men were subjected to that burden, Arpaio started chain gangs for women. When prisoners complained about the bland, boring, and repetitive food at the jail, the sheriff responded: "This ain't the Ritz Carlton. If you don't like the food, don't come back." Those incidents produced far more admirers than critics of the sheriff, and he has repeatedly won re-election by landslide margins.

But there are uglier allegations. Mexican immigrants (both illegal and legal) and Mexican Americans have repeatedly charged that Arpaio's minions engage in harassment and discriminatory law enforcement. Arpaio also strongly supported the new Arizona law (now being challenged in the courts) giving police wide latitude in questioning individuals stopped for other possible law violations about their immigration status—a position that won him few fans in the Mexican-American community.

There is no doubt that the Mexican drug cartels also loathe the man. His department is one of the most active in the southwestern states in intercepting drug shipments. Consequently, state and federal law enforcement agencies took the threat against Arpaio's life seriously. They did so perhaps even more than usual because just weeks earlier, the DEA had warned that the cartels were about to take their war from Mexico north of the border and attack U.S. law enforcement personnel.[54]

An incident in August 2009 confirmed that cartel enforcers are sometimes operating in the United States against other targets, even in generally peaceful El Paso. Police announced the arrest of three men and charged them with capital murder in what was apparently the contract killing of José Daniel González Galeana, a lieutenant in the Juárez cartel. Killers shot him to death in the front yard of his elegant Mediterranean-style home. And they clearly took no chances with their task—shooting him eight times at close range.

Three features made this case especially troubling. First, González Galeana did not operate out of Juárez, but instead lived in a quiet, upscale neighborhood in El Paso, where he ran several ostensibly legal businesses, including a freight company and a daycare center. Second, according to three U.S. law enforcement officials, González Galeana was not merely a drug trafficker, he was an informant for the U.S. Immigration and Customs Enforcement Agency. In fact, information emerged that the trafficker who allegedly ordered his execution, Rubén Rodríguez Dorado, was also an informant! That revelation infuriated officials in El Paso. "So this is how these people end up in our country," fumed El Paso police lieutenant Alfred Lowe, the city's lead homicide detective. "We bring them here."[55]

Perhaps the most disturbing aspect of the case, though, was that one of the accused assailants was a U.S. Army private based at Ft. Bliss. That raises the possibility that the cartels are now infiltrating the U.S. military. Such an achievement could give the drug lords a new source of highly trained assassins—and U.S. citizens—who would be especially useful for going after targets inside the United States.

U.S. law enforcement personnel, especially Border Patrol agents, also appear increasingly to be the targets of violence on the U.S. side of the boundary. In January 2008, agent Luis Aguilar died from injuries he suffered when a trafficker driving a Hummer loaded with drugs ran him down near the U.S.-Mexico border in southeastern

California. Robert Rosas, an agent working in a remote area of southeastern San Diego County, was gunned down in late July 2009 when he responded to a report of a border incursion near the town of Campo. A spokesman for the FBI's San Diego office stated that Rosas, a 30-year-old father of two, was ambushed and shot multiple times in the head and body. He was dead when other Border Patrol agents arrived on the scene. A few days later, Mexican authorities identified and detained five suspects in the killing.[56] At least one of them was a known trafficker in both drugs and illegal immigrants.

Anecdotal evidence of a growing danger to Border Patrol agents has been building for several years. A 2006 report by the majority staff of the House Homeland Security Committee noted that at one time, smugglers "would drop the drugs or abandon their vehicles when confronted by U.S. law enforcement." That is no longer the case. "In today's climate, U.S. Border Patrol agents are fired upon from across the river, and troopers and sheriff's deputies are subject to attacks with automatic weapons while the cartels retrieve their contraband."[57] Some attacks have come from Mexicans wearing military uniforms. It is not certain whether they are smugglers with stolen uniforms or if rogue elements of the Mexican military are attacking U.S. law enforcement personnel on behalf of traffickers.

According to a Department of Homeland Security report, in just the first nine months of 2007, there were 25 incursions by Mexican military or police personnel, some of which were in support of trafficking operations.[58] Proponents of enhanced border security contended that the situation is much worse than the DHS admits. Representative Duncan Hunter (R-CA) alleged that there were more than 200 Mexican military incursions into U.S. territory between January 2006 and August 2008.[59] Former representative Tom Tancredo (R-CO), commenting on an October 31, 2008, incident in which seven Mexican soldiers were taken into custody near Yuma, Arizona, charged: "This is not an uncommon occurrence. Often times, it is the result of the Mexican military providing cover essentially for drug transportation across into our country, and/or creating a diversion so it will draw our people away from the place where the drugs are coming across."[60]

While some of the incursions are probably innocent errors along a border that is not always well marked, others are decidedly suspicious. For example, in early August 2008, a U.S. Border Patrol agent was held a gunpoint by Mexican military personnel who retreated back into their own country only when the Patrol dispatched backup agents to the scene.[61]

A Climate of Fear

Already the miasma of fear afflicting Mexico because of the drug wars is beginning to seep across the border—especially among Mexican and Mexican-American families living in the southwestern United States. When a battle erupted between police and drug gangs in Nuevo Laredo in July 2010, frantic calls flooded into emergency dispatch centers on the U.S. side of the border in Laredo, Texas, from worried residents who could hear the gunfire and periodic explosions. Even though there were no stray bullets or other evidence of spillover, it took some time for Laredo residents to calm down. Police spokesman Joe Baeza dismissed their concerns. The drug gang members "are not Vikings," he joked. "They're not going to invade us; it doesn't work that way."[62] True enough. But as the bullets wedged in the El Paso City Hall confirm, it is unwise to assume that Mexico's drug violence will have no impact on communities in the United States.

People in Fort Hancock, Texas, and other impoverished communities along the border are clearly feeling jittery. As Associated Press correspondent Paul Weber reported from Fort Hancock: "When black SUVs trail school buses around here, no one dismisses it as routine traffic. And when three tough-looking Mexican men pace around the high school gym during a basketball game, no one assumes they're just fans. . . . Mexican families fleeing the violence have moved here or just sent their children, and authorities and residents says gangsters have followed them across the Rio Grande" in a campaign of intimidation.[63]

Many residents have either fled Mexico because of the violence or have family ties to people in Mexico that are still caught up in that turmoil. Some of those Mexican relatives are involved in the drug trade, some apparently are not, but Mexican-American communities in the United States are feeling the impact, in either case. "I have friends with fathers who've been annihilated," related Israel Morales, a high school student in Fort Hancock. "It just traumatizes you." Several school districts in south and southwest Texas have had to implement counseling programs to assist students who have lost family members in Mexico's drug violence. School administrators say that dozens of students have relatives south of the border who were killed or tortured. María Aguilar, the parent of a fourth-grade student, described how her daughter shared playground stories about how "so-and-so got killed in Mexico this weekend." [64] Paul Vranish, superintendent of the Tornillo school district near El Paso estimated that 10 percent of his students have lost a close family member in Mexico's drug warfare.

One high-school student, picked up for truancy, told a judge that he was too scared to go back to class because he had witnessed a murder in Mexico. In Fabens, Texas, fliers were circulated to faculty members asking them to watch for a gunman wanted for four killings in Ciudad Juárez. The suspect was the father of two boys at the Fabens middle school.

Texas authorities are increasingly worried that the drug violence will pursue Mexican refugees who have taken up residence in communities along the border. Local police forces have taken to escorting school buses. Authorities in other communities are nervous, even when there have been no incidents comparable to those affecting residents in Fort Hancock and other Texas towns. Manuel Paul, school superintendent in San Ysidro, California, across the border from Tijuana, stated that security concerns were not an issue, but the reason he cited offered little comfort. He concluded that most Tijuana families fleeing the fighting in that city "are running further north from the violence," bypassing San Ysidro.

Security worries among Mexican refugees and their relatives in the southwestern United States may be the canary in the coal mine about the possible spillage of violence across the border. Those communities would logically be the first to feel the effects. But even Anglo populations along the border are becoming nervous. Ranchers in the borderlands of Arizona, New Mexico, and Texas have complained for years that smugglers and illegal immigrants use their properties with impunity as routes to enter the United States. And the level of fear is rising as more and more of the uninvited seem to be involved in drug smuggling or human trafficking rather than being ordinary people looking for work and better lives in the United States.

Concerns escalated in March 2010, when Robert Krentz, a 58-year-old rancher near Douglas, Arizona, was found murdered. Although the precise motive for his slaying was unclear, authorities and the public soon concluded that an intruder from Mexico was the perpetrator. Tracks at the murder scene led back over the border into Mexico, and Krentz's ranch had long been an active route for illegal immigrants and drug shipments. The most prevalent theory is that he had stumbled upon a scout for a trafficking shipment and paid for that encounter with his life.

The death of Krentz, who was reputed to be kind to aliens moving through his land on their way north (even giving them water and food), outraged Arizonans and other Americans. Arizona's two senators, Republicans John McCain and Jon Kyl, soon asked the Obama administration to station 3,000 National Guard troops along the border. But anger and concern about the Krentz incident was not partisan in nature. Representative Gabrielle Giffords (D-AZ), whose district included the area where the rancher perished, stated that if the slaying was connected to drug smugglers, the federal government should consider all possible responses—including deploying National Guard troops.

There is also mounting uneasiness farther east in Texas. The principal trigger was an incident on Falcon Lake, which the U.S.-Mexico border bisects. On September 30, 2010, David Hartley and his wife Tiffany were jet skiing on the lake, sometimes crossing over into Mexican waters. Suddenly a speed boat approached them, and several men in the boat opened fire. The Hartleys immediately fled back toward the American side of the line, but just before they reached that point, a bullet struck David Hartley and knocked him off his jet ski. Tiffany tried to get her wounded husband onto her jet ski but soon realized that she faced a horrible choice: try to help her husband, even though he appeared to be mortally wounded, or move quickly to save her own life by continuing on toward the Texas shore. She chose the second option, but was understandably distraught, as her frantic calls to 911 revealed. Although authorities initially used the euphemism "pirates" to describe the attackers, it became rather clear that the Hartleys had encountered gunmen from a drug cartel, most likely the Zetas. Any doubt on that score disappeared a short time later when the lead Mexican investigator on the case was kidnapped and later found beheaded.[65]

The Falcon Lake killing had a similar impact on the government and people of Texas that the Krentz murder had on the people and government in Arizona. There was a surge of warnings that the situation on the border was getting alarmingly dangerous, and an equally great surge of demands from state authorities in Austin that the federal government do something to reverse the trend.

It is not just tourists along the Texas border with Mexico who apparently run risks. In one incident in early 2011, farmhands in the Rio Grande valley near the small town of La Joya were burning stalks of sugarcane for harvest when four masked men on all-terrain vehicles approached them. The armed men surrounded the crew and ordered them to leave the area. Dale Murden, the farmer who employed the crew, said he had no doubt that the masked men were drug traffickers. "They hide stuff in there," Murden said, referring to the dense fields of sugarcane, and then try to intimidate anyone who gets too close.[66] The incident on his ranch occurred just two weeks after a Hidalgo County employee was similarly threatened by masked men and ordered to stop clearing brush along a small river near the border. In early March 2011, men in a pickup truck fired shots at a foreman on a ranch adjacent to property owned by country-music star George Strait. Bullet holes pockmarked the foreman's vehicle.

Texas ranchers and farmers contend that episodes similar to the one Murden's workers experienced are growing more and more frequent, and they say that the danger began to become noticeably worse around the beginning of 2009. One farmer, Joe Aguilar, told state officials that he quit farming because of the escalating risk, saying "either you move on, or it's dangerous for your family."[67]

A few weeks after the Krentz incident, Arizona governor Jan Brewer created a flap when she asserted that most illegal immigrants crossing into the United States from Mexico were serving as drug mules. "I believe . . . that the majority of the illegal trespassers coming into the state of Arizona are under the direction and control of organized drug cartels," Brewer charged, "and they are bringing drugs in."[68] Brewer's fellow Republican, Senator John McCain, distanced himself from such an extreme allegation—but only to a limited extent, stating his belief that "there's a large number" of illegal migrants who are involved in trafficking for the cartels.[69]

Brewer's comment, and even McCain's milder version, underscores just how apprehensive political leaders in southwestern states have become about the prospect of Mexico's troubles afflicting the United States. And their views accurately reflect the concerns of their constituents. In fact, the fear and anger is spreading well beyond the southwest. A scathing editorial in the influential conservative newspaper *Investor's Business Daily* scorned President Obama's assurance that our southern border is more secure today than at any time in the past 20 years. If that's true, the paper's editors asked, "why is El Paso's City Hall taking fire from Mexico?"

The editorial went on to argue that events along the border "suggest bottoms dropping out, with horrors unimaginable in the past becoming the new norm." It then listed a series of alarming developments:

- The United States has lost control of actual U.S. territory to drug and migrant smugglers as much as 80 miles inland in Arizona. Any American who enters this area risks getting shot dead.

- The Falcon Dam on Texas' lower Rio Grande was targeted for destruction by a Mexican cartel to destroy a rival's drug smuggling route. Had the foiled plot succeeded, 4 million people could have ended up downriver with mass casualties and deaths.

- Arizona now has the second highest kidnapping rate in the world, behind only Mexico City, with all of it due to drug and migrant smugglers and their quests for cash and territory.

- Mass graves have been discovered in New Mexico, believed by lawmen to be the work of cartels.

The editorial closed by accusing the Obama administration of exhibiting no sense of urgency about the danger and, in fact, showing a "can't-do attitude."[70]

The alarm that both Governor Brewer and the *Investor's Business Daily* expressed may be excessive—and some of it may reflect a cynical strategy of taking partisan political potshots at a Democratic White House. Most of the evidence suggests that the spillage of violence over the border is not yet at a crisis point. Nevertheless, it would be a mistake to view it as a minor problem, much less as a myth.

One worrisome indicator emerged in August 2010, when the federal government posted signs along a 60-mile stretch of Interstate 8 between Casa Grande and Gila Bend, Arizona, more than 100 miles north of the border with Mexico. The signs warn motorists that they are entering an "active drug and human smuggling area," where they may encounter "armed criminals and smuggling vehicles traveling at high rates of speed." Pinal County sheriff Paul Babeu, whose jurisdiction is in the heart of that smuggling route, goes further than the federal warning signs, contending that he and his deputies are totally outnumbered and outgunned. "Mexican drug cartels literally do control parts of Arizona," Babeu stated.[71]

Such developments may be a harbinger of deterioration of the security situation on our southern border. At a minimum, that possibility deserves to be taken seriously.

8. Washington's Own War on the Cartels

The Bush administration gave strong support to President Calderón's military-led showdown with the drug cartels, and the Obama administration has not deviated in any significant way from the policy of its predecessor. Both Bush and Obama regarded Mexico's struggle against the traffickers as a mission that affects the United States almost as much as it does Mexico itself. That interpretation has become even more entrenched as Washington receives greater and greater pressure from nervous state and local officials in the southwestern states who are worried that the turmoil in Mexico will bleed across the border into their states.

U.S. officials, most notably Secretary of State Hillary Clinton, repeatedly emphasize that the drug cartels and the violence they spawn constitute a serious security threat to both countries. Even as Calderón comes under mounting criticism at home because of the large uptick in casualties associated with his campaign against the traffickers, Washington's public backing for him and his strategy remains rock solid. During a visit to Mexico in January 2011 to hold talks with Foreign Secretary Patricia Espinosa, Clinton rebuffed suggestions that Calderón's hard-line approach had failed to achieve its objective and had instead led to both a spike in killings nationwide and a rise in human-rights abuses by the Mexican military. "What President Calderón has done is absolutely necessary," Clinton stated at a news conference in Guanajuato.[1] She added: "The drug traffickers are not going to give up without a terrible fight. And when they do things that are just barbaric, like beheading people, it is meant to intimidate. It is meant to have the public say, 'Oh, just leave them alone and they won't bother me.' But a president cannot do that."[2]

The Mérida Initiative

Washington enthusiastically embraced Calderón's aggressive strategy from the outset and is backing it with a large financial-aid program, the Mérida Initiative, named after the city in Mexico's Yucatán region where the agreement was reached in October 2007. At that summit meeting between Bush and Calderón, the United States pledged to provide $1.6 billion in counternarcotics aid over a period of several years. Nearly 85 percent of that amount would go to strengthen the Mexican government's efforts, with the remainder going to similar programs in Central American countries.

The Mérida Initiative represented a quantum leap in U.S. funding for anti-drug law enforcement measures in Mexico. During the period from 2000 to 2006, U.S. assistance averaged approximately $57 million per year.[3] Beginning with the first installment of Mérida funding, which Congress approved in June 2008, that amount jumped to more than $400 million, along with additional sums for Central America. The State Department bureaucracy gradually gave implementation of the Mérida Initiative a high priority as well. During the first year, only three people in the Washington office of the International Narcotics Bureau were assigned to the program, but that total rose to 18 in 2010. Similarly, the number of people in the Narcotics Affairs Section of the U.S. Embassy in Mexico City, which has primary responsibility for implementing Mérida, soared from 19 in 2008 to 51 in March 2010, with plans eventually to reach at least 69.

But U.S. actions have sometimes not matched the promises. According to a July 2010 Government Accountability Office report, only 9 percent of the $1.6 billion promised had actually been spent by March 31, 2010. Furthermore, the GAO report concluded that U.S. officials seemed unable to determine whether the program was actually having a beneficial impact. Indeed, the GAO analysis was damning on that score, noting that the State Department's assessment methods "do not provide measurable targets, and do not measure outcomes." That conclusion irritated Representative Eliot Engel (D-NY), who along with Representative Connie Mack (R-FL) had requested the GAO study. "Nearly three years and $1.6 billion later, our counter-narcotics assistance lacks fundamental measurements of success," Engel noted caustically in a statement following the release of the report.[4]

A major part of the Mérida Initiative was to improve the hardware—everything from new helicopters to better surveillance equipment—that was available to Mexico's military and police forces. Another key component was to give those forces better training. Given the history of previous, although more limited, programs to beef-up the capabilities of anti-drug forces in Mexico, it is unclear why U.S. and Mexican authorities believe that the best answer is better equipment and training. In fact, given the disastrous program, more than a decade ago, in which the U.S. military helped train Mexican special forces personnel who later went rogue and became the Zetas (see chapter 1), one would think officials in both Washington and Mexico City would be doubly skeptical about that approach.

The GAO report does not inspire confidence that the training component of the Mérida Initiative is faring much better than that earlier fiasco. For example, after the United States spent $250,000 to train a new contingent of Mexican investigators, the unit was disbanded.[5] Other programs also had uncertain effectiveness. Some 5,000 federal police had taken courses in investigative techniques and 550 prosecutors had taken classes in various skill areas, but U.S. officials could not say whether such classes had made them even slightly more competent in counternarcotics efforts.[6]

Training efforts involving Washington's high-tech database program, eTrace, to trace gun purchases, imports, and ownership—thereby theoretically impeding the ability of the cartels to get illicit firearms—have not fared much better. That training program was first announced in Mexico in January 2008, but even the U.S. Bureau of Alcohol, Tobacco, Firearms, and Explosives conceded that the measure has not worked as well as it could or should have. A report from the inspector general of the U.S. Department of Justice was considerably more critical. The eTrace system in Mexico, the report concluded, "has yielded very limited information" of value.[7]

By the autumn of 2010, only about 20 people in Mexico had been trained to use the database, and many of them had levels of competence that were shaky, at best. In fact, the system was not even implemented in Spanish until December 2009. On October 5, 2010, U.S. and Mexican officials signed a new memorandum of understanding that pledged to train up to 30 people per month to use the system. Whether the increase in personnel quantity would be matched by an increase in the quality of performance remains to be seen.

The Obama administration is acutely aware of the corruption and competency problems in Mexico's law enforcement system—and, indeed, throughout the country's political system. That realization led to a modest, and not well-publicized, shift in U.S. drug strategy toward Mexico in May 2010. Previous aid efforts, with the Mérida Initiative as the core element, focused on beefing-up the tangible capabilities of Mexico's police and military forces. Most of the funds during the first two years of the program went to purchase airplanes, helicopters, and other high-priced equipment—purchases that, not coincidentally, benefitted the bottom line of U.S. defense firms. Critics scorned that strategy as constituting an obsession with gadgetry.

In contrast, most of the money sought in the administration's funding requests for 2011 and 2012 was aimed at judicial reforms and "good governance" programs. "We are moving away from big ticket equipment" and toward measures that support "Mexican capacity to sustain adherence to the rule of law and respect for human rights," Deputy Assistant Secretary of State Roberta Jacobsen stated in written testimony prepared for a congressional hearing.[8] A major part of the funds were earmarked for Ciudad Juárez, the current epicenter of the drug gang turmoil, to create jobs, strengthen education, and generate greater community involvement.

During her January 2011 trip to Mexico, Secretary Clinton also stressed the need for judicial reform. "A well-equipped, well-trained judicial system is essential" to winning Mexico's war on drugs, Clinton told reporters.[9] And she pledged that Washington stood ready to assist in that work.

Critics of the previous "hardware strategy" have a point that buying a few more planes, helicopters, and bullet-proof vests was not likely to have much beneficial impact on the struggle against the cartels. Some of the more sophisticated proponents of the drug war have been making that argument for some time. Former Drug Enforcement Administration chief Robert C. Bonner, writing in *Foreign Affairs*, argued that to defeat the Mexican drug gangs, "the country's law enforcement and judicial institutions must be aggressively reformed." Although he acknowledged that some of the police and military hardware can be useful, Bonner contended that "it is more important in the long run for the United States to concentrate its assistance on the development, training, and professionalization of Mexico's law enforcement officers."[10]

But there was little evidence that a mushy "institution building" approach funded by U.S. tax dollars would fare much better than did the focus on modernizing police equipment and military hardware. Institution-building efforts have been tried repeatedly over the past six decades in numerous countries to address various ills, and have amassed a thoroughly unimpressive record. The continuing corruption and incompetence of the governments in both Iraq and Afghanistan provide the latest testimony to the limitations of U.S.-sponsored reform campaigns. Proponents of the Mérida Initiative's new approach have not made the case that the outcome in Mexico will be materially different. Mexico's drug war problems lie deeper than any modest institution-building subsidy from Washington can possibly fix.

There also appear to be quiet, but very real, divisions within the Obama administration about how to best assist the drug war in Mexico. Even as the State Department advocates a greater focus on the reform of Mexico's institutions, other agencies are pushing a much more hard-line strategy. In September 2010, officials from the Pentagon's Northern Command, the Department of Homeland Security, and other departments and agencies began conducting a comprehensive review that focused on a better use (presumably a more expanded use) of military and intelligence assets to help the Mexican government's war against the cartels. Such intra-agency discussions, especially when they include the Department of Defense and the Department of Homeland Security, indicate a rising apprehension that developments in Mexico are posing a national security threat to the United States. *Wall Street Journal* correspondents Adam Entous and Nathan Hodge, who broke the story, were told that Admiral Mike Mullen, at the time Chairman of the Joint Chiefs of Staff, was "growing increasingly concerned about the security situation," and that a comprehensive intra-agency review was an implicit admission that the Mérida Initiative has been insufficient to stem the violence in Mexico.[11]

Hillary Clinton's comments to the Council on Foreign Relations in early September 2010 illustrated both the heightened worry and the depth of policy divisions within the Obama administration. Clinton asserted that the narco-violence had reached the point of being a full-blown "insurgency," and she added that Mexico was "looking more and more like Colombia looked 20 years ago."[12] That comparison drew an angry rebuttal from officials in the Calderón government, who argued that the problems their country faced, while serious, were not comparable to the large Marxist insurgency that caused so much havoc in Colombia. President Obama then undercut his own secretary of state by adopting Mexico City's view. "Mexico is vast and a progressive democracy, with a growing economy, and as a result, you cannot compare what is happening in Mexico with what happened in Colombia 20 years ago," Obama said in an interview with the Los Angeles Spanish-language newspaper *La Opinión*.[13]

A growing number of experts agree with Clinton's assessment more than Obama's. Henry Crumpton, a former CIA counterintelligence official, contends that viewing the activities of the cartels as an insurgency is the right way to frame the issue. But he concedes that the term is "particularly inflammatory to the Mexicans."[14] The vehemence of Mexico City's reaction may well have been a factor in Obama's decision to distance himself from Secretary Clinton's views. After all, a key part of Washington's strategy has been to maintain a close working relationship with Calderón's administration on the drug issue.

Washington was anxious to encourage and reward that government in any way it could. The prevailing attitude among U.S. officials was that with Calderón, the United States had, perhaps for the first time, a reliable Mexican partner in the campaign against illegal drugs. Among other signs of more effective cooperation, Mexico City extradited numerous high-level cartel suspects to the United States for prosecution. Calderón's performance was even better than that of his relatively cooperative predecessor, Vicente Fox, and far better than the record of earlier administrations.

Not surprisingly, that compliant attitude won praise from U.S. officials, past and present. One of Washington's main complaints over the years was that the Mexican government was reluctant to comply with the large number of U.S. extradition requests. Although that obstructionism was not deemed as bad as the brazen defiance that the Colombian government exhibited during the period of maximum violence in that country in the 1980s and 1990s, U.S. officials were still far from satisfied. Robert Bonner noted, in the summer of 2010, that "before Fox, there had been only six extraditions of Mexican citizens to the United States ever. During Fox's six-year tenure, there were 133. And since Calderón came to power, there have been 144."[15] And that total was in little more than half a presidential term. With Calderón's administration, the Drug Enforcement Administration, and the Justice Department officials in general, believed that they finally had found an enthusiastic ally in the war on illegal drugs.[16]

Enthusiasm is one thing; effectiveness is quite another. And it is now clear that, glowing public endorsements to the contrary, Washington was becoming very uneasy about whether Calderón's uncompromising strategy, especially his decision to use the military against the cartels, would achieve victory or even meaningful, lasting progress.

A Glimpse into a Troubling Reality: the WikiLeaks Documents

Official U.S. statements provide little hint of uneasiness about the course of the drug war in Mexico, but State Department classified cables obtained and released by WikiLeaks in 2010 and early 2011 confirm an array of private doubts. One such cable took direct aim at the Mexican army, concluding that it was outdated, cumbersome, and averse to taking necessary risks. (Another cable, though, gave significantly higher marks to Mexico's navy, especially the marines.) The judgment about the country's police and judicial systems was even more caustic than the critical assessment of the army. One cable concluded that prosecution rates for drug gang members and other organized-crime figures were "dismal,"[17] and only about 2 percent of such individuals who are detained by police are ever brought to trial. In Ciudad Juárez, only a paltry 2 percent of those arrested are even charged with a crime.

Several leaked documents suggested that the tone of optimism coming out of both Mexico City and Washington about alleged progress in the war against the cartels was unwarranted. An October 2009 memo asserted that then-undersecretary for the Interior, Gerónimo Gutiérrez Fernández, "expressed a real concern with 'losing' certain regions of Mexico to drug traffickers."[18] That comment (which Gutiérrez subsequently denied when the document became public) directly contradicted numerous public statements that Calderón and other officials made, saying that there was no portion of the country where government control was in doubt.

Policy trial balloons that Mexican officials floated before U.S. diplomats during the Calderón years also suggested a much higher level of worry about the power of the cartels, and far greater pessimism about the success of the government's anti-trafficking campaign.

An October 28, 2009, cable from the U.S. embassy in Mexico City reported that Defense Secretary General Guillermo Galván Galván proposed declaring a state of emergency that would suspend some constitutional rights in several hard-hit cities, especially Ciudad Juárez. The cable further noted that the Mexican government had not taken such action in any portion of the country since World War II. Charge d'Affaires John Freely stated that the embassy's analysis of the proposal concluded that the benefits were "uncertain at best," and the "political costs appear high."[19]

Even Washington's own policy centerpiece, the Mérida Initiative, came in for pointed criticism from both Mexican and U.S. officials in the classified documents. One cable quoted a high-ranking member of the Mexican government as saying that not enough strategic thought went into the development of that strategy, and that consequently the measure was "too hastily crafted to be effective."[20] Again, a stark contrast existed between those candid private assessments and the laudatory pronouncements about the Mérida Initiative coming out of Washington and Mexico City.

Predictably, the two governments tried to minimize the significance of the leaked documents. U.S. ambassador to Mexico, Carlos Pascual, even insisted that the cables did "not represent U.S. policy." He described them as "often impressionistic snapshots at a moment in time," and that, like some snapshots, "they can be out of focus or unflattering." Alejandro Poiré, at the time the Mexican government's spokesman on security issues, was even more dismissive, asserting that the material was "incomplete, inaccurate and out of context."[21]

But Pascual had to scramble again when WikiLeaks revealed a new batch of cables in March 2011. Those documents provided further evidence that the ambassador and other diplomats at the embassy in Mexico City had little confidence in Calderón's national security team and its conduct of the war on drugs. One cable described the appointment of Attorney General Arturo Chávez Chávez as both "unexpected" and "inexplicable." Noting Chávez's "considerable human rights baggage" from his days as state prosecutor in Chihuahua, the embassy predicted that he would be even less effective than his predecessor, Eduardo Medina Mora. That was an especially damning indictment, since an earlier cable had criticized Medina Mora for his infighting with other members of Calderón's administration and contended that his inability to successfully prosecute high-level criminals had "hindered drug enforcement efforts."[22]

The furor over the second batch of WikiLeaks documents forced Pascual to resign. Mexican officials were already furious about the earlier disclosures, and the new revelations created an irreparable breach with the Mexican government. Calderón made no secret of his distaste for Pascual. "I do not have to tell the U.S. ambassador how many times I meet with my security Cabinet. It's none of his business," the president stated in a February 2011 interview. He added, "that man's ignorance translates into a distortion of what is happening in Mexico."[23]

In any case, the view epitomized in Poiré's dismissive comment that the leaked cables were inaccurate, incomplete, and taken out of context is entirely too flippant. The WikiLeaks revelations may not provide a complete picture, but they offer insights into several important and troubling points. First, Mexican officials are considerably more worried about the actual and potential power of the drug cartels than they let on in public. Second, the military-led campaign against those organizations is not nearly as successful as the pronouncements of Mexican and U.S. leaders suggest. Third, U.S. policymakers harbor significant doubts about the capabilities of the Mexican government, not only with respect to the war on drugs, but the overall operation of the security forces and judicial system. Fourth, those policymakers are also doubtful about both the design and execution of the much-touted Mérida Initiative. Taken together, the WikiLeaks documents suggest that Calderón's war against the cartels faces the prospect of defeat, that American leaders are aware of that possibility, and that they are very worried about the implications.

Washington's Expanding Role South of the Rio Grande

Such worries may be causing the United States to pressure the Calderón government to accept more extensive U.S. involvement in the drug war on the Mexican side of the border. Washington's participation already has been fairly significant for a number of years. For example, there has been a growing willingness to use U.S. intelligence assets to directly aid Calderón's decapitation strategy. U.S. leaders have long been fond of the strategy as the best way to undermine the cartels, and they were thrilled to see the Calderón administration become more proactive on that front. When Mexican naval marines killed Arturo Beltrán Leyva in December 2009, U.S. officials were ecstatic. "We congratulate the Mexican navy and the Mexican government on a well-executed operation that was a significant blow against the drug cartels in the country," said State Department spokesman Robert Wood.[24]

The U.S. government had been far more than an interested spectator regarding that raid; American intelligence agencies apparently provided key pieces of information about Beltrán Leyva's location to the Mexican military just hours before the assault. And that was one of those rare occasions when the information, once shared with the authorities in Mexico, did not leak to the target of the raid. A few days later, information from U.S. authorities helped their Mexican counterparts strike another blow against the Beltrán Leyva organization. Police captured Jesús Basilio Araujo, known as "The Chicken," a top enforcer for the cartel that was linked to at least 109 killings.[25] Some later high-profile raids, including those against La Barbie and El Nacho Coronel, apparently also benefited substantially from assistance that U.S. intelligence agencies provided about the movements of those individuals.

Such U.S. involvement in the Mexican government's war against the cartels has been significant, but there are indications of a trend toward far more direct measures. The Obama administration has allowed Mexican police and military commandos to use U.S. territory as staging areas for raids on cartel targets inside Mexico. Officially, the reason for such "boomerang" operations is to evade the surveillance efforts of the drug gangs, since they have far greater difficulties anticipating and monitoring possible attacks from the U.S. side of the border than they would from the police or military inside Mexico. Unofficially, sequestering raid personnel inside U.S. facilities reduces the danger that information about an impending raid will leak to the targeted cartel.[26]

Some of the newer measures are so intrusive that they create considerable controversy inside Mexico and even raise questions about Washington's respect for Mexico's sovereignty. The most graphic example was the confirmation in March 2011 that U.S. Predator and Global Hawk drones were flying over Mexican territory in an effort to locate suspected drug traffickers and track their movements. What especially upset critics in Mexico's legislature—and much of the news media—was that those drones had been operating for at least two years, without anyone outside the Calderón administration being informed. Senator Ricardo Monreal, one of the more left-wing members of that chamber, blasted administration officials as being "timid, weak, servile, and subordinate" in dealing with Washington. Foreign Relations Secretary Patricia Espinosa rushed to quiet the brewing storm, insisting in a hastily called meeting with senators that Mexico's sovereignty had not been compromised. The drone flights, she said, "do not violate sovereignty because they are controlled by the government of Mexico and contribute to its capacity to fight organized crime."[27]

There wasn't much evidence of Mexican-government control—or even influence—regarding the use of the drones, however. It appeared to be a U.S.-directed operation. Furthermore, the Predators seemed to be merely one component of an increasing U.S. presence in Mexico to wage the drug war. Later revelations indicated that not only drones but manned U.S. aircraft fly over suspected cartel hideouts inside Mexico to eavesdrop on cell-phone conversations. Perhaps even more jarring, the DEA has reportedly set up an intelligence outpost, apparently staffed by CIA operatives and retired U.S. military personnel, on a Mexican military base.[28]

Brad Barker, president of HALO Corporation, a private security firm that was involved in the drone program, may have inadvertently revealed just how extensive Washington's involvement inside Mexico has become. Noting that his firm and others were tracking both vehicles and people, Barker stated: "There's been a huge spike in agents down there."[29]

Both the U.S. and Mexican governments refuse to divulge just how many U.S. agents are in Mexico to conduct anti-drug activities. But using the Freedom of Information Act, government audits, congressional testimony, and other indicators, the Associated Press was able to determine that there were "several hundred" operating in that country. And most of that information had been gathered before the murder of Jaime Zapata, which led to a new surge of U.S. personnel south of the border. That is a risky strategy, given the renowned nationalist sensitivities of the Mexican public about the "Colossus of the North." Boasts like those of one U.S. officer, that the growing surveillance and logistical operations indicated that "the military is trying to take what it did in Afghanistan and do the same in Mexico," will not likely ease those apprehensions.[30]

The escalation of the U.S. role, despite the suspicions of the Mexican people, suggests just how concerned the Obama administration has become about the extent of Mexico's drug-related disorders. Some administration officials openly express alarm at the trend in Mexico. Echoing Secretary Clinton's remarks a few months earlier that the situation in that country resembled an insurgency, Undersecretary of the Army Joseph Westphal went even a bit further. In response to a student's question following a speech at the University of Utah in early February 2011, he asserted flatly that there was "a form of an insurgency with the drug cartels that's right on our border." This wasn't "just about drugs and about illegal immigrants," Westphal emphasized, "this is about, potentially, a takeover" of the Mexican government.[31] He concluded that even a U.S. military intervention inside Mexico could not be ruled out, although he added that he never wants to see a situation where it became necessary to send troops across the border into our southern neighbor.

Westphal's comments created a political and media firestorm in Mexico. An Interior Department statement termed his comments "regrettable," and stated that the U.S. government "categorically" rejected his allegation about the existence of an insurgency. Westphal beat a hasty retreat, issuing an apology and saying that his comments "were not and have never been the policy of the Department of Defense" or any other portion of the U.S. government. "I regret that my inaccurate statements may have caused concerns for our partners and friends in the region, especially Mexico."[32]

Actions, though, speak louder than apologies issued under duress. The misgivings revealed in the WikiLeaks documents, the introduction of drones and manned aircraft for surveillance, and the rapid buildup of U.S. anti-drug personnel inside Mexico all suggest that Washington is very worried about the deteriorating security environment in that country: so much so that the Obama administration is willing to take highly controversial steps in an effort to reverse the trend.

Counterpoint: Greater U.S. Tolerance for Mexico's Drug Policy Reforms

Even as Washington has embraced Calderón's unflinching offensive against the drug gangs, the Obama administration has simultaneously shown greater flexibility and tolerance regarding his other initiatives on the drug issue. That has been the case even though U.S. officials appear to have some doubts about the wisdom of certain measures that the Mexican president is adopting. For example, the Obama administration did not reflexively oppose Mexico's drug policy reforms that drastically reduced the legal penalties for simple drug possession. That attitude was in marked contrast to the position taken by the Bush administration—and, indeed, most U.S. administrations since the end of Jimmy Carter's presidency.

Such a reform would have provoked an angry response from previous U.S. administrations. The Bush administration's vehement opposition to a measure similar to the new Mexican law caused then-president Vicente Fox to veto the bill. But Obama and his policy team did not denounce Calderón's reform, much less threaten to impose economic penalties or engage in other retaliatory actions. When asked about the measure during a visit to Mexico in July 2009, drug czar Gil Kerlikowske merely responded that the United States would "wait and see" how it worked out.[33]

At first glance, a "harm-reduction" drug law reform would seem to run counter to the overall hard-line policy that both the Calderón and Obama administrations have endorsed regarding Mexico's war on the cartels. But there is actually a rationale for the strategy of simultaneously reducing penalties for petty drug use and escalating the pressure on big-time drug trafficking operations. Indeed, Mexican officials stress that largely ignoring simple drug possession offenses frees up badly needed police and judicial resources to better focus on the real threat: the drug kingpins. (See chapter 6.)

The Obama administration seems to share that perspective. But while Washington may be more receptive than before to mild harm-reduction policy reforms in Mexico and other countries, any hint of a truce or accommodation with the Mexican cartels would be another matter entirely. Such a move would signal that Mexico City had decided to abandon—or at least greatly scale back—the goal of trying to stem the flow of drugs into the United States in exchange for a commitment from the traffickers to cool the violence inside Mexico. That step, in the view of zealous U.S. drug warriors—and even relatively moderate Obama administration policymakers—would be a devil's bargain. Calderón and his appointees undoubtedly understand the distinction between acceptable harm-reduction measures and a full-fledged appeasement policy toward the cartels, and they show no signs of venturing down the latter path. They would be unlikely ever to do so without a clear sign of encouragement from Washington, and no indication of such encouragement seems to be forthcoming.

Although the U.S. response to Mexico's harm-reduction drug law reform was relatively low-key and at least mildly supportive, officials went out of their way to reaffirm an uncompromising stance toward the trafficking gangs. "We know that Mexican law-enforcement authorities are continuing their efforts to target drug traffickers," U.S. Department of Justice spokesperson Laura Sweeny emphasized. "Our friends and partners in Mexico are waging an historic battle with the cartels, one that plays out on the streets of their communities each day. Here in the United States we will continue to enforce federal narcotics laws as we investigate, charge, and arrest cartel leaders and their subordinates in our joint effort to dismantle and disrupt these cartels."[34]

Washington's Offensive against the Cartels in the United States

The Obama administration has backed up those words not only with financial, logistical, and other assistance to the Mexican government but also with high-profile deeds at home. FBI, DEA, and other law enforcement personnel are going after the Mexican cartels on U.S. soil as well as in Mexico itself.[35] In early 2009, the Justice Department issued indictments against more than 40 leading traffickers. Then, in October 2009, U.S. law enforcement agencies launched a nationwide raid, Project Coronado, in 38 American cities that resulted in the arrests of 303 individuals.

Interestingly, the October raids were almost entirely targeted at accused operatives of La Familia, suggesting that U.S. authorities were even more worried about that organization than they were about the Sinaloa and Gulf cartels. (That point seemed to be confirmed in November 2009, when federal authorities indicted 15 members of a "command-and-control group" in charge of cocaine distribution for La Familia in Chicago.) Attorney General Eric Holder conceded as much "The sheer level and depravity of violence that this cartel has exhibited far exceeds what we, unfortunately, have become accustomed to from other cartels." He added: "While this cartel may operate from Mexico, the toxic reach of its operations extends to nearly every state within our country."[36] More recently, as La Familia has faded in prominence and splintered into rival factions, the focus of the Justice Department seems to have shifted toward giving highest priority to weakening the American partners of the extremely violent, fast-rising Zetas.[37]

As is so often the case with highly publicized drug raids, there was more symbolism than substance to Project Coronado. Authorities proudly displayed for reporters some of the $32 million in currency; 2,700 pounds of methamphetamine; 4,400 pounds of cocaine; 29 pounds of heroin; 16,000 pounds of marijuana; and various firearms that had been seized. Holder asserted, "These are drugs that were headed for our streets and weapons that often were headed for the streets of Mexico." The raids, he said, were part of a strategy of "hitting them where it hurts the most—their revenue stream. By seizing their drugs and upending their supply chains, we have disrupted their 'business-as-usual' state of operations."[38] However, even Justice Department officials had to concede that none of those arrested as a result of Project Coronado were major traffickers. Instead, they ranged from mid-level distributors to low-level street dealers and gun smugglers. That concession made Holder's boast ring hollow and the publicity campaign seem overblown.

Several journalists and policy experts interpreted Project Coronado as an effort to provide a vivid demonstration that the United States was serious about doing its part to combat the cartels. Attorney General Holder reinforced that impression when he stressed that "with the increases in cooperation between U.S. and Mexican authorities in recent years, we are taking the fight to our adversaries." College of William and Mary professor George W. Grayson noted that "many Mexican leaders have viewed the Mérida Initiative as too little and too late," and so, with the raids, "Washington is trying to make clear that we are good faith, genuine partners in the war against drugs."[39]

The administration took similar action the following year with Project Deliverance, a series of raids in 19 states. In contrast to the earlier Coronado operation, which had been directed primarily against La Familia, the new assault was an equal-opportunity venture, targeting several of the cartels. The raids netted 74 tons of illegal drugs, 501 weapons, 527 vehicles, and $154 million in cash. Some 2,200 people were arrested in the course of the dragnet. "We will not rest until we have defeated" the cartels, Holder pledged at a news conference.[40] Acting DEA administrator Michele M. Leonhart asserted that Project Deliverance inflicted a "debilitating blow" against the trafficking organizations. "The stakes are extraordinarily high," she stressed, "and this massive operation is a milestone in our tireless assault on these violent drug cartels."[41]

Apparently though, the blow wasn't all that debilitating. In late February and early March 2011, Immigration and Customs Enforcement teamed with 170 federal, state, and local law enforcement agencies to conduct a series of raids that netted some 678 gang members, most of whom were connected to the Mexican cartels.[42] Both the timing and the principal target of the "Southern Tempest" raids were not coincidental. The announcement of the arrests occurred just two weeks after the killing of ICE agent Jaime Zapata in Mexico. And a large percentage of those apprehended by Southern Tempest raids were affiliated with the Zetas—the cartel suspected in the murder of Zapata.

Such prominent programs as the Mérida Initiative and splashy raids such as Project Coronado, Project Deliverance, and Southern Tempest certainly make good media copy. They may even facilitate good feelings and greater diplomatic cooperation between the U.S. and Mexican governments. But there is little evidence that they will do anything more than annoy and mildly inconvenience the cartels. Alberto Islas, a security consultant based in Mexico City, put the underlying problem well: "They can arrest 300 guys, but 300 new guys will take their place because the market structure is intact."[43] That will be the case as long as the drug trade is so outlandishly profitable. And it will remain that profitable as long as drugs that are in high demand from consumers in the United States and other markets are illegal.

The growing frustration on both sides of the Rio Grande with the lack of meaningful progress in bringing down the cartels increases the incentive for political leaders to search for scapegoats and to grasp for policy panaceas. Both trends have become more and more apparent during the Calderón years. The temptation to seek superficial, politically comfortable answers to the severe problems bedeviling Mexico on the drug front impedes the process of finding real solutions. But politicians, being politicians, succumb all too readily to that temptation.

9. Scapegoats and Bogus Solutions

Both the Mexican and U.S. governments seem intent on indulging in fantasies about the drug violence and the power of the cartels. Perhaps the most glaring example of delusional thinking on the Mexican side was Attorney General Eduardo Medina Mora's February 26, 2009, comment that the record-setting bloodshed in Ciudad Juárez and other cities was actually a positive sign. The increased violence "is not reflecting the power of these groups," Medina Mora stated. Instead, it "is reflecting how they are melting down."[1]

American cheerleaders for Calderón's decision to attack the cartels exude a similar counterintuitive optimism about the skyrocketing violence. Writing in the pages of *Foreign Affairs*, Robert C. Bonner, who served both as head of the Drug Enforcement Administration in the early 1990s and as commissioner of U.S. Customs and Border Protection under President George W. Bush, sounded a lot like Medina Mora: "The increase in the number of drug-related homicides, although unfortunate, is a sign of progress: a consequence, in part, of government actions that are destabilizing the drug cartels and denying them access to areas in which they used to operate with complete impunity. As a result, the cartels are starting to fight one another."[2]

Calderón himself engages in similar dubious rationales and wishful thinking. Following the caustic August 2010 blog post by former president Vicente Fox, which branded the drug war as a bloody failure, Calderón, briefing leaders of the opposition Institutional Revolutionary Party at a meeting, responded that "the number of murders or the degree of violence isn't necessarily the best indicator of progress or retreat, or if the war is won or lost." The president stated, "It is [merely] a sign of the severity of the problem."[3]

Given what has happened in Mexico's northern border cities, and increasingly in other areas as well, one had better hope that the cartels don't "melt down" any more, or it soon may not be safe to venture anywhere in Mexico. The U.S. State Department has issued numerous travel alerts over the past three years, warning American businesspeople and tourists about the growing risks of travel in Mexico. Several American colleges and universities have likewise urged their students to avoid going to Mexico for spring breaks.

In 2008, Sara Carter, at the time a correspondent for the *Washington Times*, stated that a high-level source in the Pentagon had concluded that two of the leading drug trafficking organizations, the Sinaloa and Gulf cartels, could field more than 100,000 armed foot soldiers. That figure did not take into account the enforcers at the disposal of other cartels, including the rapidly rising Zetas. Adding their personnel to the mix would likely bring the total to 150,000—or perhaps even more. In short, the forces the drug gangs can deploy are now nearly as numerous as Mexico's 188,000-strong army. That sobering match-up does not support the case for optimism that the government's strategy will defeat the cartels.

Scapegoat: Lax U.S. Gun Laws

Another manifestation of dubious thinking is the belief among Mexican officials that the United States is largely to blame for the carnage. The Mexican government responds to Washington's complaints about the surging violence by blaming lenient U.S. gun laws. Medina Mora, typified that view, saying: "I think American [gun] laws are absurd," because "they make it very easy for citizens to acquire guns."[4] During his May 2010 visit to the United States, which included a summit meeting with President Obama, Calderón asserted: "If you look carefully, you will notice that the violence in Mexico started to grow a couple of years before I took office in 2006. This coincides, at least, with the lifting of the assault weapons ban in 2004."[5]

Gun-control advocates in the United States have taken up the same theme. A *New York Times* editorial encapsulated the logic of strengthening the restrictions on firearms as a way to more effectively wage the war on drugs south of the border. "Mexico has no hope of defeating the traffickers unless this country is also willing to do more to fight the drug war at home—starting with a clear commitment to stop the weapons smugglers."[6] University of Southern California scholar Pamela Starr goes even further, arguing that U.S. leaders should focus "on the southward flow of arms and ammunition that is fueling an explosion of drug-related violence in Mexico." She stresses that "an estimated 97 percent of the arms used by the Mexican cartels–including military-grade grenade launchers and assault weapons—are purchased at sporting goods stores and gun shows on the U.S. side of the border and then smuggled south, according to the Mexican government."[7] But the 97 percent estimate that she cites is so extreme that it is no longer put forth even by Mexican authorities. The most frequent figure coming out of Mexico City is now 90 percent, and sometimes a more nebulous 80 to 90 percent. Even those lower estimates are open to question.[8]

Starr's proposed solution is a "Cabinet-level initiative to attack the illicit gun trade. The departments of Homeland Security, Justice, State, Defense and Treasury all need to be involved." Echoing the arguments of Mexican political leaders, Starr asserts: "The United States is enabling the bloodshed in Mexico. We have a moral responsibility to stop arming the murderers and kidnappers—our national security demands it."[9]

A high-profile Bi-National Task Force on the United States–Mexico border urged the U.S. government to reinstate the Clinton-era ban on assault rifles to prevent such weapons from reaching the cartels. The blue-ribbon group, which included two former U.S. ambassadors to Mexico, also concluded in its October 2009 report that Washington could do more to stop the smuggling of firearms and ammunition into Mexico by expanding investigations of gun dealers and tightening regulations on gun shows. Robert Bonner, co-chairman of the task force, argued that improving such efforts would "weaken the drug cartels and disrupt their activities, and make it easier ultimately to dismantle and destroy them."[10]

Even some U.S. political leaders have accepted the Mexican government's explanation for the surging violence. In June 2008, the Bush and Calderón administrations announced a new program, the *Armas Cruzadas* (Crossed Arms), to stem the flow of guns from the United States to Mexico. Sen. Charles Grassley (R-IA) defended the initiative, saying: "As drugs come into our country, money and illegal firearms go out. We owe it to our neighbors to help cut down on outbound smuggling."[11] Despite that initiative, the southward flow of guns was again a prominent topic at the summit between Obama and Calderón 14 months later, as well as in subsequent high-level meetings between U.S. and Mexican officials.

Obama himself clearly accepts the thesis that U.S. gun laws bear heavy responsibility for the bloodshed in Mexico, and he has echoed the Calderón government's call to restore the ban on assault rifles that Congress repealed in 2004. During an April 2009 visit to Mexico, Obama apologized for the role of such weapons in that country's violence, but lamented that "none of us are under any illusion that reinstating that ban would be easy."[12] Since then, the president has retreated slightly, indicating that he would prefer to focus more on enforcing existing laws that make it illegal to send assault rifles across the border rather than expending political capital in an unpromising effort to get Congress to restore the overall ban on assault rifles.

During her January 2011 trip to Mexico, Secretary of State Clinton stated that the U.S. government was firmly committed to cracking down on weapons smuggling. She pledged $60 million in the forthcoming fiscal year for "nonintrusive" inspection equipment and other enhancements for customs agents. She also promised that the administration would push for new measures to track multiple purchases of high-powered rifles at sales sites near the border with Mexico.[13] The Bureau of Alcohol, Tobacco, Firearms, and Explosives had recently requested authority to require gun dealers to report all such purchases.

The notion that the violence in Mexico would subside if the United States had more restrictive laws on firearms is weak in terms of both logic and evidence. Many of the weapons that Mexican authorities have captured in successful raids on cartel hideouts are already illegal under U.S. law—even assuming that the weapons originated in the United States. A raid on a safe house used by enforcers of the Beltrán Leyva gang in 2008 yielded a cache that included 30 grenades and several M4 grenade launchers—weapons that cannot be bought legally in the United States.

Former U.S. drug czar Barry McCaffrey visited Mexico in late 2008 and described how well the cartels were armed: "The outgunned Mexican law enforcement authorities face armed criminal attacks from platoon-sized units employing . . . RPG's, Anti-Tank 66mm rockets, mines and booby traps, heavy machine guns, 50 caliber sniper rifles, massive use of military hand grenades, and most modern models of 40mm grenade machine guns."[14] The drug gangs clearly did not obtain most of those sophisticated, high-powered military ordnance from gun shops or gun shows in the United States.

Although some of the especially destructive weapons the drug cartels use do originate in the United States, they do not come from purchases at unethical sporting-goods stores or gun shows. One of those increasingly common weapons—grenades—typically come from military depots that the United States government helped fill for friendly Central American regimes during the Cold War.[15] Washington was so concerned about Soviet penetration of that region during the 1980s that it sent shipment after shipment of weapons to the governments of countries such as El Salvador, Honduras, and Guatemala to use against left-wing insurgents. Records indicate that at least 300,000 grenades were sent to the region during the administrations of Ronald Reagan and George H.W. Bush.

When the Cold War ended, unused grenades remained in the armories of those countries. But now, more and more of them are finding their way into the hands of Mexican drug trafficking organizations. Such weapons typically sell for $100 to $500 apiece on a vigorous black market. And they are being used with greater and greater frequency. Mexican authorities seized more than 5,800 grenades from 2007 to mid 2010, but they concede that number is a tiny fraction of the total at the disposal of the cartels. More than 90 percent of the grenades are at least 20 years old, meaning that they were manufactured during the Cold War.[16] Most of them originated in the United States, but some came from the Soviet bloc, probably part of Moscow's military-aid programs to the Marxist regimes in Cuba and Nicaragua.

Grenade attacks throughout Mexico are on the rise. Since the beginning of 2007, there have been nearly 200 attacks using grenades, including 101 attacks on government buildings. Other assaults have been directed against such targets as news media outlets, private businesses (including, in at least one case, a brothel), and police convoys. Just between July 2009 and July 2010, there were more than 72 attacks in which grenades were involved.

Even if gun laws in the United States were tightened, Mexican drug gangs would have little trouble obtaining all the guns—and far more powerful armaments—they desire from black-market sources in Mexico and elsewhere. Indeed, as the commerce in grenades indicates, there is ample evidence that they do so already. After all, drug traffickers are individuals who make their fortunes operating in a black market, and they have vast financial resources to purchase whatever they need to conduct their business.

A scathing editorial in the *Washington Times* disputed the notion that lax U.S. gun laws are responsible for the surge of bloodshed in Mexico:

> Mr. Calderón's propaganda aside, Mexican drug gangs are getting real military weapons from within Mexico, countries south of his border, and other places around the world. Reports indicate that grenades and rocket launchers in use in Mexico are not even available for sale in the United States and come from places like South Korea, Israel, and Spain. Between 2007 and 2009, 2,239 grenades were seized by the Mexican government, and those weren't from here. Markings similarly show that machine guns in Mexico largely originate from China, Israel, and South Africa.[17]

It's clear that the cartels do not have to rely on U.S. sources for their weaponry. Discussing a shootout that occurred in April 2009 between Guatemalan authorities and Mexican drug traffickers in Guatemala City that left five drug-enforcement agents dead, the country's anti-drug prosecutor, Leonel Ruíz, reported that investigators had determined that the weapons had come from military bases in Guatemala itself. And the weapons cache was quite impressive: it included nearly 4,000 rounds of ammunition; bullet-proof vests; 11 M60 machine guns; 8 anti-personnel mines; 563 grenades; and 2 armored cars.[18]

The Guatemalan episode is not the only evidence that the drug organizations have diverse sources of weaponry. A 2011 report by the National Commission for Human Rights in Honduras estimated that there were more than 850,000 weapons in circulation in that country, the majority of which were strictly illegal. A confidential cable that Secretary of State Condoleezza Rice wrote to the U.S. embassy in Tegucigalpa in 2008, which was subsequently disclosed by WikiLeaks, detailed the "possible unauthorized diversion, misuse or failure to secure" weapons that the U.S. government supplied to Honduran security forces. The cable also noted that some of those weapons, including light anti-tank weapons and grenades sent to Honduras under the U.S. Foreign Military Sales Program, were later recovered in Mexico.[19]

There are serious questions about the security of military arsenals in Mexico itself. In July 2009, federal prosecutors in Mexico City announced the arrest of a retired army captain who was accused of selling military weapons to the Beltrán Leyva cartel. Mexican officials stressed that it was the first case of a suspected weapons sale between the army and a drug organization.[20] It may have been the first case in which the government has brought charges, but only the most naive would assume that it was the first time such a transaction had taken place. Indeed, just three months later, investigators made an interesting discovery following a shootout in Tijuana between traffickers and police. In one of the vehicles used by the gunmen, there were assault rifles and bullet-proof vests—all with the insignia of the federal prosecutor's office.[21]

Enterprising analysts in the United States have also questioned the Mexican government's assertion that 90 percent of the cartels' weapons originate in the United States.[22] Even former Mexican foreign minister Jorge Castañeda is extremely skeptical of those statistics:

> The Mexican [government's] numbers unfortunately are not reliable, nor is it a reliable source. . . . The fact is that we only know for sure that 90 percent of the *traceable* weapons *actually traced* in Mexico come from the U.S., most of them from the secondary market, which is even more difficult to control than the gun store and gun show market. It is far more likely that a large majority of the weapons preferred by the cartels in Mexico—AK-47s or *cuernos de chivo* without serial numbers—come from the former Soviet Union, China, etc., and from the Central American wars of the eighties and nineties. So I do not think that enhanced weapon-flow control from north to south will make much difference, and it can wreak havoc with trade and tourism flows, which are already down and dropping.[23]

There are credible reasons for such skepticism. While the Bureau of Alcohol, Tobacco, Firearms and Explosives continues to say that many guns the cartels use are bought in the United States, primarily in Texas and Arizona, it no longer releases estimates of how many. The reason for the Bureau's reticence? Officials contend that the numbers have become "too politicized."[24] But bureaucracies are rarely shy about presenting data if they're confident that the data support their argument. The ATF's unwillingness suggests that the available evidence cannot sustain the figures previously put forth by both the Mexican and U.S. governments implying that the vast majority of cartel weapons come from sales in the United States.

Statistics that the Bureau is willing to release certainly cast doubt on the Calderón government's 90 percent figure—or anything close to that level. For example, the Mexican government submitted 21,726 requests in 2009 to trace weapons that authorities had captured. According to a report issued by the inspector general of the U.S. Justice Department, in only 31 percent of those cases could *any* source for the firearm, defined as the dealer who originally sold the gun, be identified—much less prove that it was a U.S. dealer.[25] Other analyses suggest that the percentage that could in fact be traced back to gun shops or gun shows in the United States was a very modest 17 percent.[26]

Bureau officials and some other gun-control advocates now seem to be adopting a new tack in the face of this unfavorable evidence. They argue that the specific numbers really aren't that important. "It doesn't matter if 20 percent are coming from the U.S. or 80 percent," says Kenneth Melson, the agency's deputy director. "We know a lot of guns are going to Mexico, and it's a problem."[27]

Even assuming that the Mexican government's estimate that 90 percent of the weapons used by the cartels come from stores and gun shows in the United States—and as Castañeda notes, Mexican officials are not exactly objective sources for such statistics—the traffickers rely on those outlets simply because they are easier and more convenient, not because there are no other options.

Astonishingly, it appears that the Bureau of Alcohol, Tobacco, Firearms and Explosives itself may have been a significant supplier of high-powered weapons to the drug gangs. A scandal erupted in December 2010 when information surfaced that the bureau purposefully allowed some 2,000 such firearms to be smuggled from the United States into Mexico. The plan, "Operation Fast and Furious," was to track those weapons in order to identify and gain evidence against higher-level cartel operatives. But the scheme backfired badly when some of those weapons turned up at a shoot out along the Arizona-Mexico border that left Border Patrol agent Brian Terry dead. Further investigation indicated that other weapons that Operation Fast and Furious had allowed to be smuggled were involved in drug-related killings throughout Mexico.

Mexican congressman Humberto Treviño claimed that such guns were implicated in some 150 injuries or deaths.[28]

The scandal enveloping Operation Fast and Furious built throughout the summer and fall of 2011 and into 2012 as evidence emerged that both ATF leaders and high-level officials in the Justice Department in Washington may have tried to cover up the ATF's blunders. A House investigative committee chaired by Rep. Darrel Issa (R-CA) pressed its investigation of the gun-sting fiasco while congressional Democrats scrambled to protect Attorney General Eric Holder and the Obama administration from further damage.

Despite the ongoing allegations about the role U.S. gun laws have played in arming the cartels and contributing to Mexico's drug-related violence, one point should be apparent: every sporting goods store in the southwestern states could be closed, and that measure would not disarm the drug gangs. Even restoring the assault-rifle ban would likely have little impact on the firepower the cartels can deploy. And moving beyond such a relatively narrow, restrictive measure would significantly inconvenience gun merchants and gun owners in the United States, creating a nasty political controversy with the National Rifle Association and other gun-rights organizations.

Moreover, the research on restrictive gun laws in both U.S. and foreign jurisdictions shows no correlation between tough laws and a decline in homicides and other crimes.[29] Mexico's own experience confirms that point. Following sometimes violent radical leftist challenges to the government in the late 1960s, Mexico enacted some of the strictest gun-control measures in the world. Today, it is nearly impossible for a civilian to legally possess a handgun or rifle in that country.[30] Yet such tough restrictions have done nothing to disarm the drug gangs. In fact, those measures may have made it easier for cartel enforcers to terrorize portions of the country, since they don't have to worry much about law-abiding civilians being armed and able to defend themselves and their families.

Attempts to lay the primary blame for Mexico's chaos at the door of U.S. gun laws are either naive or a cynical effort to find a scapegoat. One has to wonder whether Mexican authorities take their own arguments seriously. According to U.S. agents working in the country, Mexican prosecutors had not achieved a single conviction in a major arms-trafficking case.[31] Tightening firearms laws in the

227

United States (even if that were politically feasible) is not a solution to the violence in Mexico. At most, that step would create annoyances and minor impediments for the drug gangs.

The Calderón government's strident calls for tighter gun-control laws in the United States may reflect a broader desperation as evidence accumulates that the strategy of waging a war against the cartels is not working and has unleashed a horrifying array of side effects. Other cases of grasping at straws are even less relevant than calling for greater firearms controls in the United States.

Sometimes the suggested measures border on the bizarre. A prime example was a proposed bill, in April 2010, to crack down on the use of Twitter and Facebook. The rationale for the legislation was that drug gangs use such social networking sites to warn of police raids and to convey threats to opponents. Nazario Norberto Sánchez, the principal sponsor of the bill, said that the goal was to create an online police force to thwart cartel communications, and he stated that sharing information about actions of the police (presumably including allegations of excessive force and other abuses) ought to be illegal, especially during the country's drug war.[32]

In one sense, the proposed legislation was sinister. It emulated a pattern seen in the United States and so many other countries to use "national security" as a rationale to constrain personal conduct and even basic civil liberties. But that sinister aspect is overshadowed by the measure's sheer silliness. The notion that government law enforcement bureaucrats can effectively control a diverse and fast-changing technology is both far-fetched and reactionary. Indeed, the proposed assault on Twitter is reminiscent of the comical effort of school districts across the United States in the 1990s to ban students from possessing that new-fangled invention, the cell phone, on school property because drug pushers could use the devices to conduct business. Needless to say, that effort did not fare well. This scheme will likely suffer a similar ignominious fate in the long run.

Bogus Solution: Seal the Border

Wishful thinking about the drug-related turmoil is found north of the Rio Grande as well as in Mexico. An increasingly popular measure among Americans to stem the danger of violence seeping into the United States from Mexico is to greatly increase border security.[33] Proponents tout the alleged effectiveness of measures taken to date, even as they press for stronger initiatives. Former Rep. Duncan Hunter (R-CA) managed to encapsulate both themes:

> While we have made some progress in recent years toward creating a more enforceable border, we still have a lot of work left to do. Moving forward, we must continue strengthening security through manpower, technology and infrastructure, including the most reliable and effective enforcement tool so far: border security fencing.

> Much like many other areas of the border today, the land corridor that once existed between Tijuana, Mexico, and San Diego, Calif., was for many years considered to the most prolific and dangerous smuggling route in the nation. It was not until I wrote into law the construction of a double border fence that drug smugglers and armed gangs lost control of this corridor and conditions on both sides of the border started to improve.[34]

What Hunter did not mention is that the traffickers merely moved their preferred transit corridor a little farther to the east, crossing into California in a more remote desert region rather than through the more urbanized, visible, and better guarded San Diego metropolitan area. There was no evidence that the fence and increased surveillance did anything more than cause the traffickers a slight inconvenience.

Although the principal reason for passage of the Secure Fence Act of 2006 was anger over the flow of undocumented immigrants, concern about the drug trade and the violence accompanying it was also a factor. Representative Hunter was candid about that motive. "Recurring confrontations with Mexican soldiers, much like the drug smugglers and illegal immigrants that attempt to cross into the U.S. through Mexico each day, further illustrate why fencing and other infrastructure remains so important to the security and enforcement of our border."[35]

Those living along the border give mixed reviews, at best, regarding the effectiveness of the portion of the border fence that has been completed. Some Arizona residents believe that the segment in their area has shifted smuggling operations farther east, toward New Mexico. But others ridicule the fence. Bill Odle, who lives less than a tenth of a mile from the border, pointed out to reporters portions of the fence that traffickers had cut or scaled. In the latter case, they often brought ladders to help them speed the process. The fence "doesn't work in stopping people," Odle observed. "But it does stop wildlife."[36]

The anemic record of previous schemes to secure the border does not seem to daunt proponents, though. Following the death of Arizona rancher Robert Krentz in March 2010, probably at the hands of a scout for drug smugglers, Arizona's governor and both of that state's U.S. senators asked for the deployment of 3,000 National Guard soldiers to prevent further incursions. The Obama administration's thinking on the issue of border security appeared to be moving in the same direction. In 2009, the president announced that 1,200 National Guard personnel would be going to police the border, and the first contingents began to arrive later that year. Avid proponents of greater border security, including Arizona Senator John McCain, criticized Obama's action as inadequate. They asked for at least 3,000 personnel, and even that higher total was viewed merely as an initial step, not the final number that would be needed.

Another plan that became prominent during the first two years of the Obama administration was the creation of a "virtual fence"—the use of highly sophisticated electronic surveillance technology to vastly increase monitoring of all portions of the border. The theory was that such heightened surveillance would enable personnel guarding the border to respond to attempted incursions much faster and thereby apprehend those who were trying to enter the United States illegally. Despite the initial hype accompanying that scheme, it soon became apparent that the alleged capabilities of the virtual fence were exaggerated and that the costs would be exorbitant. The Obama administration quietly abandoned the plan in January 2011.

Proposals to seal or even "secure" the border with Mexico are unrealistic. The logistics of attempting to prevent incursions along the nearly 2,000-mile-long land border with that country would be prohibitively difficult.[37] Not only would that goal require building the North American equivalent of the Berlin Wall, it would entail stationing tens of thousands of trained military personnel to guard it and prevent breaches. Clearly, the more limited measures, such as the existence of flimsy fences and periodic appearances by the U.S. Border Patrol, have not worked. Even the limited deployment of National Guard troops makes little difference. Hundreds of thousands of unauthorized immigrants cross the border into remote sectors of the southwestern states each year. Professional drug traffickers are not going to be stymied by such systems when ordinary immigrants are not.

Even if it were possible to seal the land border at ground level, the trafficking organizations have ingenious ways of coping. On numerous occasions, U.S. authorities have detected tunnels underneath the border. Some of those facilities are incredibly sophisticated, with electric lights, rail tracks, and sometimes even air conditioning. Controlling the border above ground is no guarantee that it will be controlled below ground.

Aside from the problem of dealing with the passage of drugs and violent criminals through the land border, traffickers can bypass it entirely and enter the United States through the lengthy coastline in the Gulf of Mexico or along the California coast. Given the modest strengthening of border security since the September 11 terrorist attacks, smugglers have already focused more on the sea routes. Just between 2007 and 2009, there was a sevenfold increase in maritime drug seizures.[38] In just a one-month period in the summer of 2009, the Mexican navy made two huge seizures of cocaine from ships in the Pacific corridor, including a 7.5-ton shipment aboard two speed boats. A second incident illustrated the creativity of smugglers, in which the navy intercepted a container ship carrying 30 cocaine-laden frozen sharks.

In addition to using speed boats (the most common method) and container ships, the Mexican cartels have begun to emulate their Colombian colleagues by utilizing submarines to bring their product to market.[39] Until recently, such vessels were relatively primitive affairs—small semi-submersibles equipped with air intake and engine exhaust pipes, which meant that such craft could not fully submerge and thereby avoid radar and other technology that drug interdiction aircraft utilize. But in July 2010, it became clear that traffickers had made a huge jump in their smuggling capabilities. Ecuadorean police discovered a shipyard on a coastal estuary near the Colombian border where a new 110-foot, twin-screw diesel submarine was under construction. Not only was such a submarine capable of carrying a larger cargo than any of its predecessors, it had a conning tower, periscope, and air conditioning. It could carry 10 metric tons of cargo, with a crew of at least five, and had a range of many hundreds of miles. Most important, it was fully submersible, enabling it to evade air patrols.[40] Although one of the Colombian trafficking organizations apparently commissioned that vessel, the even better-financed Mexican cartels could easily gain access to the same technology.

There are also many low-tech methods of utilizing the sea routes. One enterprising smuggler was caught in June 2009 paddling north on a surfboard with a duffel bag full of marijuana on board. Numerous low-tech options exist with respect to getting drugs across the land border as well. Using inoffensive Mexican and Central American migrants as drug "mules" is by far the most common technique, but it's hardly the only one. Authorities discovered an especially weird scheme in January 2011 when, acting on aerial surveillance information from the U.S. Border Patrol, Mexican troops captured a metal-framed catapult along the Arizona border. This 10-foot high device, utilizing a powerful elastic band, was capable of hurling four-to-five pound bags of marijuana hundreds of feet over the border fence into U.S. territory. Some observers described it as a scene out of a Monty Python movie, and one bemused U.S. agent admitted, "I have not seen anything like that in my time as a Border Patrol agent."[41] It was assuredly not the most sophisticated smuggling technique ever devised, but it illustrated the nearly inexhaustible creativity of drug smugglers.

On the more practical front, traffickers can circumvent fences and border checkpoints by evading radar and flying over the border in small planes. Indeed, the cartels seem to maintain a veritable fleet of such planes to bring shipments into the United States.[42] That is not even a new technique. Drug trafficking organizations were utilizing such aircraft on an extensive basis at least as far back as the 1980s. Mexico's leading smuggler during the 1980s and 1990s did not earn the moniker "lord of the skies" for nothing.

And if drug shipments can filter into the United States through (or over or under) the land border or along the coastlines, so, too, can professional cartel hit men. Attempts to secure the border with Mexico to keep out drugs and criminals are akin to trying to build a modern version of the Maginot Line. That plan did not stymie mobile German military forces and save France in 1940, and schemes to seal the border will fare no better with respect to the drug cartels in the 21st century.

The immensity of the task means that proposals to seal the border are at least as futile as the calls to stop the southward flow of guns as a solution to the problems of drug trafficking and drug-related violence. There is also the matter of unintended side effects of beefing-up border security. The United States and Mexico have extensive legitimate commercial ties, with the annual bilateral trade in goods and services exceeding $400 billion. Mexico is the third-largest trading partner of the United States, and much of that flow comes through the various border crossings. If measures to greatly enhance border security lead to miles-long tie-ups at those crossings—and some of that has already occurred—there are adverse consequences to the vital economic relationship. One cannot impede traffickers from bringing their product into the United States without simultaneously impeding legal commerce. Unfortunately, most advocates of securing the border rarely address that trade-off.

Moves to tighten border security involve other unintended, and even more unpleasant, side effects. For example, putting more armed Border Patrol or National Guard personnel on the frontier with Mexico is bound to lead to incidents in which innocent civilians are injured or killed. A tragic example occurred in June 2010 with an altercation between a group of Mexican teenagers and Border Patrol officers who were trying to detain some illegal immigrants in El Paso, close to a border crossing. According to the Border Patrol, the teens directed a barrage of rocks at the officers, and the missiles chosen grew steadily in size. One agent, allegedly fearing for the safety of himself and his colleagues, responded by opening fire and hitting a 15-year-old Mexican boy, Sergio Adrián Hernández Huereca. The wounded boy staggered back across the border, dying on the Mexican side.

Both the Mexican public and the Calderón administration reacted with fury to the shooting, accusing the Border Patrol of using excessive force. And a cell-phone video surfaced that cast serious doubt on the official account.[43] Moreover, it was the second time in eight days that a Mexican citizen had been killed at the international border by U.S. authorities. On May 31, 2010, Anastasio Hernández, a Mexican migrant, died while crossing into the United States along a stretch between Tijuana and San Diego when a border agent shocked him with a stun gun. An unpleasant diplomatic incident ensued from those two killings.[44]

A proliferation of such episodes will be a likely consequence of attempting to secure the border. Militarizing the border by deploying additional National Guard troops will certainly lead to that result. Military personnel are conditioned to respond with deadly force to threatening situations. Police are trained to use the minimum force necessary; soldiers, not so much. And Mexican nationals are not the only ones who may be put at risk if the border becomes a militarized zone.

That point was demonstrated more than a decade ago by an ugly episode in south Texas. On a spring day in 1997, an 18-year-old Mexican-American named Esequiel Hernández was herding his goats when he encountered a U.S. Marine anti-drug training patrol. Members of the patrol saw that he was carrying a rifle (which is perfectly lawful in Texas). What happened next is not entirely clear. The Marines claimed that Hernández fired two shots in their direction, and when they then followed him, he again raised his rifle in a threatening manner. A corporal opened fire, killing him.

At no point did any evidence emerge that the goat herder was involved in the drug trade or any other illegal activity. Despite its initial efforts to defend the Marine's actions, the government eventually settled a wrongful-death suit with the Hernández family for $1.9 million.[45]

Even if most border security personnel do not prove trigger happy, tensions and dangers along the border are likely to rise, and innocent people are likely to die. Perhaps Americans are willing to pay that price to try to thwart the drug cartels, reduce the flow of illegal immigration, and gain greater control over our porous southern border. But it is important at least to recognize that there will be costs in blood as well as treasure. And even by militarizing the border, there is no guarantee that any of the goals—much less all of them—will be achieved.

Bogus Solution: Drastically Reduce Demand for Illegal Drugs in the United States

Equally unrealistic is the goal of massively reducing the demand for drugs in the United States. That's not to say that drug consumption is destined to head higher or even stay at current levels. Indeed, there is strong evidence that consumption levels, especially among more casual users, have already come down from peak levels in the

1970s and early 1980s for harder drugs, most notably cocaine. That general trend has been in place, marked by occasional reversals, since the early 1980s, although a majority of the decline occurred during the first decade or so of the period from 1980 to 2010.[46] According to government surveys, the number of Americans age 12 or older who used cocaine during the previous year peaked in 1982 at just over 10.45 million. By 1995, the number bottomed out at 3.66 million. The trend since then has been flat to slightly up. The number of such users in 2009 was 4.97 million. The trend line for heroin use is considerably narrower. The number of users in 2008, at 453,000, wasn't much different from the 456,000 users in 2001, or the 427,000 users in 1979—when the government first began to provide consistent data—and it was somewhat lower than the spikes of 508,000 in 1988 and 597,000 in 1997.

Despite the modest uptick in the overall consumption of hard drugs since the mid-1990s, the recreational use of those drugs, especially cocaine, is not nearly as trendy as it seemed from the late 1960s to the early 1980s. There is no credible evidence that the more cautious attitudes among casual users regarding harder drugs are going to change anytime soon.

That development is all to the good, but there are two important caveats. First, the decline in consumption has almost nothing to do with successfully stemming the supply of illegal drugs coming out of key sources like the Andean countries and Mexico. For example, the amount of cocaine produced collectively by Colombia, Peru, and Bolivia was 775 metric tons in 1990. It was 705 metric tons in 2008, and there were considerable variations in the intervening years. For instance, in the total was 715 tons in 1993, virtually the same as in 2008. But in 2005, it was 855 metric tons, considerably more than either end of the time period. In 2000, it was 727 tons, somewhat toward the lower end of the range.[47] Such gyrations aside, the bottom line is that there has been no meaningful, sustained victory from supply-side campaigns to reduce the available quantity of drugs on the retail market. The flow from drug source countries to the U.S. market is as vigorous as ever.

Instead, the decline in usage of hard drugs among casual consumers appears to have been the result of two factors that reinforced each other. The first factor was the effectiveness of campaigns to educate Americans about the very real adverse health consequences of using such drugs. For example, only the most naive individuals today believe that cocaine is a relatively harmless recreational drug; the attitude was very different three decades ago. The second factor consisted of demographic changes that facilitated the disenchantment with hard drugs. People, especially unmarried people in their teens and twenties, are the most inclined to engage in drug use or other daring, risky behavior. Older, more mature individuals are far less likely to engage in such conduct, especially if they marry and have children. Americans who may have spent some of their time in a drug-induced haze in their youth are usually a bit chagrined about that skeleton in their closet, and they're not eager to see their children follow the same path.

The demographic factor is important, because the huge population bulge known as the post–World War II baby boom passed through its teens and twenties during the 1960s, 1970s, and early 1980s. Even the youngest members of that cohort are now in their late forties, and the oldest members are in their early or mid-sixties. One would not expect a tremendous amount of illegal drug use from people in those age brackets. A modest decline in drug use was quite predictable, given the population dynamics.

A second caveat is that the majority of the decline in consumption seems to have reflected a greater wariness about hard drugs among occasional recreational users. It is a sobering reality that much of that drop has been offset by an increase in consumption by more hard-core users. And the aversion to marijuana among casual users is far less pronounced than the disenchantment with cocaine. (The children and grandchildren of the baby boomers may be more skittish about cocaine, LSD, and even meth, than their elders were, but that does not seem to apply to marijuana.) The number of marijuana users in 2009 was 28.52 million, just slightly below the peak of 29.87 million three decades earlier.

The "easy" part of the campaign to reduce the consumption of illegal drugs in the United States is largely over. Expectations that the solution to the problem of corruption and violence in Mexico lies in achieving a massive reduction in drug consumption in the United States are not likely to be realized. Given the context of the decline that has occurred, a further significant drop in usage is improbable. Among other reasons, the demographics do not favor such a trend. Indeed, a small but measurable upturn in the number of Americans in the most risk-tolerant age brackets over the next two decades suggests that a slight increase in consumption is more likely than an additional decrease. We may already be seeing that factor at work in the rebound in marijuana usage. Because that demographic growth is occurring disproportionately among lower-income groups, especially lower-income racial and ethnic minorities in which drug use rates are higher than the national average, the probability of a continuing reversal of the decline that began in the early 1980s is even more likely.

In short, those who are looking for a collapse of demand in the United States to weaken the Mexican drug cartels and reduce their power are basing their hopes on an illusion. And even in the unlikely event that U.S. demand did plummet, the beneficial impact would be far less than optimists suppose. As noted in chapter 10, the U.S. market is only one part—albeit the most important part—of a large global market for the consumption of illicit drugs. True, the U.S. market is especially important to the Mexican cartels, but the global market is growing at a brisk rate, and those organizations are moving to exploit that growth. The bottom line is that even if demand declined further in the United States, there are enough current and potential customers elsewhere in the world to make the trafficking business very profitable. Demand reduction in the United States is not a meaningful strategy for undercutting the power of the Mexican drug cartels and providing a solution to the violence in that unhappy country.

Beyond the impracticality of hoping for a decline in overall U.S. consumption, far too many crusaders against illegal drugs want to blame users for all the negative effects of the drug trade. Bill Gore, the former special agent in charge of the FBI's San Diego office, and now the county's undersheriff, typified that mentality in an interview with CBS News. American drug users should realize that they have blood on their hands because of their continuing, stubborn consumption of illegal drugs, according to Gore. "This is not a victimless crime," he thundered. "People are dying, literally hundreds of them, so they [the users] can have their recreational drugs on this side of the border."[48]

That was a classic case of missing the point. Gore apparently did not even consider the possibility that the violence in Mexico is the outcome of drug prohibition, not the mere consumption of drugs.

237

The consumption of beer and whiskey by Americans during the 1920s and early 1930s was not responsible for the bloody shootouts that took place on the streets of Chicago, New York, St. Louis, and other cities during those years. When drinking was legal, both before and after the Prohibition era, such orgies of violence did not occur. Driving the trade underground, into the hands of criminal elements, was the real cause of the carnage.

A similar dynamic applies to the drug-related violence in Mexico today. When Gore and other drug warriors in Mexico and the United States try to blame users for the bloodshed south of the border, they ignore both logic and decades of evidence. A better case can be made that prohibitionist advocates, not drug consumers, have blood on their hands.

The first step in developing a coherent strategy to dampen the violence in Mexico and weaken the power of the cartels is to bury the assortment of bogus explanations and equally bogus proposed solutions. Unfortunately, the trend seems to be in the opposite direction—to embrace multiple myths simultaneously. Secretary of State Clinton epitomized that trend during a trip to Mexico in March 2009. "Our insatiable demand for illegal drugs fuels the drug trade," she said on her arrival in Mexico City, adding that "our inability to prevent weapons from being illegally smuggled across the border to arm these criminals causes the deaths of police officers, soldiers, and civilians."[49]

The focus on superficially appealing, but ultimately fallacious, diagnoses for Mexico's corruption and violence wastes time and energy. There are no easy solutions to those terrible problems, because their roots lie in powerful economic factors combined with the country's institutional limitations and a variety of cultural factors, including a tendency in some communities to romanticize drug traffickers. Blaming Mexico's woes on U.S. gun laws or the continuing demand for illegal drugs north of the Rio Grande may be good domestic politics for that country's leaders, since it deflects at least some of the growing public dissatisfaction with the government in Mexico City. It may even be effective diplomacy for Washington to embrace those myths as a way to placate the Calderón administration and Mexican public opinion. But such use of scapegoats does not bring anyone closer to a real strategy to dampen the turmoil and weaken the dangerous, well-armed cartels. Likewise, Americans who grasp for a panacea such as schemes to seal the border merely delay the process of finding worthwhile, albeit imperfect, policies that might at least ameliorate the agony that is gripping Mexico. The wishful thinking and political posturing on both sides of the border has gone on far too long.

10. Biting the Bullet: Defunding the Cartels

The robust nature of global consumption of illegal drugs makes efforts to combat traffickers in Mexico and other source countries at best a brutally uphill struggle, and, at worst, a futile, utopian crusade. As noted in chapter four, the trade in illicit drugs is estimated to be at least $320 billion a year–and the actual amount could be much larger. Mexico is now the single most important theater in that commerce. That country is involved in almost every phase of the illegal drug trade, and dominates many of those phases. At the basic supply end, for example, Mexico is a major factor in the marijuana and cocaine business. A large region in southern Chihuahua, along the borders with Sinaloa and Durango, is now often called Mexico's Golden Triangle–reminiscent of the same term for the opium-producing center in Southeast Asia. One-third of the population in Mexico's Golden Triangle is estimated to receive its primary income from the illegal drug trade.[1]

Mexican traffickers also still derive considerable revenues from transporting and distributing cocaine and other drugs from the Andean countries, which were formerly the dominant suppliers. And Mexican entrepreneurs have become the leading purveyors of methamphetamine, which is perhaps the fastest growing drug in popularity in retail markets in the United States and some other countries. All in all, the Mexican cartels control a major chunk of the more than $300 billion a year, illicit—but very profitable—commerce.

The frustration of Mexican officials at the extent of the demand in the United States repeatedly boils over. President Calderón fumed that the demand is strengthening the cartels and fueling the violence in his country. In a June 2010 manifesto justifying his administration's military-led offensive against traffickers, Calderón asserted that "the origin of our problem of violence lies primarily with the fact that Mexico is located next to the country that has the biggest consumption of drugs worldwide. It is as if we had a neighbor next door who is the biggest addict in the world, with the aggravating factor that everyone wants to sell drugs through our house."[2] The cartels had grown rich and bold, he wrote, because of billions of dollars in profits flowing to them from U.S. consumers.[3] U.S. officials adopt a similar view. "Our insatiable demand for illegal drugs fuels the drug trade," Secretary of State Hillary Clinton told her Mexican hosts in March 2009.[4]

Yet as noted in chapter 9, U.S. demand is only one part of the equation. Even a dedicated drug warrior like former DEA chief Robert C. Bonner concedes that point, noting that the major markets for the Mexican cartels "are not just in the United States but also in Mexico itself and as far away as Europe."[5] Bonner actually understates the breadth of the problem. The Mexican organizations are taking control of trafficking routes and gaining access to potential markets in portions of sub-Saharan Africa and the Middle East, as well as in Europe.

Although the United States is the largest single retail market, U.S. demand is not the only relevant factor. The American market is actually relatively mature, with overall consumption not substantially different from what it was a decade, or even two decades, ago. The main areas of demand growth are in Eastern Europe, the successor states of the former Soviet Union, and some portions of the Middle East and Latin America. According to the United Nations, there has been a noticeable increase in the consumption of opiates throughout Eastern Europe and central Asia, especially in the former Soviet states. In Western Europe, the principal increase has been in the use of cocaine.[6] The trend of cocaine flows to Western and Central Europe is typical and sobering. In 1998, some 63 metric tons of that drug made its way to that region. By 2008, the total was 126 metric tons.[7] The Gulf cartel concluded in 2009 that market opportunities in Europe justified establishing a more extensive organizational presence on that continent. Among other steps, the cartel formed an alliance with Italy's powerful Ndrangheta organized-crime group.[8]

In the Middle East, even such a politically authoritarian and religiously conservative society as Iran is witnessing a surge in both drug trafficking and drug use, especially of heroin. Several years ago, that problem had already reached the point that the Supreme Leader's representative in one province labeled drug abuse and trafficking Iranian society's "thorniest problem."[9] Iran sometimes executes accused drug traffickers, but there is no credible evidence that even such a draconian penalty has significantly dampened drug use in that country.

The bottom line is that demand for illegal drugs on a global basis is robust and is likely to remain so. Drug cartels are profit-maximizing businesses, and the persistence of demand in the United States, combined with growth in demand elsewhere, creates an irresistible opportunity. Only if the United States abandons prohibition would at least some of the governments in other major consumer countries follow suit, thereby dramatically reducing the revenues the cartels enjoy. Without that policy change, the Mexican drug organizations will continue to operate in an extremely profitable environment.

That sobering reality has ominous implications for the strategy that advocates of a "war" on drugs continue to push. Their strategy has long had two major components. The first is to shut off the flow of drugs coming from drug source countries, through various methods of drug crop eradication, developmental aid to promote alternative economic opportunities, interdiction of drug shipments, and suppression of money-laundering activities. The second component is to significantly reduce demand in the United States through a combination of criminal sanctions, drug treatment programs, and anti-drug educational campaigns.

As discussed in chapter 9, efforts at domestic demand reduction have achieved only modest results, and most of them have come from the gradual impact of educational efforts about the dangerous health effects of hard drugs. The supply-side component of the drug war has been even less effective.[10] Moreover, with global demand continuing to increase, even if drug warriors succeeded in their goal of more substantially reducing consumption in the United States, it would have only a limited adverse impact on trafficking organizations. There is more than enough demand globally to attract and sustain traffickers who are willing to take the risks to satisfy that demand. And since the illegality of the trade creates a bloated black-market premium (depending on the drug, 90 percent or more of the retail price), the potential profits to drug trafficking organizations are astronomical. Thus, the supply-side strategy attempts to defy the basic laws of economics, with predictable results. It is a fatally flawed strategy, and Washington's insistence on continuing it causes serious problems of corruption and violence for a key drug source and drug transiting country such as Mexico.

That raises the question of whether the current strategy—or an enhanced version—has any chance at all of defeating the Mexican drug cartels. Despite mounting evidence to the contrary, drug warriors contend that the strategy can work, and they point to developments in another leading drug source country, Colombia, as a model of what should be done—and what can be accomplished—in Mexico.[11] Two questions immediately arise: Is Colombia really a shining beacon of success in the war on drugs, as admirers assert? And even if it is, are the conditions in Mexico sufficiently similar so that Colombia's success could be replicated there? There are major doubts about both points.

Colombia: Model or Illusion?

Robert Bonner, who directed the Drug Enforcement Administration during President George W. Bush's first term, makes one of the stronger arguments that Mexico can dampen the drug-related violence the same way Colombia did. His assertion is straight forward and optimistic:

> Destroying the drug cartels is not an impossible task. Two decades ago, Colombia was faced with a similar—and in many ways more daunting—challenge. In the early 1990s, many Colombians, including police officers, judges, presidential candidates, and journalists, were assassinated by the most powerful and fearsome drug-trafficking organizations the world has ever seen: the Cali and Medellín cartels. Yet within a decade, the Colombian government defeated them, with Washington's help.[12]

Bonner is correct—as far as he goes. But the success story in Colombia is neither as simple nor as complete as he (and others who make similar arguments) wants us to believe.

The overall level of violence in Colombia during the 1980s and early 1990s was indeed even greater than it is in Mexico today. But the context was different in crucial ways. Although much of the violence came from the drug cartels, especially after the Medellín cartel declared war on the Colombian state in 1984 and drug lord

Pablo Escobar surged to the height of his power, the drug traffickers were not the only source. There was also a political and ideological war being waged between the Colombian government and two radical leftist insurgent groups, the Revolutionary Armed Forces of Colombia (FARC) and the smaller, but still deadly, National Liberation Army (ELN).

During the early 1980s, the insurgency was largely confined to the countryside and jungles, so the levels of violence remained modest. But in the 1990s, at the time the power of the Medellín and Cali cartels was fading, the guerrillas expanded their assaults to the urban areas. That, in turn, led to a growth in the number and size of right-wing paramilitary organizations, and the fighting between those groups and FARC-ELN forces caused the violence to increase. While drug traffickers were often in alliance with one or more of those contending factions, the capos were not the only—or in many cases, even the primary—sources of the violence plaguing the country.

In today's Mexico, though, the drug cartels are overwhelmingly the source of the carnage. That distinction is important, because the violence in Colombia did not really subside until Álvaro Uribe became president in 2002 and went far beyond the efforts of his predecessors to wage war against the FARC and the ELN. The counterinsurgency campaigns of earlier governments had been desultory and largely defensive in nature. Uribe's campaign was vigorous and aggressive, and it produced positive results.

He was also lucky because of unusually favorable regional conditions. Not only were the leftist insurgents weakened by infighting and an aging leadership, but the external support that they had enjoyed from the Soviet Union, Cuba, and Nicaragua had faded. The Soviet Union had imploded a decade earlier, so that source was gone. Cuba's loss of Soviet support, in turn, inhibited its own ability to foment leftist revolutions in the Western Hemisphere. Nicaragua's Sandinista regime was out of power and would remain so for several more years. The left-wing government of Hugo Chávez in neighboring Venezuela would eventually become a troublesome source of support for the FARC, but during the early years of Uribe's administration, the meddling from Caracas was limited. (Now that Chávez is more proactive in aiding the FARC, its power is experiencing something of a rebound, creating growing concerns in Bogotá.)

As the threat that the Marxist groups posed started to wane, Uribe prevailed on the right-wing paramilitaries to lower their profiles and let the government take the lead in counterinsurgency efforts. Those two developments—the decline of the FARC and ELN and the restraint of the paramilitaries—led to a dramatic drop in the overall violence.

Consequently, Bonner's argument that the decline in violence was largely due to the defeat of the Medellín and Cali cartels does not hold water. As Bonner himself argues, the Medellín cartel "was obliterated by the end of 1993, and the coup de grâce was the killing of Escobar."[13] The Cali cartel was effectively destroyed by the end of 1996, yet the violence went on. Indeed, it was still so bad in 2000 that the United States proposed and funded Plan Colombia, a multibillion dollar, multiyear program to counteract the threat that drug trafficking posed to that country and its neighbors. Bonner, and others who see the defeat of the Medellín and Cali cartels as a model for defeating the Mexican cartels and ending the scourge of violence in that country, need to explain why the violence in Colombia did not substantially subside until nearly a decade after the Medellín and Cali organizations were history.

There is another problem with the assumption that the Colombian strategy can be applied to Mexico. Bonner asserts that Bogotá was wise to wage war on one cartel at a time instead of trying to take on both simultaneously. But once again, the context in Mexico is different, and it is far more daunting. The Medellín and Cali cartels dominated the illegal drug trade throughout the 1980s and early 1990s, and within Colombia itself, they had no serious competitors.

But the drug trade in Mexico is more dispersed. At the moment, the Sinaloa and Gulf cartels appear to be the leading players, but they hardly enjoy the kind of dominance the Medellín and Cali organizations did in their heyday. Indeed, both the Sinaloa and Gulf cartels are fighting several very aggressive competitors just to hold on to their leading positions. The Zetas especially seem to be on the rise, and have already significantly eaten into the territory and power of the Gulf cartel. And such groups as the Beltrán Leyva and Juárez cartels (and La Familia's successor factions), although weaker than they once were, are still serious competitors. So the task facing the Mexican government and its allies in Washington is not merely to defeat two cartels, as was the challenge in Colombia, but to defeat multiple powerful organizations.

Bonner emphasizes that in Colombia, the drug trafficking groups that filled the vacuum created when the Cali and Medellín cartels were destroyed "are smaller, more fragmented, and far less powerful—and, most important, they no longer pose a threat to Colombian national security."[14] But according to that standard, the situation in Mexico should be getting much better, not steadily worse. The illegal drug trade there is *already* fragmented in a way that it never was in Colombia during the 1980s and early 1990s.

In fact, Mexican authorities have defeated the leading cartels of the day on numerous occasions. At one time, such groups as the Guadalajara, Tijuana, and Juárez cartels were the most powerful players. They are now either secondary factors or have completely unraveled, yet their successors are just as successful. And the newer lead players seem to be even more violent and pose an even greater threat to the Mexican state. The notion that Mexico can duplicate Colombia's victory over the Medellín and Cali cartels in a very different, much more challenging, environment is at best overly optimistic.

Yet U.S., Mexican, and Colombian officials act as though the Colombian model that extinguished those cartels can be used as a template for dealing with the situation in Mexico. "Mexico has what we had some years ago, which are very powerful cartels," Colombian president Juan Manuel Santos stated. "What we can provide is the experience that we have had dismantling those cartels."[15] Over the past few years, some 7,000 Mexican security forces have received training from their Colombian counterparts. Much of that training has been conducted by Colombia's police commandos, who had leading roles in the armed struggles against leftist guerrillas and drug traffickers. Washington is paying for part of that training, apparently as an alternative to sending large numbers of U.S. police and military personnel to Mexico for such a mission—something that most Mexicans would regard as politically very sensitive.

To his credit, Bonner does not overstate the breadth of the "success" in Colombia the way some others do, who insist that Colombia can be a model for defeating the drug cartels in Mexico.[16] He emphasizes that in Colombia, "the objective was to dismantle and destroy the Cali and Medellín cartels—not to prevent drugs from being smuggled into the United States or to end their consumption." He fully acknowledges that "there are still drug traffickers in Colombia, and cocaine is still produced there."[17]

That is something of an understatement. A 2008 report from the Government Accountability Office showed that cocaine exports from Colombia had actually *increased* since the end of the 1990s, and that flow eased just marginally over the next three years, from 2008 to 2010. Overall coca cultivation in 2010 (116,000 hectares) was just slightly below what it was in 1999 (125,500 hectares).[18] Moreover, even that modest drop was more than offset by the increase in crop yields from the acreage that was planted.

But the distinction between drug trafficking and drug violence may point the way to at least a partial solution to Mexico's problem. By focusing on containing the violence, rather than trying to stem the flow of drugs, the Uribe government managed to bring at least some measure of peace to Colombia. It certainly appears that throughout Uribe's administration, Bogotá did just enough on the anti-trafficking front to placate Washington without provoking the traffickers to the extent of disrupting a relatively stable domestic environment. Even with such restraint, the level of violence in Colombia is beginning to rebound. According to a February 2011 UN report, there was a 40 percent rise in massacres in 2010, mostly attributed to new drug gangs that have arisen.[19]

There is one other problem with the Colombian model, especially the version that emerged following the adoption of Plan Colombia in 2000 and the election of Álvaro Uribe in 2002. A widening investigation by the Colombian attorney general's office has uncovered some disturbing information about Plan Colombia and the conduct of Uribe's administration. An August 20, 2011, story by Karen De Young and Claudia J. Duque in the *Washington Post* stated, "American cash, equipment and training, supplied to elite units of the Colombian intelligence service over the past decade to help smash cocaine-trafficking rings, were used to carry out spying operations and smear campaigns against Supreme Court justices, Uribe's political opponents, and civil society groups."[20]

Indeed, six former high-level officials of Colombia's Department of Administrative Security had already confessed to such abuses of power, and more than a dozen others were currently on trial. The investigation keeps expanding, now bringing several top political aides of Uribe—and even the former president himself—under scrutiny. The burgeoning scandal in Colombia should be a cautionary tale to those who advocate using the same approach to bring down the Mexican drug cartels.

Is an Appeasement Policy Feasible in Mexico?

Another suggested approach to tame the drug violence in Mexico is the adoption of a policy of accommodation or appeasement. That was the essence of the proposal put forth in 2008 by Calderón's former director of communications, Rubén Aguilar, which former president Vicente Fox now urges the government to consider. (See chapter 6.) Doing so would be an attempt to return the country to the situation that existed during the era of political dominance by the Institutional Revolutionary Party (PRI). Yet prospects for a successful deal along those lines are not favorable, even if Calderón and other hard-line types would countenance it—which seems very unlikely.

First of all, the Mexican cartels are extremely powerful, and several of them seem intent on achieving both dominance in the illegal drug trade and invulnerability from the authority of the Mexican government. Reaching even an implicit agreement with such strong and violent actors would be a major challenge. After all, Bogotá was never able to achieve a modus vivendi with the Medellín and Cali organizations. During their heyday, neither cartel was interested in a compromise with the Colombian government. Only their weaker and fragmented successors seem willing to mute their challenge to the state. It's hard to imagine that Mexico's leading cartels, which are growing ever more powerful, would have much interest in such a deal with the Mexican government.

Mexico's fractious multiparty system makes it even less likely that officials can engineer a return to the status quo ante under the PRI. That arrangement worked precisely because the PRI was the only meaningful political actor in the country. Drug lords knew that as long as they kept the money flowing to PRI appointees, they could conduct their commercial activities with a minimum of disruption. The current and prospective political environments make such calculations far less reliable. Even if a cartel successfully bribes a PAN official in a city or state, for example, the next election could bring a PRI or PRD leader to power with a whole new set of appointees, and the process would have to begin all over again. Hedging political bets requires traffickers to bribe multiple political factions, significantly raising the financial costs, and making that approach less secure. Given the underlying political uncertainty, the cartels are not likely to let their robust enforcement branches atrophy merely based on a promise—and perhaps a purely temporary one at that—of government restraint.

Mexico's political leaders could perhaps act as the brokers in a market-sharing arrangement among the cartels. But the existence of so many powerful trafficking organizations would make such an arrangement inherently unstable—even in the unlikely event that that bloody rivals could reach an initial agreement. The number of powerful players is too large, the Mexican political system too multipolar, and the prize of the U.S. consumer market for illegal drugs is both too large and too near to make an appeasement policy a workable option over the long term. There are huge obstacles to returning to the relatively stable period of accommodation between the Mexican government and the drug traffickers during the PRI era. Too much has changed—politically, economically, and socially—in the past decade.

At best, an appeasement policy, even if it could be reached, would probably buy Mexico a precarious, short-lived truce. And even that would require the tacit consent of the United States, something that is not likely to be forthcoming from Washington. After all, the adoption of an appeasement policy by Mexican authorities would mean that the flow of illegal drugs into the United States would be unimpeded. It would also mean that the drug kingpins that U.S. drug warriors have pursued for years would effectively be off-limits. It is hard to imagine the U.S. government accepting, much less approving, such an arrangement.

Other "Band-Aid" Solutions

Even without an appeasement policy by Mexico City, though, there are other developments that could lead to a temporary decline in the country's awful violence. One scenario would be if the cartels agreed to a truce among themselves and at least moderated their turf fights. There are precedents for that step, although just local ones. Perhaps the most notable episode was a tacit truce in 2007 between the Sinaloa and Gulf cartels that led to a sharp drop off in killings in Nuevo Laredo. As one analyst put it, the warring factions "weakened by their own casualties" and under pressure from the Calderón government, "made a prudent business decision." Will Glasby, a special agent for the U.S. Drug Enforcement Administration, concluded, "They weren't making money at that point." Consequently, the cartels realized that they were spending more time waging a war against each other instead of focusing on getting their product to market and "they were losing members on a daily basis through executions [and] assassinations."[21] According to Glasby, under the cease-fire agreement, the Sinaloans paid a tax to the Gulf cartel to use the border crossing between Nuevo Laredo and Laredo, Texas.

But as Glasby and others admit, the cartels have certainly not gone away, and the flow of drugs through that area remains as brisk as it ever was. Indeed, Nuevo Laredo "reverted to an earlier model: The traffickers smuggle their cocaine and marijuana across the river, mostly mind their own business, and Mexican authorities—some of whom are on the take—look the other way."[22] Even so, the inter-cartel fighting in and around Nuevo Laredo has heated up again in the past year or so.

Similar truces and informal market-sharing agreements have occurred from time to time in U.S. cities over the years. And as the turf fights wane, the number of killings go down as well. That pattern occurred in Washington, D. C., beginning in the early 1990s. The homicide rate peaked in 1991 with 474 deaths and then declined throughout the next two decades. By 2010, the number of murders was down to 131.

The main problem with hoping that such truces solve the problem of drug violence is that they rarely last. Either one faction (or more) cheats and the turf fights resume, or a new entrant tries to forcibly gain a share of the market. That would likely prove to be the pattern in Mexico as well—even assuming that the leading cartels were able to broker a nationwide truce.

A final possibility for a temporary fix would be if one Mexican cartel became utterly dominant and could control the trafficking routes without having to fend off rivals. But that is unlikely, since there are multiple very strong organizations in the mix. The Sinaloa cartel, Gulf cartel, and the Zetas are all roughly equal in power at the moment, and each one controls a major chunk of territory that gives it a reliable base of operations. The Mexican government's earlier focus on the Gulf cartel, and its more recent focus on the Zetas, has strengthened the relative position of the Sinaloa cartel, but even so, the latter organization is still a long way from having a de facto monopoly over the illegal drug trade. It is hard to picture a situation in which one of those three leading cartels could eliminate the other two—plus the smaller, but still relevant, outfits such as the Juárez and Tijuana cartels and the splintered La Familia/Knights Templar.

Furthermore, a peaceful interlude created by the emergence of one cartel as a near monopoly would likely break down—just as a market-sharing agreement among rival gangs would do. Sooner or later, the dominant cartel would likely split, which is what happened when the Beltrán Leyva branch broke off from El Chapo Guzmán's Sinaloa organization a few years ago. Or entirely new, ambitious competitors would emerge to seek the vast profits that exist in the global black market, and the cycle of violence would begin again. Tens of billions of dollars per year in potential revenues is a mighty powerful temptation.

The reality is that as long as the global (especially U.S.) prohibitionist policy remains intact, there is no good outcome for Mexico. But are U.S. officials and opinion leaders prepared to consider abandoning drug prohibition? And even if they were, would they be wise to do so?

The Legalization Model: Snare or Solution?

Given the healthy state of global demand for illegal drugs, there is little prospect of ending—or even substantially reducing—the trade in them. And prospects for fragmenting or otherwise weakening the Mexican cartels to the point that they pose a lesser security threat to Mexico and the United States are just marginally better. The disappointing four-decade-old record of the war on drugs has led more and more knowledgeable people to argue that there is only one policy change that would have a meaningful beneficial impact: ending the prohibitionist strategy and legalizing currently illegal drugs. Needless to say, though, that remains an extremely controversial proposal.

The brutal reality is that prohibition simply drives commerce in a product underground, creating an enormous black-market potential profit that attracts violence-prone criminal elements. Even the U.S. State Department has conceded that point, although it remains staunchly committed to a prohibitionist strategy:

> Drug organizations possess and wield the ultimate instrument of corruption: money. The drug trade has access to almost unimaginable quantities of it. No commodity is so widely available, so cheap to produce, and as easily renewable as illegal drugs. They offer dazzling profit margins that allow criminals to generate illicit revenues on a scale without historical precedent.[23]

That is the depressing, unassailable point. And it needs to be asked whether a policy that puts literally hundreds of billions of dollars per year on a global basis into the hands of organized crime is a sensible policy, whatever the rationale or motives.

Defenders of the current policy, when pressed, usually concede that there are problems, but they insist that the unintended side effects of legalization would be even worse. The Drug Enforcement Administration contends that legalization would lead to much greater drug use and levels of addiction. An especially worrisome aspect of the DEA's reasoning is the agency's emphasis that use rates (and societal costs from addiction) are much higher for alcohol and tobacco, which are legal, than they are for currently illegal drugs.[24]

Such reasoning is flawed on multiple levels. The notion that usage rates among currently illegal drugs would rival those of alcohol and tobacco if prohibition were abandoned is shockingly simplistic. Personal preferences and cultural influences have major impacts on use rates for any substance; the legality-illegality aspect is only one factor among many. DEA analysts do not explain why usage levels for cocaine and heroin are much lower than those for marijuana, even though all of those drugs are strictly illegal. Clearly, some other factor plays a role.

Measuring societal costs of different mind-altering substances solely with respect to problems of addiction is also inherently misleading. That sort of analysis even leads the DEA to dismiss the widely held perception that the Prohibition era of the 1920s did not work as nothing more than a "myth." The agency arrives at that astonishing conclusion by emphasizing statistics showing that alcohol consumption levels and rates for drunkenness and alcohol-related diseases declined during Prohibition.[25]

But stressing those benefits without a full, candid acknowledgement of the societal "collateral damages" of Prohibition is akin to measuring the strength of a corporation by listing its assets while ignoring the liabilities side of the ledger. By that standard, Enron, WorldCom, Bear-Stearns, and AIG were all well-run, fabulously profitable enterprises. Yes, Prohibition "worked"—if one ignores the surge of corruption and violence that accompanied the "Noble Experiment." The DEA tries to finesse that problem by asserting that organized crime was around both before and after Prohibition, implying that outlawing alcohol had little effect on that problem. Such an impression is misleading at best. Rates of both corruption and violence at the hands of organized crime were dramatically higher during the 1920s than in the decades immediately preceding and following the Prohibition period.

The DEA's obsession with the social costs of legal drugs like alcohol and tobacco, combined with the agency's idealized version of the Prohibition era, creates the suspicion that at least some drug warriors might like to have another fling at banning liquor. At a minimum, their reasoning provides an insight into why they seem impervious to the ugly negative consequences of the current war on drugs.

Even the DEA's core argument—that use and addiction rates would soar if drugs were legalized—is deeply flawed. The most comprehensive drug reform—the one in Portugal, which is now a decade old, rebuts that thesis. After Portugal decriminalized the possession of all drugs, including cocaine and heroin, in July 2001, the predicted surge in usage and associated problems did not materialize. Glenn Greenwald, whose 2009 Cato Institute White Paper is a thorough study of Portugal's reform, notes that the empirical data "indicate that decriminalization has had no adverse effect on drug use rates in Portugal, which, in numerous categories, are now among the lowest in the EU, particularly when compared with states with stringent criminalization regimes." Moreover, while "postde-criminalization usage rates have remained roughly the same or even decreased slightly when compared with other EU states, drug-related pathologies—such as sexually transmitted diseases and deaths due to drug usage—have decreased dramatically."[26]

Those results stand in marked contrast to the parade of horrors that the DEA and other supporters of prohibition trot out every time even modest steps toward legalization or decriminalization are proposed. Moreover, even if there were a modest uptick in drug use following legalization, one would need to measure the resulting negative consequences against the array of negative consequences under drug prohibition. Even though our society has serious problems with alcoholism and drunk driving, few people outside the DEA and other citadels of drug war zealotry would argue that the system in the 1920s was, on balance, a better policy. By the same token, given the awful effects of the drug war in the United States and internationally, it is hard to imagine a system that would be worse.

Waning Support Around the World for the War on Drugs

Governments around the world seem to be gradually awakening to the problems caused by a strict prohibitionist strategy. Such countries as the Netherlands and Portugal have adopted decriminalization measures (de facto or de jure) for possession and use of small quantities of drugs.[27] Sentiment for such harm-reduction approaches is taking hold in the Western Hemisphere as well. The president of Argentina has endorsed the decriminalization of drug consumption, and the then-president of Honduras, Manuel Zelaya, went even further, embracing the legalization of drug use.[28]

A 2010 report by the Latin American Commission on Drugs and Democracy, the roster of which included more than a dozen former political leaders, diplomats, and other dignitaries, strongly criticized the war on drugs. Three leaders of that commission, former Brazilian president Fernando Henrique Cardoso, former Colombian president César Gaviria, and former Mexican president Ernesto Zedillo, subsequently published an op-ed in the *Wall Street Journal* highlighting those criticisms. They stated their thesis categorically: "The war on drugs has failed. And it's high time to replace an ineffective strategy with more humane and efficient drug policies. . . . Prohibitionist policies based on eradication, interdiction and criminalization of consumption simply haven't worked. Violence and the organized crime associated with the narcotics trade remain critical problems in our countries."[29]

A comprehensive report published in June 2011 by the Global Commission on Drug Policy reached a similar conclusion.[30] "The global war on drugs has failed, with devastating consequences for

255

individuals and societies around the world," the report stated flatly. The report went on: "Vast expenditures on criminalization and repressive measures directed at consumers of illegal drugs have clearly failed to effectively curtail supply or consumption. Apparent victories in eliminating one source or trafficking organization are negated instantly by the emergence of other sources and traffickers."[31] The commissioners urged governments to "break the taboo on debate and reform. The time for action is now."[32] Members of that blue-ribbon panel included four former heads of state, including President Cardoso; the then-prime minister of Greece, George Papandreou; former U.S. secretary of state George P. Shultz; former UN secretary general Kofi Annan; and former chairman of the Federal Reserve Paul Volcker.

Ernesto Zedillo's byline on the *Wall Street Journal* op-ed is just one indication that disenchantment with the drug war is growing within Mexico's political elite. The PRD, the third major political party in Mexico, has called for drug legalization, and even President Calderón embraced more-limited reform measures.[33] That campaign bore fruit in April 2009 when the Mexican congress enacted a bill that decriminalized possession of small amounts of illegal drugs, including not only marijuana but cocaine, ecstasy, heroin, and crystal meth. Calderón signed that bill into law in mid August. Under the new law, anyone caught with the equivalent of about as many as five marijuana joints or four lines of cocaine can no longer be arrested or fined—much less imprisoned. Police simply give them the address of a rehabilitation clinic and urge them to overcome their habit.[34]

Less than two weeks after Calderón signed Mexico's drug reform legislation, a similar result occurred in Argentina through the judicial process. In a case involving a criminal conviction for marijuana possession, the Argentine supreme court ruled that possession of a small quantity of the drug for personal consumption was an activity protected by a privacy-rights clause in the country's constitution. Any law to the contrary was deemed unconstitutional.

Former president Vicente Fox took the debate to a new level in August 2010—and stunned both Mexican and U.S. political leaders who had long considered him an adamant drug warrior. Bush administration officials had repeatedly praised Fox's cooperation with Washington's anti-drug efforts as significantly better than those of his predecessors. Writing in his blog on August 8, 2010,

Fox broke sharply with his previous positions. "We should consider legalizing the production, distribution, and sale of drugs," he wrote. Then he added a succinct, damning indictment of both Calderón's drug policies and those of his own administration: "Radical prohibition strategies have never worked."

Fox stressed that legalization did not imply that drugs were good or that they didn't harm those who consume them (although he did note that countries that had adopted serious drug law reforms had not experienced an explosion of either drug use or crime rates). But his reason for abandoning prohibition was based on a realistic assessment of economic realities. People should look at legalization, Fox argued, "as a strategy to strike at and break the economic structure that allows gangs to generate huge profits in their trade, which feeds corruption and increases their areas of power."[35]

Advocates of reform in the United States are understandably encouraged by such developments. Allen St. Pierre, who heads the National Organization for the Reform of Marijuana Laws, argued that Mexico's legislation reflects changing global attitudes regarding the criminalization of drug use. "Cultural social norms are shifting around the world and in the United States. There will likely come a point when the majority see that prohibition is expensive and simply doesn't work."[36]

Expensive it certainly is—for the taxpayers of the United States. Harvard University senior lecturer in economics Jeffrey A. Miron and New York University scholar Katherine Waldock estimate that legalizing drugs would save more than $41.3 billion per year in government expenditures on enforcing drug prohibition statutes. Some $25.7 would be saved at the state and local level, and $15.6 billion at the federal level. They also estimate that legalizing drugs would yield tax revenues of some $46.7 billion. Merely legalizing marijuana would put $8.7 billion into the tax coffers.[37] The prospect of major savings in law enforcement costs, combined with a significant new source of revenue, ought to have considerable appeal to lawmakers, especially in those states facing chronic budget problems. It ought to have even more appeal to hard-pressed taxpayers who have seen hundreds of billions of their hard-earned dollars wasted over the decades in the futile war on drugs.

The reforms in such countries as Portugal, Mexico, and Argentina are modest steps in the right direction, and they certainly are more sensible than a knee-jerk adherence to comprehensive prohibition. Legalizing, or even decriminalizing, drug possession has the beneficial effect of not stigmatizing (and sometimes ruining) the lives of users. And such reforms have the salutary effect of not filling prisons with nonviolent offenders. Even more limited liberalization measures, such as the medical marijuana statutes that are now in effect in 16 states, are an improvement on the previous rigid system of a comprehensive ban on that drug.

But those reforms, desirable as they are, do not get to the causal root of the violence that accompanies the drug trade. Mexico's 2009 reform, for example, made no change regarding the penalties for drug sales. Indeed, the new law stated explicitly that any person convicted selling any quantity of any drug would be sent to prison. Experts speculated that a key motive for the measure was to divert police attention and resources away from pursuing small-time users, thereby enabling authorities to escalate their campaign against traffickers—and Mexican government officials conceded as much.[38] Even Portugal's otherwise bold drug reform regarding possession and use kept trafficking in drugs strictly illegal.

Yet unless the production and sale of drugs is also legalized, the black-market premium will still exist and law-abiding businesses will still stay away from the trade. In other words, drug commerce will remain in the hands of criminal elements that do not shrink from engaging in bribery, intimidation, and murder. *Wall Street Journal* columnist Mary Anastasia O'Grady aptly makes that distinction with respect to Mexico's drug law reform:

> Mexican consumers will now have less fear of penalties and, increasingly in the case of marijuana, that's true in the United States as well. But trafficking will remain illegal, and to get their product past law enforcement the criminals will still have an enormous incentive to bribe or to kill. Decriminalization will not take the money out of the business, and therefore will not reduce corruption, cartel intimidation aimed at democratic-government authority or the terror heaped on local populations by drug lords."[39]

Because of its proximity to the huge U.S. market, Mexico will continue to be a cockpit for that drug-related violence. By its domestic commitment to prohibition, the United States is creating the risk that the drug cartels may become powerful enough to destabilize its southern neighbor. Their impact on Mexico's government and society has already reached worrisome levels. Worst of all, the carnage associated with the black-market trade in drugs does not respect national boundaries. The frightening violence now convulsing Mexico could become a feature of life in American communities, if the cartels begin to flex their muscles north of the border on something more than a limited, sporadic basis.

When the United States and other countries ponder whether to persist in a strategy of drug prohibition, they need to consider all of the potential societal costs, both domestic and international. On the domestic front, American's prisons are bulging with people who have run afoul of the drug laws. Approximately one-third of inmates in state prisons, and nearly 60 percent of those in federal prisons, are incarcerated for drug trafficking offenses. Most of those inmates are small-time dealers. Prohibition has created or exacerbated a variety of social pathologies, especially in minority communities where drug use rates are higher than the national average and rates of arrests and imprisonment are dramatically higher.

John McWhorter, an African-American scholar who is a contributing editor to the *New Republic*, points to two especially destructive effects of the war on drugs in black neighborhoods. "The War on Drugs destroys black families," he states bluntly. "It has become a norm for black children to grow up in single-parent homes, their fathers away in prison for long spells, and barely knowing them." The drug war, he McWhorter contends, "plays a large part in this."[40]

He also points to the skewed economic incentives. "The War on Drugs discourages young black men from seeking legal employment. Because the illegality of drugs keeps the prices high, there are high salaries to be made in selling them. This makes selling drugs a standing tempting alternative to seeking lower-paying legal employment. The result is usually spells in jail, as well as a failure to build the job skills for legal employment that serve as a foundation for a productive existence in middle and later life."

Perhaps the most insidious and destructive effect is that drug prohibition creates a large number of dubious role models. "The War on Drugs makes spending time in prison a badge of honor," McWhorter concludes. The ex-con is seen "as a hero rather than someone who went the wrong way. In the 1920s, before the War on Drugs, black

Americans, regardless of class level, did not view black ex-cons as heroes."

Drug abuse is certainly a major public health problem, and its societal costs are considerable. But banning the drug trade creates ugly social and economic distortions. Worst of all, prohibition provides an opportunity for some of the most unsavory individuals and organizations to gain dominant positions in that commerce. Drug prohibition leads inevitably to an abundance of corruption and violence, both inside the United States and in drug source or drug transiting countries, which are even worse societal costs, and that reality is now becoming all too evident in Mexico.

Changing Attitudes in the United States Regarding Drug Policy

There are tentative signs of at least modest changes regarding drug policy in the United States, as well as in such countries as Portugal, Argentina, and Mexico. The Obama administration's low-key, largely noncommittal response to Mexico's reform legislation stood in marked contrast, not only to the Bush administration's vehement opposition to a similar proposal in 2006 but also Washington's long-standing posture of hostility and intimidation toward any government that dared to flirt with drug policy reform.

There were also indications early in the Obama administration that the president and his advisers wanted to move away from the "war" model and instead deal with drug use as primarily a public-health issue. At least rhetorically, the administration stressed the importance of drug education and drug treatment programs while reducing the long-standing emphasis on arresting and imprisoning drug law violators. The Obama Justice Department also instructed federal prosecutors in jurisdictions where medical marijuana laws were in effect not to trample on those statutes by authorizing raids on, or prosecutions of, marijuana clinics—unless there were especially flagrant violations of federal law.[41]

Unfortunately, those early signs of a more tolerant approach had virtually disappeared by 2011. Washington authorized more and more raids on medical marijuana dispensaries in California and other states, displaying an arrogant indifference to the wishes of the voters in those states.[42] Increasingly, the Obama administration's drug policies resembled the hard-line policies of its predecessors.

That regression is especially puzzling and unfortunate, because public attitudes in the United States seem to be shifting in a more liberal direction regarding drug issues. Several states began to pass medical marijuana initiatives in the 1990s and the early years of the new century, and by 2009, 13 states had gone even further and decriminalized the personal possession of that drug.

Reformers in California sought to go still further, putting Proposition 19 on the ballot in the November 2010 election. Approval of Prop 19 would have created the "Regulate, Control and Tax Cannabis Act." Under its provisions, the possession of limited quantities of marijuana would no longer have been illegal under state law. In addition, residents could legally grow marijuana plants for personal use in plots as large as 25 square feet. The measure also would have added additional protections to the operators of medical marijuana clinics. It appeared for a time that voters would approve Proposition 19. Public-opinion polls taken in the weeks leading up to the election showed support as high as 52 percent, with margins over opponents of 8 to 10 percent.

On election day, though, the measure went down to defeat, with 56 percent of those voting casting "no" votes. Several factors probably contributed to the negative vote, most notably the differential turnout between older voters, who tended to oppose legalization, and younger voters, who tended to favor it. The vote was certainly a set back for opponents of drug prohibition. But it was mildly encouraging that nearly 45 percent of Californians were willing to vote in favor of a measure legalizing marijuana. It is hard to imagine a robust legalizative initiative even getting on the ballot two or three decades ago, much less attracting that level of support.

There are indications that the fading of enthusiasm for prohibition is not confined to California. In April 2009, the results of a nationwide Zogby poll provided evidence of changing attitudes: 52 percent of respondents thought that marijuana should be legal, taxed, and regulated. An earlier ABC News/*Washington Post* poll found 46 percent in favor of legalization.[43] An October 2011 Gallup poll confirmed that there was growing support for legalizing marijuana—some 50 percent favored legalization, while only 46 percent opposed it. As recently as 2006, only 36 percent endorsed legalization, with 60 percent opposed. And Gallup surveys taken in the 1970s, 1980s, and 1990s consistently showed opposition

261

between 66 and 84 percent, with pro-legalization sentiment languishing in the low to mid 20s.[44]

A deeper analysis of the 2011 Gallup survey provided even more encouragement for advocates of legalization. Opposition was strongest among respondents over the age of 65. Conversely, support for legalization was strongest among respondents 18 to 29 (a whopping 62 percent.) Given the realities of the mortality tables, the portion of the population supportive of the drug war is certain to diminish, even if that trend might be offset somewhat by the tendency of people to become more socially conservative as they age. It was also significant that solid majorities of both Democrats and Independents (57 percent in both cases) embraced legalization of marijuana.

All of this suggests that Americans are at least wavering in their support for drug prohibition. That trend puts the option of legalization on the table and could lead to a much-needed national discussion about the ramifications, both domestic and international, of Washington's current drug policy. Such a debate would have special relevance for Mexico.

Biting the Bullet and Helping Our Neighbor

The most feasible and effective strategy to counter the mounting turmoil in Mexico is to drastically reduce the potential revenue flows to the trafficking organizations. In other words, the United States could substantially defund the cartels through the full legalization (including manufacture and sale) of currently illegal drugs. If Washington abandoned the prohibition model, it is very likely that other members of the international community would do the same, although there would be some thorny diplomatic issues to overcome, since the United States and most other countries have obligations under a number of international treaties.[45] The United States exercises disproportionate influence on the issue of drug policy, as it does on so many other global issues, and a signal from Washington of a decisive shift away from the drug war would be extremely significant.

If prohibition were rescinded, the profit margins for the drug trade would be similar to the margins for other legal commodities, and legitimate business personnel would become the principal players. That is precisely what happened when the United States ended its quixotic crusade against alcohol in 1933. To help reverse the burgeoning tragedy of drug-related violence in Mexico, Washington must seriously consider adopting a similar course today with respect to illegal drugs.

Even taking the first step away from prohibition by legalizing marijuana, indisputably the mildest and least harmful of illegal drugs, could cause problems for the Mexican cartels. Experts provide a wide range of estimates about how important the marijuana trade is to those organizations. The high-end estimate, from a former DEA official, is that marijuana accounts for approximately 55 percent of total revenues. Other experts dispute that figure. Edgardo Buscaglia, who was a research scholar at the conservative Hoover Institution until 2008, provides the low-end estimate, contending that the drug amounts to "less than 10 percent" of total revenues. Officials in both the U.S. and Mexican governments contend that it's more like 20 to 30 percent.[46]

Whatever the actual percentage, the marijuana business is financially important to the cartels. It also is crucial to cementing the loyalties of farmers who grow the crops, especially in the mountains of western Mexico. Most of them are able to make significantly more from marijuana cultivation than they can from competing crops, such as maize (corn). The Mexican marijuana trade is already under pressure from competitors in the United States. One study concluded that the annual harvest in California alone equaled or exceeded the entire national production in Mexico, and that output for the United States was more than twice that of Mexico.[47] As sentiment for hard-line prohibition policies fades in the United States, and the likelihood of prosecution diminishes, one could expect that domestic growers, both large and small, will become bolder about starting or expanding their business.

Legalizing pot would strike a nasty blow against Mexican traffickers. It would be difficult for them to compete with American producers in the American market, given the difference in transportation distances and other factors. There would be little incentive for consumers to buy their product from unsavory Mexican criminal syndicates when legitimate domestic firms could offer the drug at a competitive price—and advertise how they are honest enterprises. Indeed, for many Americans, they could just grow their own supply—a cost advantage that the cartels could not hope to match.

Legalizing all drugs would cause even more problems for the cartels. That is not to say that the inevitable decline in revenues would put them out of business. They do have other sources of income, most notably kidnapping, prostitution, smuggling of illegal migrants into the United States, and extortion rackets. Just as the end of alcohol prohibition did not eliminate organized crime in the United States, drug legalization is not a panacea that would obliterate the Mexican cartels. But it would strike a major financial blow and significantly weaken them, just as the end of Prohibition in 1933 eroded the alarming power that bootlegging organizations had acquired during the 1920s.

It is increasingly apparent, in any case, that both the U.S. and Mexican governments need to make a drastic change in their efforts to combat Mexico's drug cartels. George Grayson aptly summarizes the fatal flaw in the existing strategy: "It is extremely difficult—probably impossible—to eradicate the cartels. They or their offshoots will fight to hold on to an enterprise that yields Croesus-like fortunes from illegal substances craved by millions of consumers."[48]

Felipe Calderón's military-led offensive is not just a futile, utopian crusade. That would be bad enough, but the reality is much worse. It is a futile, utopian crusade that has produced an array of ugly, bloody side effects. A different approach is needed—and one hopes that Calderón's successor has the wisdom to abandon the disastrous military offensive. One also hopes that Washington will not pressure the new administration in Mexico City to continue the foolish course that Calderón established.

The most effective way to deal with the murderous traffickers is to greatly reduce the "Croesus-like" fortunes available to the cartels. And the only realistic way to do that is to bite the bullet and end the policy of drug prohibition—preferably in whole—but at least in part, starting with the legalization of marijuana.

A failure to move away from prohibition in the United States creates the risk that the already nasty corruption and violence next door in Mexico may get even worse. The danger grows that our southern neighbor could become, if not a full-blown failed state, at least a de facto narcostate in which the leading drug cartels exercise parallel or dual political sovereignty with the government of Mexico. We may eventually encounter a situation—if we haven't already—where the cartels are the real power in significant portions of the country.

And we must worry that the disorder inside Mexico will spill over the border into the United States to a much greater extent than it has to this point.

The fire of drug-related violence is flaring to an alarming extent in Mexico. We already can smell the smoke and sometimes see the flames. U.S. leaders need to take constructive action now, before that fire consumes our neighbor's home and threatens our own.

Notes

Foreword

1. United Nations Office on Drugs and Crime, *World Drug Report 2011* (New York: United Nations, 2011), p. 125.
2. David Luhnow, "Saving Mexico," *Wall Street Journal*, December 26, 2009.
3. Cited in "México: 12,000 muertes vinculadas a la lucha antidrogas," *El Nuevo Herald*, January 3, 2012.

Introduction

1. Quoted in Sara Miller Llana, "Prominent Politician Diego Fernández de Cevallos Freed in Mexico," *Christian Science Monitor*, December 20, 2010.
2. Quoted in James C. McKinley Jr., "Fleeing Drug Violence, Mexicans Pour Into U.S.," *New York Times*, April 17, 2010.
3. Quoted in Lizbeth Díaz, "Children Traumatized by Mexico Drug War Killings," Reuters, March 31, 2009.
4. Sam Quiñones, "State of War," *Foreign Policy*, February 16, 2009, http://www.foreignpolicy.com/articles/2009/02/16/state_of_war.
5. Quoted in "Top Mexican Drug Cartel Suspect Arrested, Officials Say," CNN.com, April 2, 2009, http://articles.cnn.com/2009-04-02/world/mexico.drug.arrest_1_drug-cartel-juarez-cartel-cartel-leader?_s=PM:WORLD.
6. Robert C. Bonner, "The New Cocaine Cowboys: How to Defeat Mexico's Drug Cartels," *Foreign Affairs* 89, no. 4 (July–August 2010): 40.
7. George W. Grayson, *Mexico: Narco-Violence and a Failed State?* (New Brunswick, NJ: Transaction, 2010), p. 272.
8. Quoted in "Embattled Mexican Mayor Sent Family to Live in U.S.," Associated Press, November 23, 2009.
9. Bonner, "The New Cocaine Cowboys," p. 35.
10. Kevin G. Hall, "U.S. Consulate Employee Slain in Drug-Ridden Mexican City," *McClatchy Newspapers*, March 14, 2010.
11. Quoted in Jerry Markon, "2,200 Arrested in U.S. Crackdown on Mexican Drug Cartels," *Washington Post*, June 11, 2010.
12. Quoted in Randal C. Archibold, "Hired by Customs, but Working for the Cartels," *New York Times*, December 18, 2009.
13. Gabriel Arana, "The Border Violence Myth," *Nation*, May 27, 2009.
14. Quoted in Tim Johnson, "Mexico Rethinks Drug Strategy as Death Toll Soars," as in *McClatchy Newspapers*, August 12, 2010.
15. "Sugiere Rubén Aguilar Negociar Con El Narco," *Reforma*, December 20, 2008.
16. Quoted in William Booth and Steve Fainaru, "New Strategy Urged in Mexico," *Washington Post*, July 28, 2009.

267

17. Quoted in E. Eduardo Castillo, "Ex-Mexico President Calls for Legalizing Drugs," Associated Press, August 8, 2010.

18. Quoted in Mayolo López, "Descarta Calderón Negociar Con Carteles," *Reforma*, December 20, 2008.

19. Quoted in "Calderon's Shot at American Guns," editorial, *Washington Times*, May 24, 2010.

20. Quoted in "Mexico Slams 'Absurd' U.S. Gun Laws as Drug War Rages," Reuters, June 14, 2008.

21. Quoted in Juan Forero, "Colombia Shares Its Cartel-Fighting Expertise with Mexican Forces," *Washington Post*, January 22, 2011.

22. Quoted in Castillo, "Ex-Mexico President Calls for Legalizing Drugs."

23. Ibid.

24. Drug Enforcement Administration, *Speaking Out Against Drug Legalization* (Washington: Drug Enforcement Administration, 2010), http://www.justice.gov/dea/demand/speak_out_101210.pdf, p. 46.

Chapter 1

1. Ioan Grillo, "Drug Dealing for Jesus: Mexico's Evangelical Narcos," *Time.com*, July 19, 2009, http://www.time.com/time/world/article/0,8599,1911556,00.html. For Grillo's detailed discussion of the culture that has grown up around the drug trade and the leading traffickers, see his book *El Narco: Inside Mexico's Criminal Conspiracy* (New York: Bloomsbury Press, 2011), especially chapter 10.

2. Quoted in Mark Stevenson, "Paying for Protection," Associated Press, September 8, 2009.

3. Terrence E. Poppa, *Drug Lord: The Life and Death of a Mexican Kingpin* (Seattle: Demand Publications, 1998), pp. 322–26.

4. Quoted in George W. Grayson, *Mexico: Narco-Violence and a Failed State?* (New Brunswick, NJ: Transaction, 2010), p. 77.

5. Quoted in Chris Kraul, "Turf War Crosses the Line," *Los Angeles Times*, October 1, 2004.

6. Elijah Wald, *Narcocorrido: A Journey Into the Music of Drugs, Guns, and Guerrillas* (New York: HarperCollins, 2002), p. 2.

7. Quoted in Kraul, "Turf War Crosses the Line."

8. Chris Hawley, "Mexico Drug Ballads Hit Sour Note with Government," *USA Today*, December 27, 2009.

9. Wald, *Narcocorrido*, p. 294.

10. Quoted in Poppa, *Drug Lord*, p. 315.

11. Catherine E. Shoichet, "Mexico: Grammy Winner Sang at Drug Cartel's Party," Associated Press, December 15, 2009.

12. "Mexico Mayhem," *Latin American Herald Tribune*, June 28, 2010.

13. Quoted in Theunis Bates, "Mexican Singer Killed Hours after Denying He'd Died," AOL News, June 28, 2010, http://www.aolnews.com/2010/06/28/mexican-singer-killed-hours-after-denying-hed-died/.

14. "Despite Death Threat, Jenni Rivera Does Not Up Security," Celestrellas.com, July 2, 2010, http://entretenimiento.aollatino.com/2010/07/02/jenni-rivera-death-threat-twitter/.

15. Mark Stevenson, "Mexican Drug Lords Sport Flashy, Goofy Nicknames," Associated Press, July 23, 2009.

16. Ibid.

17. Quoted in John Quiñones, "Modern Mobster: American Drug King," ABC News, May 19, 2010, abcnews.go.com/WNT/video/high-school-star-mexican-drug-cartel-1069429.

18. "Reclutan Zetas a Mujeres," *El Norte*, March 27, 2009.

19. Quoted in "Mexico Drug Gang Hiring 'Pretty Hitwomen,'" Agence France Presse, August 17, 2010.

20. David Luhnow and José De Córdoba, "The Drug Lord Who Got Away," *Wall Street Journal*, June 13, 2009.

21. Quoted in Ioan Grillo, "Guns, Germs, and Recession: The Curse of Mexican Tourism," *Time.com*, June 11, 2009.

22. Quoted in Julie Watson, "Forbes: Mexico Kingpin among World's Most Powerful," Associated Press, November 12, 2009. For a discussion of Guzmán's influence and charisma, and the efforts to apprehend him in the years following his escape from prison, see Malcolm Beith, *The Last Narco: Inside the Hunt for El Chapo, The World's Most Wanted Drug Lord* (New York: Grove Press, 2010).

23. Useful discussions of the various cartels, large and small, past and present, can be found in Grayson, *Mexico: Narco-Violence and a Failed State?*, pp. 55–92; Sylvia Longmire, *Cartel: The Coming Invasion of Mexico's Drug Wars* (New York: Palgrave MacMillan, 2011), pp. 15–28; and Jerry Langton, *Gangland: The Rise of the Mexican Drug Cartels from El Paso to Vancouver* (Mississauga, ON: Wiley, 2012), pp. 59–71.

24. Good recent studies of the drug cartels and their territorial rivalries include Bob Killebrew and Jennifer Bernal, *Crime Wars: Gangs, Cartels, and U.S. National Security*, Center for a New American Security, September 2010, pp. 14–21; and June S. Beittel, "Mexico's Drug Trafficking Organizations: Source and Scope of the Rising Violence," Congressional Research Service Report to Congress, January 7, 2011, pp. 6–12.

25. Tracy Wilkinson, "Leading Mexico Drug Suspect Arrested," *Los Angeles Times*, June 22, 2011.

26. For a summary of the involvement of Mexican smuggling groups in drug trafficking before the 1980s, see Grayson, *Mexico: Narco-Violence and a Failed State?*, pp. 20–35.

27. Poppa, *Drug Lord*, pp. xii–xv, 123–34.

28. Peter Andreas, "The Political Economy of Narco-Corruption in Mexico," *Current History* 97, no. 618 (April 1998): 161–62.

29. Tim Golden, "Mexican Connection Grows as Cocaine Supplier to U.S.," *New York Times*, July 30, 1995; and Andreas, "The Political Economy of Narco-Corruption in Mexico."

30. Statement by Thomas A. Constantine, administrator, Drug Enforcement Administration, U.S. Department of Justice, before the National Security, International Affairs and Criminal Justice Subcommittee of the House Government Reform and Oversight Committee, regarding Cooperation with Mexico, February 26, 1998, http://www.justice.gov/dea/pubs/cngrtest/ct980226.htm; and "Organized Crime and Terrorist Activity in Mexico, 1999–2002," Federal Research Division, Library of Congress, February 2003, http://www.loc.gov/rr/frd/pdf-files/OrgCrime_Mexico.pdf.

31. Poppa, *Drug Lord*, p. 322.

32. "Organized Crime and Terrorist Activity in Mexico, 1999–2002," pp. 6–7.

33. Luhnow and De Córdoba, "The Drug Lord Who Got Away."

34. Patrick McDonnell, Ken Ellingwood, and Hector Tobar, "Officials Link Ensenada Massacre to Drug Feud," *Los Angeles Times*, September 19, 1998.

35. "Organized Crime and Terrorist Activity in Mexico, 1999–2002," p. 4; and Laurie Freeman, "State of Siege: Drug-Related Violence and Corruption in Mexico," Washington Office on Latin America, June 2006, p. 3.

36. Richard Boudreaux, "Mexico's Master of Illusion," *Los Angeles Times*, July 5, 2005.

37. Freeman, "State of Siege: Drug-Related Violence and Corruption in Mexico," pp. 3–6; Ginger Thompson, "Rival Drug Gangs Turn the Streets of Nuevo Laredo Into a War Zone," *New York Times*, December 4, 2005; and Chris Kraul, "Mexican Official Says Tijuana, Gulf Cartels Have United," *Los Angeles Times*, January 14, 2005.

38. For a discussion of the reasons for the feud between El Chapo and the Beltrán Leyva brothers, as well as the bloody escalation of that struggle, see Beith, *The Last Narco*, pp. 139–50.

39. Chris Arsenault, "U.S.-Trained Cartel Terrorizes Mexico," Al Jazeera, October 20, 2010.

40. Alberto Najar, "Desertaron 100 Mil Militares Con Fox," *Milenio*, July 20, 2007.

41. Quoted in Arsenault, "U.S.-Trained Cartel Terrorizes Mexico."

42. Quoted in Olga R. Rodríguez, "Mexico: Cartels Team Up to Destroy Hit Men Gang," Associated Press, April 12, 2010.

43. A good, comprehensive treatment of La Familia can be found in George W. Grayson, *La Familia Drug Cartel: Implications for U.S.-Mexican Security* (Carlisle, PA: U.S. Army War College, Security Studies Institute, December 2010).

44. On the origins of La Familia, see Grayson, *Mexico: Narco-Violence and a Failed State?* pp. 198–200.

45. "Toma 'La Familia' Ley en Michoacán," *Reforma*, November 22, 2006.

46. Quoted in Grillo, "Drug Dealing for Jesus."

47. Quoted in Steve Fainaru and William Booth, "A Mexican Cartel's Swift and Grisly Climb," *Washington Post*, June 13, 2009.

48. Ibid.

49. The religious component may have been the result of Nazario Moreno's stint as a laborer in California and Texas, where he came into close contact with evangelical Christians and may have even undergone a conversion experience. See Grillo, *El Narco*, p. 197.

50. Quoted in Grillo, "Drug Dealing for Jesus."

51. Grillo, "Drug Dealing for Jesus."

52. Quoted in Steve Fainaru and William Booth, "A Test of Faith in Mexico's Drug War," *Washington Post*, August 11, 2009.

53. Grillo, *El Narco*, p. 198.

54. Marc Lacey, "Mexico's Drug Traffickers Continue Trade in Prison," *New York Times*, August 11, 2009.

55. Fainaru and Booth, "A Mexican Cartel's Swift and Grisly Climb."

56. Quoted in Jennifer González, "No End to Violence in Blood-Soaked Mexican State," Agence France Presse, July 27, 2009.

57. Gustavo Ruíz, "Signs Announce New Gang in Western Mexico State," Associated Press, March 10, 2011.

58. Ibid.

59. Wilkinson, "Leading Mexico Drug Gang Suspect Arrested."

60. Robin Emmott, "Cartel Inc.: In the Company of Narcos," Reuters, January 14, 2010.

61. Quoted in William Booth, "New Adversary in U.S. Drug War: Contract Killers for Mexican Cartels," *Washington Post*, April 4, 2010.

62. Lacey, "Mexico's Drug Traffickers Continue Trade in Prison."

63. Ibid.

64. Quoted in Mica Rosenberg, "Corrupt, Insecure Prisons Undermine Mexico's Drug War," Reuters, August 18, 2010.

Chapter 2

1. E. Eduardo Castillo, "Mexican Governor Candidate Killed, Cartels Blamed," Associated Press, June 28, 2010; Tim Johnson, "Assassins Hit Leading Candidate in Key Mexican Border State," McClatchy Newspapers, June 28, 2010; and Ioan Grillo, "Mexico: Where Bullets Are Intimidating the Ballot," Time.com, June 29, 2010, http://www.time.com/time/world/article/0,8599,2000511,00.html.

2. Sara Miller Llana, "Mexico Drug War Death Toll Up 60 Percent in 2010. Why?" Christian Science Monitor, January 13, 2011.

3. "Mexico: Drug Violence Kills More Than 47,000 People," Associated Press, January 11, 2012.

4. George W. Grayson, Mexico: Narco-Violence and a Failed State? (New Brunswick, NJ: Transaction, 2010), p. 48.

5. See Ted Galen Carpenter, Bad Neighbor Policy: Washington's Futile War on Drugs in Latin America (New York: Palgrave Macmillan, 2003), chapter 7.

6. E. Eduardo Castillo, "Mexican Cartel Recruiting Hitmen," Associated Press, April 14, 2008.

7. Sam Quiñones, "State of War," Foreign Policy, February 16, 2009, http://www.foreignpolicy.com/articles/2009/02/16/state_of_war.

8. Stratfor.com, "Drug Cartels: The Growing Violence in Mexico," October 2006.

9. Tim Padgett, "On the Bloody Border," Time, May 4, 2009, p. 39.

10. Sylvia Longmire, Cartel: The Coming Invasion of Mexico's Drug Wars (New York: Palgrave Macmillan, 2011), p. 25.

11. Quoted in Steve Fainaru and William Booth, "A Mexican Cartel's Swift and Grisly Climb," Washington Post, June 13, 2009.

12. Quoted in Elliot Spagat, "Mexico's Drug Cartels Slay Rival Street Dealers," Washington Times, June 23, 2009.

13. Ibid.

14. Ibid.

15. For a graphic, detailed account of how bad the situation has become since the upsurge in killings started in early 2008, see Charles Bowden, Murder City: Ciudad Juárez and Global Economy's New Killing Fields (New York: Nation Books, 2010)

16. Andrew Rice, "Life on the Line," New York Times Magazine, July 28, 2011.

17. "17 Dead, Including Prosecutor, in Mexico Border Attacks," Agence France Presse, July 29, 2009.

18. John Burnett, "Nuevo Laredo Returns to Normal as Violence Slows," NPR transcript, January 23, 2009, http://www.npr.org/templates/story/story.php?storyId=99742620.

19. "Gunbattles Paralyze Mexican City Across from Texas," Associated Press, July 22, 2010.

20. Quoted in Mark Stevenson, "Mexico Says Cartels Turning Attacks on Authorities," Associated Press, April 25, 2010.

21. "Mexican State Security Chief Wounded in Ambush," Agence France Presse, April 24, 2010.

22. Quoted in Steve Fainaru and William Booth, "As Mexico Battles Cartels, The Army Becomes the Law," *Washington Post*, April 2, 2009.

23. William Booth, "Warrior in Drug Fight Soon Becomes Victim," *Washington Post*, February 9, 2009.

24. "10 Arrested in Police Chief's Killing," Associated Press, November 7, 2009.

25. Jerry Langton, *Gangland: The Rise of the Mexican Drug Cartels from El Paso to Vancouver* (Mississauga, ON: Wiley, 2012), pp. 131–39.

26. "Mexico's 'La Familia' Cartel Declares War on Police," Agence France Presse, July 15, 2009.

27. "At Least 40 People Killed in Drug-Related Mexico Violence," Agence France Presse, September 3, 2009.

28. Quoted in Sara Miller, "Drug Cartels Launch Mexico's 'Tet Offensive,'" *Christian Science Monitor*, July 15, 2009.

29. "16 Dead, 2 Bodies Chopped Up, in Latest Mexico Violence," Agence France Presse, April 1, 2009.

30. "9 Decapitated Bodies Found in Western Mexico," Associated Press, October 16, 2009.

31. Fainaru and Booth, "A Mexican Cartel's Swift and Grisly Climb."

32. Ibid.

33. "Severed Heads in Cooler Found Outside Mexican Town Hall," Agence France Presse, January 21, 2009.

34. Olga R. Rodríguez, "11 Bodies Found Inside Abandoned Car in Mexico," Associated Press, June 5, 2009.

35. Olga R. Rodríguez, "Mexico Cartel Stitches Rival's Face on Soccer Ball," Associated Press, January 8, 2010.

36. Quoted in Marc Lacey, "Mexico Lawmen Outmatched by Drug Violence," *New York Times*, October 17, 2009.

37. Lizbeth Díaz, "Mexico Suspect Says He Dissolved 300 Bodies," Reuters, January 23, 2009.

38. Rick Jervis, "YouTube Riddled with Drug Cartel Videos, Messages," *USA Today*, April 9, 2009.

39. Mica Rosenberg, "Mexico Drug Cartels Use Gory Videos to Spread Fear," Reuters, August 4, 2010.

40. Jervis, "YouTube Riddled with Drug Cartel Videos, Messages."

41. Pamela Starr, "Mexico's Spreading Drug Violence," *Los Angeles Times*, October 22, 2008.

42. U.S. Department of State, Bureau of Consular Affairs, "Travel Alert," April 14, 2008. It appears that the original travel alert is no longer available; however, there is a statement from the U.S. Embassy in Mexico. See, instead, Embassy of the United States, Mexico City, "State Department Issues Updated Travel Alert," Statement by Ambassador Antonio O. Garza, http://mexico.usembassy.gov/eng/releases/ep080414travelalert.html.

43. Manuel Roig-Franzia, "Tijuana Strip Turns Ghostly in Wake of Drug Violence," *Washington Post*, June 16, 2008.

44. Rice, "Life on the Line."

45. Quoted in Johnson, "In Mexico's Murder Capital, Residents, Businesses Suffer," *McClatchy Newspapers*, April 14, 2010.

46. Carol Cullar, "Mexico's Drug War, My Backyard," *USA Today*, July 21, 2010.

47. Ibid.

48. Quiñones, "State of War."

49. Joseph Contreras, "A Future City of Knowledge or a Killing Field?" *Globalist*, April 17, 2009.

50. Quoted in Contreras, "A Future City of Knowledge or a Killing Field?"

51. Tim Johnson, "Grisly Mass Graves in Mexico Yield 50 Casualties of Drug War," *McClatchy Newspapers*, July 24, 2010; and Mark Stevenson, "51 Bodies Found at Northern Mexico Dumping Ground," Associated Press, July 24, 2010.

52. Quoted in Nicholas Casey, "Mexico Under Siege," *Wall Street Journal*, August 19, 2010.

53. Dudly Althaus, "Mexico Arrests 5 in Fatal Casino Blaze," *Houston Chronicle*, August 29, 2011.

54. Natalia Parra, "Shootout Kills 18 Near Mexican Resort," Associated Press, June 7, 2009. The final total turned out to be 17, not 18. See Marc Lacey, "Dotted With Tourists, and Now Bullets, Mexican Resort Town is Home to Drug War," *New York Times*, June 9, 2009.

55. Quoted in Parra, "Shootout Kills 18 Near Mexican Resort."

56. Grayson, *Mexico: Narco-Violence and a Failed State?* p. 108.

57. Nicholas Casey, "Killings Hit Mexico Tourist Hub," *Wall Street Journal*, January 10, 2011.

58. "Eight Killed in Attack on Cancún Bar," Agence France Presse, August 31, 2010.

59. "Mexico: 6 Bodies in Cave, 3 with Hearts Cut Out," Associated Press, June 6, 2010.

60. "Six Shot Dead in Mexico Disco in Likely Drug Attack," Reuters, February 6, 2010.

61. "3 Bodies Found Hanging from Bridges in Mexico," Associated Press, July 14, 2010.

62. Sara Miller Llana, "Mexico Mass Grave Highlights Gruesome Drug War," *Christian Science Monitor*, June 8, 2010; "55 Bodies Found Dumped in Mexican Mine: Officials," Agence France Presse, June 7, 2010. (Ultimately, authorities believed that there were 64 bodies in that mine.) See also William Booth, "Mass Grave in Taxco, Mexico, Is Largest Discovered in Violent Drug War," *Washington Post*, June 24, 2010.

63. Quoted in José Cortazar, "Drug Violence Scares Off Tourists to Mexico," Reuters, April 13, 2010.

64. Tim Johnson, "Mexico Seeks More Tourists–But Is it Safe to Go?" *McClatchy Newspapers*, August 3, 2010.

65. Marc Lacey, "Mexican Candidate and Family Are Killed in Apparent Drug Hit," *New York Times*, September 7, 2009.

66. Quoted in Robin Emmott, "Mexican Cartels Break Open New Front in Drugs War," Reuters, May 21, 2009.

67. Quoted in William Booth and Steve Fainaru, "New Strategy Urged in Mexico," *Washington Post*, July 28, 2009.

Chapter 3

1. Marc Lacey, "Mexico Lawyer Who Defended Drug Traffickers Is Shot Dead," *New York Times*, August 10, 2009.

2. Alicia A. Caldwell, "Gunmen Kill 10 at Mexico Drug Treatment Center," Associated Press, September 16, 2009.

3. Olivia Torrest and Danica Coto, "Mexican Police Say 20 Killed in Drug-Plagued City," Associated Press, June 11, 2010.

4. "Mexico: 9 Killed in Drug Rehab Center," Reuters, June 26, 2010.

5. Quoted in Julian Cardona, "Army Feeble as Murders Surge in Mexico Drug War City," Reuters, July 8, 2009.

6. Quoted in Julie Wolf, "New Reason for Mexican Immigration to U.S.: Drug Violence," McClatchy Newspapers, May 20, 2009.

7. William Booth, "Ambushed by a Drug War," Washington Post, July 23, 2009.

8. Quoted in Booth, "Ambushed by a Drug War."

9. Howard Campbell, Drug War Zone: Frontline Dispatches from the Streets of El Paso and Juárez (Austin: University of Texas Press, 2009), pp. 214–26.

10. For a summary of the assaults on journalists, see George W. Grayson, Mexico: Narco-Violence and a Failed State? (New Brunswick, NJ: Transaction, 2010), pp. 97–101; and Sylvia Longmire, Cartel: The Coming Invasion of Mexico's Drug Wars (New York: Palgrave Macmillan, 2011), pp. 104–06.

11. "Journalist Found Dead in Acapulco," Washington Post, July 30, 2009.

12. "Body of Online Journalist found in Northern Mexico," Associated Press, August 25, 2011; and Tracy Wilkinson, "2 Mexican Journalists Found Slain," Los Angeles Times, September 1, 2011.

13. Quoted in Julian Cardona and Chris Wilson, "Gunmen Kill Mexican Reporter in Front of Colleagues," Reuters, September 24, 2009.

14. E. Eduardo Castillo, "Reporter Kidnapped and Killed in Northern Mexico," Associated Press, November 3, 2009.

15. Wilkinson, "2 Mexican Journalists Found Slain."

16. William Booth, "Violence Against Journalists Grows in Mexico's Drug War," Washington Post, November 25, 2008.

17. Quoted in Olga R. Rodríguez, "Mexico Cartel Stitches Rival's Face on Soccer Ball," Associated Press, January 8, 2010.

18. Quoted in Jason Beaubien, "Mexico's Drug Cartels Use Force to Silence Media," National Public Radio, transcript, August 3, 2010, p. 3.

19. William Booth, "In Mexico's Nuevo Laredo, Drug Cartels Dictate Media Coverage," Washington Post, August 2, 2010.

20. Beaubien, "Mexico's Drug Cartels Use Force to Silence Media," p. 2.

21. Quoted in Olga R. Rodríguez, "Narco-Blogger Beats Mexico Drug War News Blackout," Associated Press, August 13, 2010.

22. Olga R. Rodríguez, "Mexican Police Free Reporters Nabbed by Drug Gang," Associated Press, July 31, 2010; Jason Lange, "Mexican Police Free Journalists Seized by Drug Gangs," Reuters, July 31, 2010; and "Mexico Rescues Two Kidnapped Journalists in Drug Gang Row," Agence France Presse, July 31, 2010.

23. Quoted in Lange, "Mexican Police Free Journalists Seized by Drug Gangs."

24. Quoted in Mica Rosenberg, "Mexico Drug Cartels Use Gory Videos to Spread Fear," Reuters, August 4, 2010.

25. "Amenaza Narco a Periodistas y Soldados," Reforma, May 28, 2009.

26. William Booth, "Gunmen Attack TV Offices in Mexico," Washington Post, January 8, 2009.

27. Quoted in "Mexico Media on High Alert After Drug-Gang Attack on Televisa," Time.com, January 15, 2009.

28. Booth, "In Mexico's Nuevo Laredo, Drug Cartels Dictate Media Coverage."

29. Alberto Fajardo, "Car Bomb Explodes Outside Mexico TV Studio," Reuters, August 27, 2010.

30. Quoted in "Gunmen Kill Priest, 2 Seminarians in Mexico," Associated Press, June 15, 2009.

31. Grayson, *Mexico: Narco-Violence and a Failed State?* pp. 122–24.

32. Michael Miller, "The Age of Innocents," *Newsweek*, October 24, 2008, http://www.thedailybeast.com/newsweek/2008/10/24/the-age-of-innocents.html.

33. For a chilling account of the incident, see Chris Hawley, "Mexican Civilians Caught in Crossfire," *USA Today*, August 31, 2010.

34. Olga R. Rodríguez and Mark Walsh, "Soldiers Fire on Family's Car in Mexico, Killing 2," Associated Press, September 6, 2010.

35. "15 People Killed in 1 Day in Mexican Border City," Associated Press, November 14, 2009; and Mariano Castillo, "Texas Boy, 7, Gunned Down While Visiting His Father in Mexico, Officials Say," CNN.com, November 18, 2009.

36. Quoted in Tim Johnson, "In Mexico's Murder Capital, Residents, Businesses Suffer," *McClatchy Newspapers*, April 14, 2010.

37. Quoted in James C. McKinley Jr., "Fleeing Drug Violence, Mexicans Pour Into U.S.," *New York Times*, April 17, 2010.

38. Elisabeth Malkin, "Drug Gang Suspected in Mexico Party Massacre," *New York Times*, July 19, 2010.

39. Longmire, *Cartel*, pp. 83–93.

40. Mark Stevenson and E. Eduardo Castillo, "Drug Cartel Suspected in Massacre of 72 Migrants," Associated Press, August 26, 2010.

41. "Mexico Probes Hitmen Motive in Migrant Killings," Agence France Presse, August 26, 2010.

42. Quoted in Lizbeth Díaz, "Children Traumatized by Mexico Drug War Killings," Reuters, March 31, 2009.

43. Ibid.

44. Quoted in Chris Hawley, "Mexico Schools Teach Lessons in Survival," *USA Today*, July 8, 2010.

45. Ibid.

46. "6 Dead as Drug Violence Hits Heart of Acapulco," Associated Press, April 15, 2010.

Chapter 4

1. United Nations Office on Drugs and Crime, *2007 World Drugs Report* (2007), p. 176, http://www.unodc.org/pdf/research/wdr07/WDR_2007.pdf; and Ioan Grillo, "Mexico's Cocaine Capital," *Time.com*, August 14, 2008.

2. Joel Millman and José De Córdoba, "Drug Cartel Links Haunt an Election South of Border, *Wall Street Journal*, July 3–5, 2009.

3. Ibid.

4. Ibid.

5. Shannon O'Neil, "The Real War in Mexico: How Democracy Can Defeat the Drug Cartels," *Foreign Affairs* 88, no. 4 (July–August 2009): 72.

6. Millman and De Córdoba, "Drug Cartel Links Haunt an Election South of Border."

7. Ibid.

8. Tim Padgett, "Is Mexico's Fearsome La Familia Dead or Just Lurking?" *Time.com*, January 31, 2011, http://www.time.com/time/world/article/0,8599,2044696,00.html.

9. David Luhnow, "Questions Over Tape Face Mexico Politician," *Wall Street Journal*, October 16, 2010.

10. Quoted in Millman and De Córdoba, "Drug Cartel Links Haunt an Election South of Border."

11. Quoted in Martha Mendoza, "Mexico Mayor Announces Death Before Body Is Found," Associated Press, November 3, 2009.

12. Quoted in Alexandra Olson, "Candidates Threatened in Local Mexico Elections," Associated Press, May 15, 2010.

13. Mary Jordan, "Inquiry Reignites Talk of Church's Drug Ties," *Washington Post*, October 1, 2003.

14. Quoted in "Bishop's Admission on Drug-Tainted Donations Causes Uproar," CNN.com, October 4, 2005. See, Lisa J. Adams, "Mexican Church under Fire for Admitting it Accepts Money from Drug Dealers," *Associated Press*, http://www.banderasnews.com/0510/nr-mexchurch.htm.

15. Robin Emmott, "Cartel Inc.: In the Company of Narcos," Reuters, January 14, 2010.

16. Robert C. Bonner, "The New Cocaine Cowboys: How to Defeat Mexico's Drug Cartels," *Foreign Affairs* 89, no. 4 (July–August 2010): 37.

17. Ibid.

18. See Ted Galen Carpenter, *Bad Neighbor Policy: Washington's Futile War on Drugs in Latin America* (New York: Palgrave Macmillan, 2003), p. 177.

19. Ibid., p. 178.

20. Mary Jordan and Kevin Sullivan, "Border Police Chief Only Latest Casualty in Mexico Drug War," *Washington Post*, June 16, 2005, p. A1.

21. John Authers, "Police Return to Mexico Frontier Town to do Battle with Drug Cartels," *Financial Times*, July 30, 2005, p. 7.

22. Mark Stevenson, "27 Cancún Policemen Face Drug Charges," Associated Press, March 1, 2005.

23. Quoted in Mary Jordan and Kevin Sullivan, "Mexican Police Held in Killings; Work for Drug Traffickers Suspected," *Washington Post*, January 30, 2004, p. A11.

24. Emmott, "Cartel Inc.: In the Company of Narcos."

25. Quoted in Catherine E. Shoichet, "Mexican Official: Disband Local Police Forces," Associated Press, October 31, 2009.

26. Chad Deal, "Mexican Drug Cartels: You Want Silver or Lead?" *San Diego Reader*, September 22, 2010.

27. Olga R. Rodríguez, "11 Bodies Found Inside Abandoned Car in Mexico," Associated Press, June 5, 2009.

28. Mark Stevenson, "Mexico: Prison Guards Let Killers Out, Lent Guns," Associated Press, July 25, 2010; and Robert Campbell, "Hitmen Behind Mexico Massacre Were Prisoners: Government," Reuters, July 25, 2010.

29. Olga R. Rodríguez, "Mexico Agents Arrest Border Police Chief," Associated Press, April 17, 2008.

30. E. Eduardo Castillo, "Mexico Reveals Drug Corruption Network," *Washington Times*, October 27, 2008.

31. Chris Hawley, "In Mexico's Drug Wars, Local Police Stepping Up," *USA Today*, September 16, 2009.

32. Quoted in Robin Emmott, "Police Corruption Undermines Mexico's War on Drugs," *Reuters*, May 23, 2007.

33. CNN.com, "Mexico Officers Arrested, Accused of Ties to Drug Cartel," September 15, 2009, http://articles.cnn.com/2009-09-15/world/mexico.officials.arrested_1_drug cartel-hidalgo-state-municipal-police-officers.

34. Quoted in Gabriel Alcocer, "Mexico Arrests Cancún Mayor on Drug Charges," *Associated Press*, May 26, 2010.

35. Marc Lacey, "In Sweeping Move, Mexico Replaces Customs Agents," *New York Times*, August 17, 2009.

36. Quoted in Eduardo Castillo, "Another Protected Witness Dies in Mexico," *Associated Press*, December 1, 2009.

37. Ibid.

38. Jason Lange, "From Spas to Banks, Mexico Economy Rides on Drugs," *Reuters*, January 22, 2010. For a discussion of the increasing diversification of the cartels as they seek to raise more revenue, see Ioan Grillo, *El Narco: Inside Mexico's Criminal Insurgency* (New York: Bloomsbury Press, 2011), pp. 259–71.

39. Ioan Grillo, "Stolen Oil: A Gusher of Cash for Mexican Drug Cartels," *Time.com*, March 9, 2011, http://www.time.com/time/world/article/0,8599,2058007,00.html.

40. Ibid.

41. Quoted in Steve Fainaru and William Booth, "Mexico's Drug Cartels Siphon Liquid Gold," *Washington Post*, December 13, 2009.

42. Quoted in Robert Campbell, "Mexican Drug Gangsters Menace Natural Gas Drillers," *Reuters*, February 15, 2011.

43. Quoted in "Mexican Cartels Diversify," *Latin American Herald Tribune*, October 21, 2010.

44. Lange, "From Spas to Banks, Mexico Economy Rides on Drugs."

45. Ibid.

46. Quoted in Mark Stevenson, "Paying for Protection," *Associated Press*, September 8, 2009.

47. Ioan Grillo, "Drug Dealing for Jesús: Mexico's Evangelical Narcos," *Time.com*, July 19, 2009, http://www.time.com/time/world/article/0,8599,1911556,00.html.

48. Quoted in Jennifer González, "No End to Violence in Blood-Soaked Mexican State," *Agence France Presse*, July 27, 2009.

49. Stevenson, "Paying for Protection."

50. Hope Yen, "Fewer Mexicans Heading to U.S.," *Washington Times*, July 23, 2009.

51. Lange, "From Spas to Banks, Mexico Economy Rides on Drugs."

52. Quoted in Tim Johnson, "In Mexico's Murder Capital, Residents, Businesses Suffer," *McClatchy Newspapers*, April 14, 2010.

53. Quoted in Bill Whitaker, "Tijuana's Top Cop Wages War on Drug Gangs," *CBS News*, transcript, December 2, 2009, p. 1.

54. Quoted in Bill Whitaker, "Brutal Drug War Fueled By U.S. Appetite," *CBS News*, transcript, December 16, 2008, p. 5.

55. Quoted in Whitaker, "Tijuana's Top Cop Wages War on Drug Gangs."

56. For an account of this episode, see Andrew Becker, "Mexican Police Fleeing Cartels Find U.S. Reluctant to Grant Asylum," *Los Angeles Times*, June 15, 2009.

57. Quoted in Byron Pitts, "'Silver or Lead' in Mexico: Bribes or Death," *60 Minutes*, CBS News, January 9, 2011.

58. Ibid.

59. Ibid.

60. Ioan Grillo and Dolly Mascarenas, "Mexico Shaken by Top Politician's Feared Murder," *Time.com*, May 17, 2010, http://www.time.com/time/world/article/0,8599,1989557,00.html.

61. Alexandra Olson, "Mexico Suspends Search for Missing Ex-Candidate," Associated Press, May 22, 2010.

62. Sara Miller Llana, "Prominent Politician Diego Fernández de Cevallos Freed in Mexico," *Christian Science Monitor*, December 20, 2010.

63. Ibid.

Chapter 5

1. Christopher Paul, Agnes Gereben Schaefer, and Colin P. Clarke, "The Challenge of Violent Drug-Trafficking Organizations: An Assessment of Mexican Security Based on Existing RAND Research on Urban Unrest, Insurgency, and Defense Sector Reform," RAND Defense Research Institute, 2011, p. 64.

2. Barry R. McCaffrey, "Narco-Violence in Mexico: A Growing Threat to U.S. Security," December 2008, pp. 5–7, http://www.unc.edu/depts/diplomat/item/2009/0103/comm/mccaffery_mexico.html.

3. Quoted in "Top Mexican Drug Cartel Suspect Arrested, Officials Say," CNN.com, April 2, 2009, http://articles.cnn.com/2009-04-02/world/mexico.drug.arrest_1_drug-cartel-juarez-cartel-cartel-leader?_s=PM:WORLD.

4. Fernando Escalante Gonzalbo, "Homicidios 2008–2009 La Muerte Tiene Permiso," *Nexos*, March 1, 2011, http://www.nexos.com.mx/?P=leerarticulo&Article=1943189.

5. Human Rights Watch, *Neither Rights Nor Security: Killings, Torture and Disappearances in Mexico's "War on Drugs,"* (New York: Human Rights Watch, November 2011), p. 4.

6. Shannon O'Neil, "The Real War in Mexico," *Foreign Affairs* 88, no. 4 (July–August 2009): 64.

7. Robert C. Bonner, "The New Cocaine Cowboys: How to Defeat Mexico's Drug Cartels," *Foreign Affairs* 89, no. 4 (July–August 2010): 40.

8. George W. Grayson, *Mexico: Narco-Violence and a Failed State?* (New Brunswick, NJ: Transaction, 2010), p. 272.

9. Richard Marosi, "Mexico Convoy Threads Its Way through Strange Drug War in Sonora State," *Los Angeles Times*, October 16, 2010.

10. Bonner, "The New Cocaine Cowboys," p. 35.

11. "Catholic Church Warns of Cartel Control in Mexico," Associated Press, June 20, 2010.

12. Quoted in David Luhnow, "Mexico's Drug War Spreads," *Wall Street Journal*, April 19, 2010.

13. Olga R. Rodríguez, "Getaway for Mexican Elite Now Cartel Battleground," Associated Press, April 28, 2010.

14. Quoted in Mark Stevenson and Alicia A. Caldwell, "Mexico Cartels Empty Border Towns," Associated Press, April 16, 2010.

15. Ibid.

16. Mica Rosenberg, "Mexico's Refugees: A Hidden Cost of the Drugs War," Reuters, February 17, 2011.

17. Quoted in James C. McKinley Jr., "Fleeing Drug Violence, Mexicans Pour Into U.S.," *New York Times*, April 17, 2010.

18. See Molly Molloy and Charles Bowden, eds., *El Sicario: The Autobiography of a Mexican Assassin* (New York: Nation Books, 2011.)

19. Quoted in Chris Hawley, "Drug Cartels Outmatch, Outgun Mexican Forces," *USA Today*, June 16, 2010.

20. Quoted in Diana Washington Valdez, "Report: Mexican Drug Cartels Adopting Military Tactics," *El Paso Times*, August 7, 2011.

21. Mark Potter, "Mexican Government Struggling with Escalating Violence in Four-Year Drug War," NBC Nightly News, transcript, September 7, 2010, p. 2.

22. Sara Miller Llana, "Mexico Car Bomb: 'Colombianization' of Mexico Nearly Complete," *Christian Science Monitor*, July 18, 2010; and Alicia A. Caldwell, "U.S. Official: Mexican Car Bomb Likely Used Tovex," Associated Press, July 19, 2010.

23. Quoted in "Attorney General Says No 'Narcoterrorism' in Mexico," Agence France Presse, July 16, 2010.

24. Quoted in Kevin Johnson, "Mexican Cartels Rely More on Explosives in Drug War," *USA Today*, July 22, 2010.

25. "Congresswoman Raises Red Flag on Hezbollah-Cartel Nexus on U.S. Border," FoxNews.com, June 25, 2010, http://www.foxnews.com/politics/2010/06/25/congresswoman-raises-red-flag-hezbollah-cartel-nexus-border/; and "Report: Hizbullah on U.S.-Mexico Border," *Jerusalem Post*, July 20, 2010.

26. Alberto Fajardo, "Car Bomb Explodes Outside Mexico TV Studio," Reuters, August 27, 2010; and E. Eduardo Castillo, "Car Bomb Explodes in Mexico Where 72 Bodies Found," Associated Press, August 27, 2010.

27. Robin Emmott, "Hitmen Kill Mexican Mayor in Drug War State," Reuters, August 29 2010; and Jorge Vargas, "Mayor in Violent Mexican Border State Killed," Associated Press, August 29, 2010.

28. Quoted in Martha Mendoza, "Mexico Opens 2010 with One of its Deadliest Days," Associated Press, January 11, 2010.

29. Julian Cardona, "Mexicans Flee Drug War City in Fear of Killings," Reuters, February 18, 2010.

30. Ibid.

31. Quoted in David Luhnow, "Elite Flee Drug War in Mexico's No. 3 City," *Wall Street Journal*, September 10, 2010.

32. Ibid.

33. Ibid.

34. Rosenberg, "Mexico's Refugees: A Hidden Cost of the Drugs War."

35. Ricardo Chavez, "Mexico Town's Police Force Quits after Attack," Associated Press, August 4, 2011.

36. Quoted in Andrew Becker, "Mexican Police Fleeing Cartels Find U.S. Reluctant to Grant Asylum," *Los Angeles Times*, June 15, 2009.

37. Julian Cardona, "Mexican Student Takes Over Police in Drug War Town," Reuters, October 21, 2010.

38. Quoted in Jesús Alcázar, "Young Mother Becomes Mexican Town's Police Chief," Agence France Presse, October 20, 2010.

39. Juan Carlos Llorca, "Young Mexican Police Chief Seeks U.S. Asylum," Associated Press, March 9, 2011.

40. "Embattled Mexican Mayor Sent Family to Live in U.S.," Associated Press, November 23, 2009.

41. Quoted in Tim Johnson, "Along Mexico's Border, Just Going to Work Can Risk Death," *McClatchy Newspapers*, April 14, 2010.

42. Luhnow, "Elite Flee Drug War in Mexico's No. 3 City."

43. Michelle Roberts, "Media CEO: Journalist Safety a Challenge in Mexico," Associated Press, March 25, 2010.

44. Sara Miller Llana, "Ciudad Juárez Mobilizes to Protect Children from Mexico's Drug War," *Christian Science Monitor*, March 23, 2010.

45. Quoted in Tim Johnson, "In Mexico's Murder Capital, Residents, Businesses Suffer," *McClatchy Newspapers*, April 14, 2010.

46. Quoted in George W. Grayson, "Vigilantism: Increasing Self-Defense against Runaway Violence in Mexico," *Foreign Policy Institute E-Note*, October 23, 2009, http://www.fpri.org/enotes/200910.grayson.vigilantismmexico.html. For a more extensive discussion of Mexico's vigilante activity, see George W. Grayson, *Threat Posed by Mounting Vigilantism in Mexico*, U.S. Army War College Strategic Studies Institute, September 2011, pp. 29–46.

47. Julian Cardona, "Shadow of Vigilantes Appears in Mexico," Reuters, January 19, 2009; and Grayson, "Vigilantism: Increasing Self-Defense against Runaway Violence in Mexico."

48. Ricardo González, "Mexican Shooting Kills 8; Vigilantes Suspected," Associated Press, August 31, 2009.

49. "Mexico Police, Angry Residents Clash Over Suspects," Associated Press, November 11, 2009.

50. "Official's Body Found Hanging from Tijuana Bridge," Associated Press, October 9, 2009.

51. "Bodies Dumped with Vigilante Warnings in Mexico," Associated Press, January 17, 2010.

52. The record of the right-wing paramilitary groups regarding the drug trade is a murky one. They did attack some traffickers, especially those that seemed to be working with the FARC, but some of the paramilitaries were themselves heavily involved in drug trafficking.

53. Quoted in Mark Stevenson, "Mexican Border City Groups Call for UN Peacekeepers," Associated Press, November 12, 2009.

54. Quoted in Julian Cardona, "Mexicans in Drug War City Call on Army to Leave," Reuters, December 6, 2009.

55. Nicholas Casey, "Inside Mexico's Drug War, Americans Allege Abuse," *Wall Street Journal*, July 15, 2010.

56. Ibid.

57. Steve Fainaru and William Booth, "Mexico Accused of Torture in Drug War," *Washington Post*, July 9, 2009.

58. Ibid.

59. Amnesty International, *Mexico: New Reports of Human Rights Violations by the Military* (London: Amnesty International, December 2009), p. 8.

60. Ibid.

61. Ibid., p. 11.

62. Ibid.

63. Ibid., p. 14.

64. Ibid., p. 15.

65. Casey, "Inside Mexico's Drug War, Americans Allege Abuse."

66. Nicholas Casey, "Pair Convicted of Drug Trafficking in Mexico," *Wall Street Journal*, September 3, 2010.

67. Human Rights Watch, *Neither Rights Nor Security*, (New York: Human Rights Watch, 2011), pp. 5–6.

68. Quoted in David Luhnow, "Mexico's President Calderón Ousts Controversial Minister," *Wall Street Journal*, July 15, 2010.

Chapter 6

1. Shannon O'Neil, "The Real War in Mexico: How Democracy Can Defeat the Drug Cartels," *Foreign Affairs* 88, no. 4 (July–August 2009): 65.

2. Ibid.

3. For discussions of Calderón's strategy and how it has evolved, see Sylvia Longmire, *Cartel: The Coming Invasion of Mexico's Drug Wars* (New York: Palgrave Macmillan, 2011), pp. 111–34; Jerry Langton, *Gangland: The Rise of the Mexican Drug Cartels from El Paso to Vancouver* (Mississauga, ON: Wiley, 2012), pp. 103–30, 159–68; and Ioan Grillo, *El Narco: Inside Mexico's Criminal Insurgency* (New York: Bloomsbury Press, 2011), pp. 109–30.

4. Quoted in John Lyons, "Mexico's Cops Seek Upgrade," *Wall Street Journal*, October 24, 2009.

5. Robert Beckhusen, "Mexico Launches New Offensive against Cartel, Ratcheting Up Drug War," *Wired.com*, January 27, 2012.

6. Tim Johnson, "For Mexican Cartels, Marijuana Is Still Gold," *McClatchy Newspapers*, September 2, 2010.

7. Quoted in Alexandra Olson, "Calderón: Violence Price Worth Paying in Drug War," Associated Press, September 2, 2010.

8. Marc Lacey, "Mexico Lawmen Outmatched by Drug Violence," *New York Times*, October 17, 2009.

9. Julie Watson and Alexandra Olson, "Mexico Justice Means Catch and Release," Associated Press, July 28, 2010.

10. Quoted in Julie Watson, "Mexican Kingpin's Death Could Spark More Bloodshed," Associated Press, December 17, 2009.

11. Ibid.

12. "Mexico Arrests Drug Kingpin 'the Barbie,'" Agence France Presse, August 30, 2010.

13. Quoted in Missy Ryan and Cynthia Barrera, "Mexicans Hope 'La Barbie' Arrest May Turn Tide," Reuters, August 31, 2010.

14. Quoted in Adriana Barrera, "Mexican Marines Capture Top Drug Lieutenant," Reuters, September 13, 2010; and E. Eduardo Castillo, "Mexican Marines Arrest Presumed Drug Kingpin," Associated Press, September 12, 2010.

15. "Outsmarted by Sinaloa," *The Economist*, January 7, 2010.

16. John Burnett, Marisa Penalosa, and Robert Benincasa, "Mexico Seems to Favor Sinaloa Cartel in Drug War," National Public Radio, transcript, May 19, 2010, p. 1.

17. Ibid., p. 3.

18. Beckhusen, "Mexico Launches New Offensive against Cartel."

19. David Luhnow and José De Córdoba, "Hit Men Kill Mexican Hero's Family," *Wall Street Journal*, December 23, 2009.

20. Olga R. Rodríguez, "Top Mexican Drug Lord Killed in Clash with Army," Associated Press, July 29, 2010; and Alberto Fajardo, "Mexico Kills Kingpin in Drug War Coup," Reuters, July 29, 2010.

21. Quoted in Tracy Wilkinson, "Leading Mexico Drug Gang Suspect Arrested," *Los Angeles Times*, June 22, 2011.

22. González Armendez and Martínez, both quoted in Martha Mendoza and Elliott Spagat, "Violence Expected as Mexican Drug Lord Arrested," Associated Press, January 13, 2010.

23. Quoted in Sara Miller Llana, "In Mexico, Skepticism That Arrest of Edgar Valdez Villarreal–'La Barbie'–Will Stem Drug Trade," *Christian Science Monitor*, August 31, 2010.

24. Ibid.

25. Quoted in Robert Campbell, "Mexican Cartels Cannot be Defeated, Drug Lord Says," Reuters, April 4, 2010.

26. Catherine Bremer, "Mexico's Drug War Leaves a Generation of Narco Widows," Reuters, January 20, 2010.

27. Quoted in Robin Emmott, "Mexicans Mourn Drug War Victims on Day of the Dead," Reuters, November 2, 2009.

28. Quoted in Elisabeth Malkin, "In Mexican Vote, Nostalgia for Past Corruption," *New York Times*, July 7, 2009.

29. "Sugiere Rubén Aguilar Negociar Con El Narco," *Reforma*, December 20, 2008.

30. Quoted in William Booth and Steve Fainaru, "New Strategy Urged in Mexico," *Washington Post*, July 28, 2009.

31. Olga R. Rodríguez and Alexandra Olson, "Vote Shows Mexicans Have Little Faith in Any Party," Associated Press, July 5, 2010.

32. Tim Johnson, "Drug Violence Casts Dark Shadow Over Mexican Vote," *McClatchy Newspapers*, July 4, 2010; and Rodríguez and Olson, "Voters Show Mexicans Have Little Faith in Any Party."

33. Quoted in Booth and Fainaru, "New Strategy Urged in Mexico."

34. "Critican Propuesta de Rubén Aguilar," *Reforma*, December 19, 2008.

35. Quoted in Mayolo López, "Descarta Calderón Negociar Con Carteles," *Reforma*, December 20, 2008.

36. Quoted in Booth and Fainaru, "New Strategy Urged in Mexico."

37. Quoted in William Booth, "Mexico's Drug Violence Claims Hundreds of Lives in Five Days," *Washington Post*, June 16, 2010.

38. Quoted in Robin Emmott, "Calderón Says More Drug Violence Likely Ahead," Reuters, August 24, 2010.

39. Quoted in "Ex-Mexico Prez Suggests Truce with Drug Cartels," Associated Press, August 26, 2011.

40. Quoted in Olga R. Rodríguez, "Point Man in Mexico's War on Drug Cartels Resigns," Associated Press, September 8, 2009.

41. Quoted in Julie Watson, "With New AG, Mexico Tries to Revamp Drug War," Associated Press, September 9, 2009.

42. Quoted in Luhnow and De Córdoba, "Mexico Eases Ban on Drug Possession," *Wall Street Journal*, August 22, 2009.

43. Quoted in Watson, "With New AG, Mexico Tries to Revamp Drug War."

44. Mark Stevenson, "Mexican President Says Crime Now Third Priority," Associated Press, January 7, 2010.

45. Quoted in E. Eduardo Castillo, "Ex-Mexico President Calls for Legalizing Drugs," Associated Press, August 8, 2010.

46. Mary Anastasia O'Grady, "Mexico's Hopeless Drug War," *Wall Street Journal*, September 13, 2009.

47. A version of this section appeared as "Drug Mayhem Moves South," *National Interest* 117 (January–February 2012): 32–37.

48. Shannon O'Neil, "The Real War in Mexico," 66.

49. O'Grady, "Mexico's Hopeless Drug War."

50. Quoted in Ioan Grillo, "Behind the Murder of a Drug Czar," *Time.com*, December 17, 2009.

51. Nick Miroff and William Booth, "Violence Accompanies Cartels in Move South," *Washington Post*, July 27, 2010.

52. Ibid.

53. Ibid.

54. Hal Brands, *Crime, Violence, and the Crisis in Guatemala: A Case Study in the Erosion of the State*, (Carlisle, PA: U.S. Army War College, Strategic Studies Institute, May 2010). The situation has grown even worse in the two years since Brand prepared his study.

55. Herbert Hernández, "Outgunned Guatemala Army Extends Battle with Drug Gangs," Reuters, January 18, 2011.

56. Katherine Corcoran, "Mexican Drug Cartels Move Into Central America," Associated Press, March 13, 2011.

57. Quoted in Oakland Ross, "The Shifting Epicenter of Drug Violence in Central America," *TheStar.com*, August 28, 2011.

58. William Booth, "Central America Asks U.S. for Help with Drug Cartels," *Washington Post*, June 22, 2011.

59. Monica Villamizar, "A Drug Trafficker's Paradise," Aljazeera.net/Americas, August 15, 2011, http://blogs.aljazeera.net/americas/2011/08/15/drug-traffickers-paradise.

60. Lauren Mathae, "Drug Trafficking: Central America's Dark Shadow," Council on Hemispheric Affairs Report, August 16, 2011.

61. "Drug Traffickers Capitalize on Permissive and Weak Governments of Central America," *Inside Costa Rica*, August 5, 2011.

62. "Mexico and Costa Rica Vow to Fight Drug Cartels," FoxNews Latino, August 23, 2011.

63. Quoted in Mathae, "Drug Trafficking: Central America's Dark Shadow."

64. "Alvaro Colom: 'Huge Aggression' by Cartels," Aljazeera.net, August 14, 2011, http://www.aljazeera.com/indepth/spotlight/drugscentral/2011/08/201181454515250330.html.

65. Colom interview with Agence France Presse, August 2, 2011, *Ticotimes.net.*, August 3, 2011.

66. Corcoran, "Mexican Drug Cartels Move Into Central America."

67. Quoted in Booth, "Central America Asks U.S. for Help With Drug Cartels."

68. Ibid.

69. Quoted in Marianella Jiménez, "Costa Rica Wants U.S. Anti-Drug Program for CentAm," Associated Press, August 17, 2010.

70. Booth, "Central America Asks U.S. for Help with Drug Cartels."

Chapter 7

1. Quoted in Jerry Markon, "2,200 Arrested in U.S. Crackdown on Mexican Drug Cartels," *Washington Post,* June 11, 2010.

2. Sylvia Longmire, *Cartel: The Coming Invasion of Mexico's Drug Wars* (New York: Palgrave Macmillan, 2011), pp. 161–68.

3. Stephanie Simon, "Pot 'Plantations' on the Rise," *Wall Street Journal,* September 3, 2009.

4. Alicia A. Caldwell and Manuel Valdes, "Drug Gangs Taking Over U.S. Public Lands," Associated Press, March 1, 2010.

5. See Bob Killebrew and Jennifer Bernal, *Crime Wars: Gangs, Cartels, and U.S. National Security* (Washington: Center for a New American Security, September 2010).

6. Malcolm Beith, *The Last Narco: Inside the Hunt for El Chapo, the World's Most Wanted Drug Lord* (New York: Grove Press, 2010), pp. 176–80.

7. Evan Peréz and David Luhnow, "Sweep Strikes Blow Against Mexican Cartel," *Wall Street Journal,* October 23, 2009.

8. Quoted in Mark Strassmann, "Exclusive: Mexican Drug Cartels in Atlanta," CBS Evening News, October 21, 2009.

9. Christopher Sherman, "Texas Sheriff Among Those Sentenced in Drug Ring," Associated Press, August 27, 2009.

10. Edwin Mora, "127 Border Patrol and Customs Workers Arrested for Corruption," CNSNews.com, June 9, 2011.

11. Quoted in Randal C. Archibold, "Hired by Customs, but Working for the Cartels," *New York Times,* December 18, 2009.

12. An excellent account of Martha Garnica and her corrupt activities on behalf of traffickers is the long feature article by Ceci Connolly, "The Inside Woman," *Washington Post,* September 12, 2010.

13. Ibid.

14. Quoted in Archibold, "Hired by Customs."

15. Archibold, "Hired by Customs."

16. Mora, "127 Border Patrol and Customs Workers Arrested for Corruption."

17. Quoted in Connolly, "The Inside Woman."

18. "Travel Warning," U.S. Department of State, Bureau of Consular Affairs, Mexico, April 22, 2011, p. 3.

19. U.S. Department of State, "Current Report of Non-Natural Death Causes Abroad, July 1, 2005–June 30, 2008, Mexico," http://travel.state.gov/law/family_issues/death/death_600.html.

20. Ben Conery and Jerry Seper, "Border Violence Threatens Americans," *Washington Times,* April 1, 2010.

21. "Travel Warning," U.S. Department of State, p. 2.

22. "Mexican Police Say They Freed U.S. Kidnap Victim," Associated Press, November 9, 2009.

23. Bill Whitaker, "Brutal Drug War Fueled By U.S. Appetite," CBS News, transcript, December 16, 2008, p. 3.

24. Mariano Castillo, "Texas Boy, 7, Gunned Down While Visiting His Father in Mexico, Officials Say," CNN.com, November 18, 2009.

25. Quoted in William Booth, "Ambushed by a Drug War," *Washington Post,* July 23, 2009.

26. Quoted in Julian Cardona, "U.S. Soldier Dies in Drug Attack in Mexico Strip Bar," Reuters, November 4, 2009.

27. Quoted in José De Cordoba and Joel Millman, "Mexico Gunbattle Spurs U.S. Warning," *Wall Street Journal*, August 24, 2010.

28. Quoted in Robin Emmott and Missy Ryan, "U.S. Staff Told to Send Children Out of Mexican City," Reuters, August 27, 2010.

29. Morgan Lee, "Mexican Murder Suspect: U.S. Consulate Infiltrated," Associated Press, July 3, 2010.

30. William Booth, "Gang Formed in Texas Prison Tied to Contract Killings," *Washington Post*, April 4, 2010; and James C. McKinley Jr., "Suspect Says Juárez Killers Had Pursued Jail Guard," *New York Times*, March 31, 2010.

31. "U.S. Consulate in Ciudad Juárez Closes For Security," Associated Press, July 29, 2010.

32. "Explosive Device Tossed at U.S. Consulate in Mexico," Reuters, April 10, 2010.

33. "FBI, Police Raid Gang in Texas after Mexico Murders," Agence France Presse, March 18, 2010.

34. Jerry Langton, *Gangland: The Rise of the Mexican Drug Cartels from El Paso to Vancouver* (Mississauga, ON: Wiley, 2012), p. 235.

35. Quoted in Danna Harman, "Mexican Drug Cartels's Wars Move Closer to U.S. Border," *USA Today*, August 17, 2005.

36. CNN, "Lou Dobbs Tonight," transcript, June 4, 2008, p.1.

37. Quoted in Megan Basham, "Cartel Assassins," *American Spectator*, August 17, 2005.

38. Ioan Grillo, *El Narco: Inside Mexico's Criminal Insurgency* (New York: Bloomsbury Press, 2011), p. 243.

39. Gabriel Arana, "The Border Violence Myth," *Nation*, May 27, 2009.

40. Daniel Pastrana and Aprille Muscara, "Little Spillover of 'Narco-Deaths,'" Inter Press Service, March 19, 2011.

41. Andrew Rice, "Life on the Line," *New York Times Magazine*, July 28, 2011.

42. Quoted in Kevin Johnson, "Violence Drops in U.S. Cities Neighboring Mexico," *USA Today*, December 27, 2009.

43. Fox Business Network, "America's Nightly Scoreboard," August 19, 2010.

44. Quoted in William Booth, "Mayhem Crosses the Border with Informers," *Washington Post*, August 17, 2009.

45. Ibid.

46. Alicia A. Caldwell, "Bullets from Mexican Shootout Hit Texas City Hall," Associated Press, June 30, 2010; Maggie Ybarra and Adriana Gómez Licon, "Mexican Authorities: Federal Agents Could Have Fired Bullets that Struck City Hall," *El Paso Times*, July 2, 2010; and "Gunfire Hitting City Hall Prompts Texas AG to Ask for More Troops on Border," *El Paso Times*, June 30, 2010.

47. Grillo, *El Narco*, pp. 251–55.

48. CBS 11 TV, "Drug Violence Spills over the Border from Mexico," October 27, 2008. See Ed Lavandera, "Police: U.S. Teens Were Hit Men for Mexican Cartel," CNN.com, March 12, 2009, articles.cnn.com/2009-03-12/justice/cartel.teens_1_drug-cartels-los-zetas-mexican-gulf-cartel.

49. "Mexico: The Iraq Next Door," editorial, *Investor's Business Daily*, November 12, 2008.

50. Alicia Caldwell, "4 Accused of Nabbing Texas Man Later Found Slain," Associated Press, February 18, 2010.

51. Alicia A. Caldwell, "Mexican Cartel List Targets Americans, Police Say," Associated Press, June 20, 2008.

52. Tim Gaynor, "Mexico Drug Gang Threatens Arizona Police," Reuters, June 23, 2010.

53. Thomas Gutiérrez and Wayne Drash, "Being a Cop in Border Town More Perilous as Drug Cartels Issue Threats," CNN.com, June 24, 2010.

54. "An Illegal Bounty," editorial, *Investor's Business Daily*, August 3, 2010.

55. Quoted in Booth, "Mayhem Crosses the Border with Informers."

56. "Mexico Extradites Man Accused of Killing U.S. Agent," Associated Press, January 28, 2010; and "Mexico Police Name Suspect in Border Agent Death," Associated Press, July 27, 2009.

57. Majority Staff of the House Committee on Homeland Security, Subcommittee on Investigations, "A Line in the Sand: Confronting the Threat at the Southwest Border," Interim Report, October 2006, p 19.

58. Department of Homeland Security, Customs and Border Protection, Office of Border Patrol, "Mexican Government Incidents," Fiscal Year Report, 2007, pp. 4, 7–15.

59. Jerry Seper, "Official Questions Mexico at Border," *Washington Times*, August 11, 2008.

60. Quoted in Casey Wian, "U.S. Border Agents Detain Mexican Troops," CNN.com, November 1, 2008.

61. Jerry Seper, "Border Patrol Agent Held at Gunpoint," *Washington Times*, August 6, 2008.

62. Quoted in "Gunbattles Paralyze Mexican City Across from Texas," Associated Press, July 22, 2010.

63. Paul J. Weber, "In Texas, Fear Follows Mexicans Who Flee Drug War," Associated Press, March 29, 2010.

64. Ibid.

65. For an analysis of the Falcon Lake shooting and its probable larger context, see Scott Stewart, "The Falcon Lake Murder and Mexico's Drug Wars," *Security Weekly*, Stratfor.com, October 21, 2010, http://www.stratfor.com/weekly/20101020_falcon_lake_murder_and_mexicos_drug_wars?utm_source=SWeekly&utm_medium=email&utm_campaign=101021&utm_content=readmore&elq=957c21f7de0742a18c24b9413f009e7c.

66. Quoted in Paul J. Weber, "Texas Farmers Say Drug War Making Job Dangerous," Associated Press, March 11, 2011.

67. Ibid.

68. Quoted in Paul Davenport, "Ariz. Gov.: Most Illegal Immigrants Smuggling Drugs," Associated Press, June 25, 2010.

69. Liz Goodwin, "McCain Disputes Governor's Claim on Drug Mules," *Yahoo! News*, June 28, 2010.

70. "Shootout at El Paso City Hall," editorial, *Investor's Business Daily*, July 2, 2010.

71. Quoted in Jerry Seper and Matthew Cella, "Signs in Arizona Warn of Smuggler Dangers," *Washington Times*, September 1, 2010.

Chapter 8

1. Quoted in Diego Urdaneta, "Clinton Says Mexico Drug Crackdown 'Absolutely Necessary,'" Agence France Presse, January 24, 2011.

2. Quoted in Nacha Cattan, "Why Hillary Clinton Flagged Judicial Reform as 'Essential' to Mexico's Drug War," *Christian Science Monitor*, January 25, 2011.

3. United States Government Accountability Office, *Mérida Initiative: The United States Has Provided Counternarcotics and Anticrime Support but Needs Better Performance Measures*, Report to Congressional Requesters, GAO-10-837, July 2010, p. 2.

4. Quoted in Marc Lacey, "Report Says U.S. Fails to Assess Drug Aid to Mexico," *New York Times*, July 20, 2010.

5. GAO July 2010 report, p. 18.

6. Alexandra Olson, "GAO report: Mexico Drug Aid Needs Better Oversight," *U-T San Diego*, July 20, 2010, http://www.signsonsandiego.com/news/2010/jul/20/gao-report-mexico-drug-aid-needs-better-oversight/.

7. Quoted in Katherine Corcoran, "ATF: New Accord with Mexico Will Boost Gun Traces," Associated Press, October 6, 2010.

8. Quoted in E. Eduardo Castillo and Martha Mendoza, "U.S. Officials Seek Drug War Change," Associated Press, May 26, 2010.

9. Quoted in Cattan, "Why Hillary Clinton Flagged Judicial Reform as 'Essential to Mexico's Drug War.'"

10. Robert C. Bonner, "The New Cocaine Cowboys: How to Defeat Mexico's Drug Cartels," *Foreign Affairs* 89, no. 4 (July–August 2010): 44–45.

11. Quoted in Adam Entous and Nathan Hodge, "U.S. Sees Heightened Threat in Mexico," *Wall Street Journal*, September 10, 2010.

12. "Mexico Facing 'Insurgency,' Clinton Says," National Public Radio, September 9, 2010.

13. Quoted in Mica Rosenberg, "Mexico Drug War Not Comparable to Colombia: Obama," Reuters, September 9, 2010.

14. Quoted in Entous and Hodge, "U.S. Sees Heightened Threat in Mexico."

15. Bonner, "The New Cocaine Cowboys," p. 39.

16. William Booth and Steve Fainaru, "New Strategy Urged in Mexico," *Washington Post*, July 28, 2009.

17. Quoted in Katherine Corcoran, "U.S. Cables: Mexico Drug War Lacks Clear Strategy," Associated Press, December 3, 2010.

18. Ibid.

19. Ibid.

20. Ibid.

21. Ibid.

22. Quoted in "Leaked Cables Suggest U.S. Doubted Mexico Prosecutor," Associated Press, March 9, 2011.

23. Quoted in Alexandra Olson, "U.S. Ambassador to Mexico Quits Amid WikiLeaks Furor," Associated Press, March 20, 2011.

24. Quoted in "Washington Hails Killing of Mexican Drug Lord," Agence France Presse, December 17, 2009.

25. "Mexico Catches Cartel Suspect Linked to 109 Deaths," Associated Press, December 19, 2009.

26. Mark Mazzetti and Ginger Thompson, "U.S. Widens Role in Mexican Fight against Crime," *New York Times*, August 25, 2011.

27. Quoted in E. Eduardo Castillo, "Mexico's Top Diplomat Defends U.S. Drone Flights," Associated Press, March 18, 2011.

28. Mazzetti and Thompson, "U.S. Widens Role in Mexican Fight against Crime."

29. Quoted in E. Eduardo Castillo and Martha Mendoza, "U.S. Law Enforcement Role in Mexico's Drug War Surges," Associated Press, March 20, 2011.

30. Quoted in Mazzetti and Thompson, "U.S. Widens Role in Mexico's Fight against Crime."

31. Quoted in Matthew D. La Plante, "Army Official Suggests U.S. Troops Might be Needed in Mexico," *Salt Lake City Tribune*, February 8, 2011.

32. Quoted in "Mexico Angry at U.S. Officials 'Insurgency' Remarks," Associated Press, February 9, 2011.

33. Quoted in Ioan Grillo, "In Decriminalizing Much Drug Use, Mexico May Be Setting an Example," *Time.com*, August 26, 2009.

34. Quoted in David Luhnow and José De Córdoba, "Mexico Eases Ban on Drug Possession," *Wall Street Journal*, August 22, 2009.

35. For a description of the offensive inside the United States against the Mexican cartels and the various federal and state agencies involved, see Sylvia Longmire, *Cartel: The Coming Invasion of Mexico's Drug Wars* (New York: Palgrave Macmillan, 2011), pp. 141–56, 194–98.

36. Quoted in James C. McKinley Jr., "U.S. Arrests Hundreds in Raids on Drug Cartel," *New York Times*, October 3, 2009.

37. Ioan Grillo, *El Narco: Inside Mexico's Criminal Insurgency* (New York: Bloomsbury Press, 2011), pp. 253–55.

38. Quoted in McKinley, "U.S. Arrests Hundreds in Raids on Drug Cartel."

39. Quoted in Spencer S. Hsu, "Raid Targets Mexican Cartel; 303 Arrested," *Washington Post*, October 23, 2009.

40. Quoted in Jerry Markon, "2,200 Arrested in U.S. Crackdown on Mexican Drug Cartels," *Washington Post*, June 11, 2010.

41. Quoted in Jerry Seper, "Massive Bust Nets Suspects, Drugs in 18 States," *Washington Times*, June 10, 2010.

42. Karin Zeitvogel, "U.S. Arrests 678 Gang Members, Many Tied to Mexico Cartels," Agence France Presse, March 1, 2011.

43. Quoted in Evan Pérez and David Luhnow, "Sweep Strikes Blow against Mexican Cartel," *Wall Street Journal*, October 23, 2009.

Chapter 9

1. Traci Carl, "Progress in Mexico Drug War Is Drenched in Blood," Associated Press, March 10, 2009, http://www.msnbc.msn.com/id/29620369/ns/world_news-americas/t/progress-mexico-drug-war-blood-drenched/.

2. Robert C. Bonner, "The New Cocaine Cowboys: How to Defeat Mexico's Drug Cartels," *Foreign Affairs* 89, no. 4 (July–August, 2010): 41.

3. Quoted in Tim Johnson "Mexico Rethinks Drug Strategy as Death Toll Soars," *McClatchy Newspapers*, August 12, 2010.

4. Quoted in "Mexico Slams 'Absurd' U.S. Gun Laws as Drug War Rages," Reuters, June 14, 2008.

5. Quoted in "Calderón's Shot at American Guns," editorial, *Washington Times*, May 24, 2010.

6. "Mexico at the Brink," editorial, *New York Times*, June 4, 2008.

7. Pamela Starr, "Mexico's Spreading Drug Violence," *Los Angeles Times*, October 22, 2008.

8. The fall-back position for those who blame U.S.-origin weapons for much of Mexico's violence is that, regardless of the specific percentage, a substantial portion of those weapons come from U.S. gun stores and gun shows. See Ioan Grillo, *El Narco: Inside Mexico's Criminal Insurgency* (New York; Bloomsbury Press, 2011), pp. 212–17. Grillo's account actually is much more balanced than those produced by most analysts who subscribe to that theory.

9. Starr, "Mexico's Spreading Drug Violence."

10. Catherine E. Shoichet, "U.S.-Mexico Group Urges New Assault Weapons Ban," Associated Press, October 14, 2009.

11. CNN, "Lou Dobbs Tonight," transcript, June 9, 2008, p.1, http://transcripts.cnn.com/TRANSCRIPTS/0806/09/ldt.01.html.

12. Quoted in Ioan Grillo, "Obama's Mexico Mission: Keep Guns El Norte," *Time.com*, August 10, 2009.

13. Nacha Cattan, "Why Hillary Clinton Flagged Judicial Reform as 'Essential' to Mexico's Drug War," *Christian Science Monitor*, January 25, 2011.

14. Quoted in Sam Quinones, "State of War," *Foreign Policy* 171 (March/April 2009): 78.

15. See Nick Miroff and William Booth, "Mexican Drug Cartels' Newest Weapon: Cold War-Era Grenades Made in U.S.," *Washington Post*, July 17, 2010.

16. Ibid.

17. "Calderón's Shot at American Guns," *Washington Times*.

18. Juan Carlos Llorca, "Mexico Drug Cartel's Grenades from Guatemalan Army," Associated Press, June 4, 2009.

19. Ronan Graham, "Honduran Guns Feeding Central American Arms Trade," *Honduras Weekly*, August 13, 2011.

20. E. Eduardo Castillo, "Mexico Sends More Police, Army after Gang Attacks," Associated Press, July 16, 2009.

21. "Tijuana Police Find 2nd Body Hanging from Bridge," Associated Press, October 17, 2009.

22. A report by the international consulting firm STRATFOR provides the most detailed critique of that figure and explains why it is inflated. See Scott Stewart, "Mexico's Gun Supply and the 90 Percent Myth," *Security Weekly*, February 10, 2011, *stratfor.com*, http://www.stratfor.com/weekly/20110209-mexicos-gun-supply-and-90-percent-myth.

23. Jorge Castañeda, "A Response to Roberts, Carpenter, and Hanson," *Cato Unbound*, August 14, 2009, http://www.cato-unbound.org/2009/08/14/jorge-castaneda/a-response-to-roberts-carpenter-and-hanson/. *Cuernos de chivo* (literally "goat's horns") are named for the curved ammunition magazines on the weapons.

24. Katherine Corcoran, "ATF: New Accord with Mexico Will Boost Gun Traces," Associated Press, October 6, 2010.

25. Ibid.

26. David Rittgers, "Mexican Criminals, American Guns," *National Review Online*, March 21, 2011.

27. Quoted in Corcoran, "ATF: New Accord with Mexico Will Boost Gun Traces." For another example of that argument, see Grillo, *El Narco*, pp. 213–15.

28. Nacha Cattan, "Mexico Lawmakers Livid Over U.S. 'Operation Fast and Furious,'" *Christian Science Monitor*, March 9, 2011.

29. John C. Moorhouse and Brent Wanner, "Does Gun Control Reduce Crime or Does Crime Increase Gun Control?" *Cato Journal* 26, no.1 (Winter 2006): 103–24; C. E. Moody and T. B. Marvell, "Guns and Crime," *Southern Economic Journal* 71, no. 4 (2005): 720–36; and Gary A. Mauser and Don B. Kates, "Would Banning Firearms Reduce Murder and Suicide? A Review of International Evidence," *Bepress Legal Series*, Working Paper 1413, August 17, 2006, http://law.bepress.com/expresso/eps/1564.

30. See Robert Farago, "Fewer Firearms, More Crimes: Gun Control Set Off Explosion of Drug-Cartel Violence," *Washington Times*, October 1, 2010.

31. William Booth, "U.S. Struggles to Stop Flow of Guns to Mexico," *Washington Post*, October 7, 2010.

32. Alexis Okeowo, "To Battle Drug Lords, Mexico Weighs a Crackdown on Twitter," *Time.com*, April 14, 2010.

33. Lou Dobbs, former CNN and now Fox News host, is one of the most outspoken advocates of that approach, both to reduce the amount of illegal immigration and to stop the spread of drug trafficking and its associated violence spilling across the border. See, for example, his comments on two programs. CNN, "Lou Dobbs Tonight," transcript, May 14, 2008, pp.1–2, and CNN, "Lou Dobbs Tonight," transcript, June 9, 2008, p. 2.

34. Duncan Hunter, "National Security = Border Security," *Washington Times*, June 12, 2008.

35. Quoted in Jerry Seper, "Official Questions Mexico at Border," *Washington Times*, August 11, 2008.

36. Quoted in Randal C. Archibold, "Ranchers Alarmed by Killing Near Border," *New York Times*, April 4, 2010.

37. For a good overview of the logistical challenges involved in securing the border, see Will Weissert, "Promises, Promises: Securing U.S. Border Impossible," Associated Press, December 6, 2011.

38. Randal C. Archibold, "As U.S. Tightens Mexico Border, Smugglers Are Taking to the Sea," *New York Times*, July 18, 2009.

39. Kevin G. Hall, "U.S. Intelligence Prompted Mexico's Seizure of Drug Sub," McClatchy News Service, July 18, 2008. According to the U.S. military's Southern Command, at least 40 drug submarines had been spotted since 2006, mostly off the Pacific coast of Central America or Mexico.

40. Frank Bajak, "DEA: Seized Submarine Quantum Leap for Narcos," Associated Press, July 4, 2010.

41. Quoted in Lauren Frayer, "Soldiers Seize Drug Slingshot on U.S.-Mexico Border," *AOL News*, January 27, 2011.

42. Robin Emmott, "Mexico Captures 19 Suspected Drug Gang Planes," Reuters, November 13, 2008.

43. Sara Miller Llana, "U.S. Border Patrol Shooting Threatens Mexico Drug War Cooperation," *Christian Science Monitor*, June 10, 2010.

44. Olivia Torres and Christopher Sherman, "Mexico Anger High as U.S. Border Patrol Kills Teen," Associated Press, June 9, 2010; and Nicholas Casey, "FBI Probes Mexican Border Death," *Wall Street Journal*, June 9, 2010.

45. Ted Galen Carpenter, *Bad Neighbor Policy: Washington's Futile War on Drugs in Latin America* (New York: Palgrave Macmillan, 2003), p. 4.

46. Data for drug use trends in the United States are taken from the U.S. Department of Health and Human Services website. See "Results from the 2009 National Survey on Drug Use and Health: Volume II. Technical Appendices and Selected Prevalence Tables," http://www.oas.samhsa.gov/NSDUH/2k9NSDUH/2k9ResultsApps. htm; "Results from the 2009 National Survey on Drug Use and Health: Detailed Tables," http://oas.samhsa.gov/NSDUH/2k9NSDUH/tabs/Sect7peTabs29to31.pdf; "Results from the 2002 National Survey on Drug Use and Health: Detailed Tables," http://oas.samhsa.gov/nhsda/2k2nsduh/Sect4peTabs1to14.pdf; "Results from the 2001 National Household Survey on Drug Abuse: Volume II. Technical Appendices and Selected Data Tables," http://oas.samhsa.gov/NHSDA/2k1NHSDA/vol2/appendixh_1.htm; "Summary of Findings from the 2000 National Household Survey on Drug Abuse," http://oas.samhsa.gov/NHSDA/2kNHSDA/2knhsda. htm; "1998 National Household Survey on Drug Abuse," http://oas.samhsa.gov/NHSDA/98DetailedTables/sumtab98.pdf; "Office of Applied Studies, National Household Survey on Drug Abuse," Advance Report #18 (1995), http://oas.samhsa. gov/nhsda/ar18ttoc.htm; and "National Survey on Drug Abuse: Main Findings 1982," http://www.eric.ed.gov/PDFS/ED237844.pdf.

47. U.S. Department of State, Bureau of International Narcotics and Law Enforcement Affairs, *International Narcotics Control Strategy Report, 1998*, February 1999, http://www.state.gov/www/global/narcotics_law/1998_narc_report/index.html; and *International Narcotics Control Strategy Report, 2005*, March 2005, http://www.state.gov/j/inl/rls/nrcrpt/2005/.

48. Quoted in Bill Whitaker, "Brutal Drug War Fueled by U.S. Appetite," CBS News, transcript, December 16, 2008, p. 2.

49. Quoted in Mark Landler, "Clinton Says U.S. Feeds Mexico Drug Trade," *New York Times*, March 26, 2009.

Chapter 10

1. Tim Johnson, "For Mexican Cartels, Marijuana Is Still Gold," *McClatchy Newspapers*, September 2, 2010.

2. Quoted in Mexico, Presidency of the Republic, Felipe Calderón Hinojosa, "The Fight for Public Safety," June 13, 2010. Also see William Booth, "Mexico's Drug Violence Claims Hundreds of Lives in Five Days," *Washington Post*, June 16, 2010.

3. His tendency to blame U.S. drug consumption for Mexico's woes has not softened with time. Following the bloody attack on the Casino Royale in Monterrey in August 2011, Calderón again blamed the "insatiable" U.S. consumer demand for drugs. Miguel Ángel Gutíerrez, "Mexico's Calderon Berates U.S. after Casino Attack," Reuters, August 26, 2011.

4. Quoted in Mark Landler, "Clinton Says U.S. Feeds Mexico Drug Trade," *New York Times*, March 26, 2009.

5. Robert C. Bonner, "The New Cocaine Cowboys: How to Defeat Mexico's Drug Cartels," *Foreign Affairs* 89, no. 4 (July–August, 2010): 37.

6. United Nations, International Narcotics Control Board, *Report of the International Narcotics Board for 2007* (New York: United Nations, 2007), pp. 95, 100, http://www.incb.org/incb/en/annual-report-2007.html.

7. Lisa Haugaard, Adam Isacson, and Jennifer Johnson, *A Cautionary Tale: Plan Colombia's Lessons for U.S. Policy Toward Mexico and Beyond* (Washington: Latin America Working Group Education Fund, Center for International Policy, and Washington Office on Latin America, November 2011), p. 7.

8. Robin Emmott, "Cartel Inc.: In the Company of Narcos," Reuters, January 14, 2010.

9. Quoted in A. William Samii, "Drug Abuse: Iran's Thorniest Problem," *Brown Journal of World Affairs* 9, no. 2 (Winter/Spring 2003): 283.

10. For an overall discussion of the failure of supply-side campaigns in the Western Hemisphere, see Ted Galen Carpenter, *Bad Neighbor Policy: Washington's Futile War on Drugs in Latin America* (New York: Palgrave Macmillan, 2003), pp. 5–7, 21–23, 97–98, 118–21, and 230–31. For a recent study of the extreme difficulties involved in dampening the global supply of just one drug, heroin, see Letizia Paoli, Victoria A. Greenfield, and Peter Reuter, *The World Heroin Market: Can Supply Be Cut?* (New York: Oxford University Press, 2009).

11. Shannon K. O'Neil, "How Mexico Can Win the Drug War, Colombia's Way," Bloomberg.com, June 17, 2011.

12. Bonner, "The New Cocaine Cowboys," pp. 35–36.

13. Ibid., p. 43.

14. Ibid., p. 42.

15. Quoted in Juan Forero, "Colombia Shares Its Cartel-Fighting Expertise with Mexican Forces," *Washington Post*, January 22, 2011.

16. O'Neil, "How Mexico Can Win the Drug War, Colombia's Way." For a more restrained assessment of the Colombia model, and especially the performance of Plan Colombia, see Haugaard, Isacson, and Johnson, *A Cautionary Tale*. Also see Daniel Mejia, "Evaluating Plan Colombia," in Philip Keefer and Norman Loayza, eds., *Innocent Bystanders: Developing Countries and the War on Drugs* (New York: Palgrave Macmillan, 2010), pp. 135–64.

17. Bonner, "The New Cocaine Cowboys," p. 42.

18. Haugaard, Isacson, and Johnson, *A Cautionary Tale*, p. 8.

19. Jack Kimball, "Colombia Crime Gangs Spur More Massacres in '10: UN," Reuters, February 24, 2011.

20. Karen De Young and Claudia J. Duque, "U.S. Aid Implicated in Abuses of Power in Colombia," *Washingtonpost.com*, August 20, 2011. Also see Haugaard, Isacson, and Johnson, *A Cautionary Tale*, pp. 8–9, 19.

21. John Burnett, "Nuevo Laredo Returns to Normal as Violence Slows," NPR transcript, January 23, 2009, http://www.npr.org/templates/story/story.php?storyId=99742620.

22. Ibid.

23. U.S. Department of State, Bureau for International Narcotics and Law Enforcement Affairs, *International Narcotics Control Strategy Report*, March 2006, pp. 18–19.

24. Drug Enforcement Administration, *Speaking Out Against Drug Legalization* (2010), pp. 46–47, 54.

25. DEA, *Speaking Out Against Drug Legalization*, p. 9.

26. Glenn Greenwald, "Drug Decriminalization in Portugal: Lessons for Creating Fair and Successful Drug Policies," Cato Institute White Paper, April 2, 2009.

27. However, the Netherlands seems to be waffling on its reforms. See Toby Sterling, "Amsterdam Moves to Close a Fifth of 'Coffee Shops,'" Associated Press, November 21, 2008.

28. "Legalize Drugs to Fight Trafficking: Zelaya," Agence France Presse, October 13, 2008. For a concise analysis of Zelaya's proposal and the growing sentiment for the liberalization of drug laws in the Western Hemisphere, see Juan Carlos Hidalgo, "President of Honduras Calls for Drug Legalization," Cato-at-Liberty, October 14, 2008, http://www.cato-at-liberty.org/president-of-honduras-calls-for-drug-legalization/.

29. Fernando Henrique Cardoso, César Gavria, and Ernesto Zedillo, "The War on Drugs Is a Failure," *Wall Street Journal*, February 23, 2009.

30. *War on Drugs*, Report of the Global Commission on Drug Policy, June 2011.

31. Ibid., p. 2.

32. Ibid., p. 3.

33. Miguel Ángel Gutiérrez, "Mexico Seeks to Decriminalize Small-Time Drug Use," Reuters, October 3, 2008.

34. David Luhnow and José De Córdoba, "Mexico Eases Ban on Drug Possession," *Wall Street Journal*, August 22, 2009; and Ioan Grillo, "In Decriminalizing Much Drug Use, Mexico May Be Setting an Example," *Time.com*, August 26, 2009, http://www.time.com/time/world/article/0,8599,1918725,00.html.

35. Quoted in E. Eduardo Castillo, "Ex-Mexico President Calls for Legalizing Drugs," Associated Press, August 8, 2010.

36. Quoted in Grillo, "In Decriminalizing Much Drug Use, Mexico May Be Setting an Example."

37. Jeffrey A. Miron and Katherine Waldock, "The Budgetary Impact of Ending Drug Prohibition," Cato Institute White Paper, September 27, 2010.

38. Luhnow and De Córdoba, "Mexico Eases Ban on Drug Possession."

39. Mary Anastasia O'Grady, "Mexico's Hopeless Drug War," *Wall Street Journal*, September 13, 2009.

40. John McWhorter, "How the War on Drugs Is Destroying Black America," *Cato's Letter* 9, no. 1 (Winter 2011), p. 2

41. David Johnson and Neil A. Lewis, "Obama Administration to Stop Raids on Medical Marijuana Dispensers," *New York Times*, March 3, 2009.

42. "Feds Cracking Down on California Medical Marijuana Dispensaries," *Los Angeles Times*, October 6, 2011.

43. Luhnow and De Córdoba, "Mexico Eases Ban on Drug Possession"; and Ryan Grim, "Majority of Americans Want Pot Legalized: Zogby," *Huffington Post*, May 6, 2009.

44. "Record-High 50% of Americans Favor Legalizing Marijuana Use," Gallup Survey, October 17, 2011, http://www.gallup.com/poll/150149/record-high-americans-favor-legalizing-marijuana.aspx.

45. For a discussion of the international legal and diplomatic issues involved in ending drug prohibition, see Ted Galen Carpenter, "Ending the International Drug War," in Jefferson Fish, ed., *How to Legalize Drugs* (London: Aronson, 1998), pp. 293–309.

46. Johnson, "For Mexican Cartels, Marijuana Is Still Gold."

47. Ibid.

48. George W. Grayson, *Mexico: Narco-Violence and a Failed State?* (New Brunswick, NJ: Transaction, 2010), p. 254.

Index

About the Author

Ted Galen Carpenter is a senior fellow at the Cato Institute and previously served as the institute's vice president for defense and foreign policy studies. Dr. Carpenter is the author of nine books and more than 500 articles and studies on international affairs. His previous books include *Bad Neighbor Policy: Washington's Futile War on Drugs in Latin America* (2003) and *Smart Power: Toward a Prudent Foreign Policy for America* (2008). His articles have appeared in *Foreign Affairs*, the *New York Times*, the *Washington Post*, the *Wall Street Journal*, the *National Interest*, and many other publications. He is a frequent guest expert on radio and television programs in the United States and throughout the world. Dr. Carpenter received his Ph.D. in history from the University of Texas at Austin in 1980. He is a contributing editor to the *National Interest* and serves on the editorial board of the *Journal of Strategic Studies*.

Cato Institute

Founded in 1977, the Cato Institute is a public policy research foundation dedicated to broadening the parameters of policy debate to allow consideration of more options that are consistent with the traditional American principles of limited government, individual liberty, and peace. To that end, the Institute strives to achieve greater involvement of the intelligent, concerned lay public in questions of policy and the proper role of government.

The Institute is named for *Cato's Letters*, libertarian pamphlets that were widely read in the American Colonies in the early 18th century and played a major role in laying the philosophical foundation for the American Revolution.

Despite the achievement of the nation's Founders, today virtually no aspect of life is free from government encroachment. A pervasive intolerance for individual rights is shown by government's arbitrary intrusions into private economic transactions and its disregard for civil liberties.

To counter that trend, the Cato Institute undertakes an extensive publications program that addresses the complete spectrum of policy issues. Books, monographs, and shorter studies are commissioned to examine the federal budget, Social Security, regulation, military spending, international trade, and myriad other issues. Major policy conferences are held throughout the year, from which papers are published thrice yearly in the *Cato Journal*. The Institute also publishes the quarterly magazine *Regulation*.

In order to maintain its independence, the Cato Institute accepts no government funding. Contributions are received from foundations, corporations, and individuals, and other revenue is generated from the sale of publications. The Institute is a nonprofit, tax-exempt, educational foundation under Section 501(c)3 of the Internal Revenue Code.

CATO INSTITUTE
1000 Massachusetts Ave., N.W.
Washington, D.C. 20001
www.cato.org